THE WAY TO CHRISTIANITY
In Search of Spiritual Growth

by Richard Chilson, C.S.P.

Top cover photo: Arlene Blum, American Women's Himalayan Expedition
Lower cover photo: Jean-Claude Lejeune

Library of Congress Catalog Card Number: 79-64652
ISBN: 0-03-053426-7

Printed in the United States of America

5 4 3 2 1

Winston Press, Inc.
430 Oak Grove
Minneapolis, Minnesota 55403

To Mary
who not only helped
but walked the journey with me

And to Jac
my best student
my best teacher

Other Books by the Author:
An Introduction to the Faith of Catholics
A Believing People
I Can Pray, You Can Pray
A Creed for Young Catholics

Table of Contents

Whan that Aprile with his shoures soote
The droghte of March hath perced to the roote,
And bathed every veyne in swich licour
Of which vertu engendred is the flour;
Whan Zephirus eek with his sweete breeth
Inspired hath in every holt and heeth
The tendre croppes, and the yonge sonne
Hath in the Ram his halve cours yronne,
And smale foweles maken melodye,
That slepen al the nyght with open ye
(So priketh hem nature in hir corages);
Thanne longen folk to goon on pilgrimages,
And palmeres for to seken straunge strondes,
To ferne halwes, kowthe in sondry londes;
And specially rom every shires ende
Of Engelond to Caunterbury they wende,
The hooly blisful martir for to seke,
That hem hath holpen whan that they were seeke.

Geoffrey Chaucer

INTRODUCTION

For one reason or another the wonderful people Chaucer describes in his *Canterbury Tales* have undertaken a sacred, spiritual journey for healing or wholeness. Their destination is a shrine famous in the Middle Ages for healing and cures. On their way to that shrine, the pilgrims will entertain one another with stories that reveal to themselves and to one another who they are.

Our society is also intrigued by the spiritual journey. Now that we have "all that money can buy," we are beginning to look inward in our search for peace and happiness. We want to become more fully realized. We seek a wholeness beyond our current grasp. We thirst for a peace and harmony that will refresh us and strengthen us for our daily tasks. We ache for a depth in our relationships with one another that will enable those relationships to be truly nourishing and challenging. We, too, are ready to embark upon a sacred journey or pilgrimage.

Many of us have turned East to the spiritualities and disciplines of Buddhism and Hinduism. Others of us look to the burgeoning growth psychologies for techniques of spiritual development. But what of the traditional spiritual path of the West, the path of Chaucer's pilgrims? Christianity, too, affords not only an understanding of human life and development but a way of growth as well. If we do not immediately look to Christianity for such helps, it is perhaps because in our culture Christianity is too close to us. We cannot see the forest for the many trees.

What might we learn if we came upon Jesus and his message afresh, uncluttered by our own ideas of what he means and by our history of what he has meant to our society? Can we step outside our accustomed faith or lack of faith and meet him first as a teacher and spiritual guide rather than as the fully developed Christ of the Christian churches? By walking again or for the first time the path toward Jesus we might discover in this man and in his teaching a response to our yearning for wholeness.

Our starting point will be our search for wholeness in whatever way this thirst has arisen in our life. All we need is a willingness to put aside temporarily all our inherited notions of this man Jesus so that we can truly see him and then decide whether he can guide us toward the wholeness we seek.

Even if we have never been Christians, we may have come to suspect that Jesus has something to say to us. Or we may have left off our formal affiliation with the Christian religion and yet have caught a glimpse of Jesus different from the one we found inadequate. Or we may be committed Christians who simply want to deepen our faith; we feel there is something more to life than we have been able to experience thus far. So let's step back and outside the boundaries of Christianity. Let's meet Jesus much as the first people in the gospels did. What does he teach? What does he offer? Can we trust him to fulfill what he promises?

Our initial goal in reading this book might be merely to learn about the Christian experience. In that case we read from a safe distance about a pilgrimage of self-discovery and growth that many in the West have walked over the last two thousand years. We are reading, of course, about *their* pilgrimage, not about our own.

However, our goal in reading this book might be more encompassing than mere knowledge, valuable as that is. We might want to explore the impact of Jesus' message on our own lives and experience. How does he help us understand our life? What way of transformation does he offer? What would it be like to live as Jesus suggests?

But suppose we want to make our own pilgrimage now by encountering Jesus. This pilgrimage obviously cannot be described in a book written by another. After all, the real pilgrimage is the quest of our own life for wholeness, and the book we read is our own life experience. So our pilgrimage would have to take some shape in a journey (and a book) of our own creation. Then of what use is this present book? It becomes a guide and companion.

To read the present book as a guide is different from reading it simply as a book to be understood. While we might read an ordinary book in a few sittings, we cannot hope to read the book of our own pilgrimage in less time than it takes to make the journey. As a guide, the present book meets us at a certain point in our life journey and invites us to walk a certain path toward wholeness. In doing so it will guide us a considerable distance and be our companion for the better part of a year.

A year might seem a long time to spend on just one book. But it is not so much a year with a book as a year with our own life. Whether we are aware of it or not, we are already on a pilgrimage between birth and death, and the book of our journey is being written with or without our awareness. The question is whether we choose to take an active hand in its writing or not.

During this next year another chapter of our own pilgrimage book, and perhaps a crucial one at that, will be written. Do we want to help in creating that chapter? If so, we can look on this book as a writer's manual for that other book. In spite of the time it will take to "read" *The Way to Christianity*, it is not difficult to read, and it may make the reading and the writing of that other book easier and more enjoyable.

Besides, since the book in your hand is only a guide, it need not be your constant companion. Use it when you want to explore further in your life and its pilgrimage. When you arrive at a place where you would like to investigate further, when you find yourself stuck at a certain point, or when you need a rest, put this guide down and return to it when the time seems right. Although you may put *The Way to Christianity* down for a while, your pilgrimage and your exploration can still continue.

In its earliest days Christianity depended upon adult converts rather than the offspring of Christian parents to increase its ranks. The process by which a person became a Christian was called catechumenate. Today the catechumenate is being resurrected, at least in the Roman Catholic communion. In this book we will use the format of the catechumenate as our own method of investigating the Christian way of life. For whether we are already committed Christians or not, the catechumenate process enables us to test Jesus and his message.

Indeed the present book can be used by Christian churches as a modern catechumenate during which the inquirer can come to encounter Jesus and his power to transform human life. The catechumenate is not so much a teaching in the "traditional" sense as an encounter with a way of living and with a process of life transformation.

Employed in its fullest potential, this book becomes a tool by which we can not only investigate Jesus but also come to know his community. Some of the explorations are done in the context of a group of people so that we can become aware of the importance of the community in shaping the Christian experience.

The book is ecumenical in its content. Drawing from the various Christian traditions, it provides a truly catholic perspective on the faith. Individual churches can use it and easily expand upon its explorations by showing how its vision is assimilated into their particular tradition.

In a group context it is best that one member of the group be a leader. This leader ideally will have already made the pilgrimage so that he or she can offer help to the group. But the leader is not called upon to be the expert or the teacher. Each member of the group should have opportunity to lead the group in the explorations and contribute to the overall experience of the group.

4

o o o

If you are leading a group and have already made the pilgrimage, you will return to this journey on a slightly deeper level. You will be able to explore more deeply than before. And you can give more attention to the process of the pilgrimage so that you can aid the others in your own group.

You will notice a section in the journal on the process itself. As a group leader you will want to observe this overall process intently. You can make entries in this section concerning the experience of the group with the meditations. As you continue the pilgrimage explorations for a second time with your group, be aware of the process of meditation. The skills you develop in meditation and journal work can then allow you to help your group.

The Way to Christianity initiates the reader into both the Christian life and the Christian year. Although the book may be "done" at any time, there is a way to journey so that the work of the book reflects the passage of the Christian year. Ideally Parts One and Two are done in the summer or early fall. Here at the beginning it is good to take your time so that the group members can acquire the necessary skills in meditation, reading, and journal writing. Let the group set its own tone and pace. Use the group meeting to process the work and to do group meditations. Allow time for the participants to share their experience and to inquire about the process itself.

The time after Pentecost—summer and fall—is called Kingdomtide in some Christian communities. Part Three, which explores the idea of Kingdom, is best done at this time, probably in the fall. This season comes to fulfillment in Advent as we look forward to the full coming of the Kingdom; and the great feast of Christmas—the end of Part Three—looks back to the first coming of Jesus as well as forward to the second coming and the full realization of God's Kingdom.

Part Four ideally occupies the time between Christmas and the beginning of Lent. Part Five, in which the pilgrim makes a decision whether or not to follow Jesus, could take place during Lent and climax with Easter. Then in Part Six, we spend the time between Easter and Pentecost reflecting upon the dynamics and shape of Christian existence as we prepare and work for the full coming of the Kingdom.

Invitation to a Pilgrimage

One day King Arthur and his knights were sitting at the Round Table when they heard of the quest for the Holy Grail, that cup from which Jesus drank at the Last Supper. The Grail had been preserved, so went the story, by Joseph of Arimathaea, who had brought it to England. But soon afterwards it had disappeared—some said because of the wickedness of the world. What if one of the knights of the Round Table should find the Grail and bring it back into Arthur's kingdom? The Grail would guarantee the peace and perfection that Arthur dreamed of for Camelot. But this journey in search of the Grail was no ordinary quest. For only he whose life became perfect and holy itself would be able to see that holy vessel and come into its presence.

The knights, fired by the thought of such a mission, agreed to devote all of their energies in search of the sacred chalice. And so the next day all donned their armor, mounted their steeds, and rode away from the castle. When they arrived at the entrance to the forest, each knight took leave of his fellows and entered the forest where it seemed to him darkest.

This search for the Grail is often understood as the Western version of the spiritual journey; it provides a model for the shape of the Western world's quest for fulfillment, peace, perfection, and happiness. It might also be the story of each one of us and might speak of our own longing for wholeness.

For there is a tradition in the West that has shaped the way we see ourselves and the way we live in our world. Perhaps that tradition, which helps form our roots as Western people, is today largely forgotten, unknown, or put aside; but that is not to say it no longer exists or is incapable of nourishing us. Many today are excited by the thought of just such a journey as those knights undertook. We know that we must make such a journey alone through the forest of our own interior life, but we also hope we might be sustained, inspired, and guided by the ideal of a common quest whose vision might sustain us all.

Since the day Arthur's knights rode in search of the Grail, many others have undertaken this quest for wholeness. Have we ourselves heard this call in our own lives? Stories of other pilgrims who have gone before us into the dark wood might help us recognize this longing in our own lives.

There are two children we know who have made such a journey. The first is a most extraordinary child named Alice. One day Alice fell into a rabbit hole, or through the looking glass; she's a little confused now and thinks she might have done both. But when she fell, or passed through, she left behind the cozy little world where she could pass the afternoon under a great tree listening to her older sister read a story. Instead she found herself in a crazy world of adults. And in this looking-glass world she found that in order to survive she had to paint white roses red—something Alice considers quite silly. But not only did she have to paint them red; she also had to say they had been red all along. Otherwise the crazy Queen would shout, "Off with her head!" All the other people in this wonderland seem to have accepted the craziness and silliness and to live as though it were true. But Alice will not accept such a compromise. This mad world is upside down and inside out, just the reverse of the real world, and she will not give up her search for a way back out of this madness.

We all know about another young woman, named Dorothy, who says she comes from Kansas. One day Dorothy and her little dog are whisked up into a tornado and find themselves far from home in a strange, somewhat frightening world called Oz. Strange and wonderful as that world is, Dorothy would prefer to go back to the ordinary world of Kansas, for that is where her home is. So she, too, is on a pilgrimage, walking down a yellow brick road in search of the wizard of this world who, Dorothy has been told, is wise and powerful, able to do anything.

There are other people who journey along with Dorothy and Alice. They are grown up, but they haven't surrendered the hope that there is a way back home out of Oz and Wonderland. As they journey they keep their strength up by telling stories of worlds such as Middle Earth and of other quests such as those for rings of power. They speak of other powerful people—superpeople—who are said to have the power to make all things well again.

Other people call these pilgrims escapists; but the searchers do not consider themselves to be running away. They say they take our world seriously but cannot take it ultimately. They remember other and better worlds that they glimpsed in childhood and have seen again in fantasy. When asked if those fantasy worlds could possibly be real, they say they are willing to go on a pilgrimage—to meet the wizard with Dorothy, to speak to the crazy Queen with Alice. For only by journeying on this quest is there any chance to find out for sure whether their childhood dreams are just airy dreams or are actually visions of a better world than the topsy-turvy looking-glass world we adults believe is real.

Another famous pilgrim is a man who at his life's midpoint found himself exiled from family and lost in a dark wood—a wood very similar to the one the knights entered. To find his way again, this man must make a long, fantastic voyage through hell, purgatory, and heaven. We might describe the first stage of his journey as a stripping of his illusions and defenses so that he can no longer shirk the ugliness and alienation of his existence. From that hell of self-discovery he ascends a steep mountain of transformation where he learns—from his teachers, his friends embarked upon the same journey, and his

7

dreams—how he might find his true self and recreate his life. This path, though arduous, is nonetheless possible, for it is created out of his everyday life and builds upon his natural being.

Love for a woman draws him to continue the journey. The pilgrimage itself becomes a discovery of true love, not lust, not passion, not dependency, but the rich overflowing of that charity by which the cosmos is sustained. And finally, to aid him along that path of union in love, he is granted a vision of something beyond his beloved—a vision of the harmony, joy, and beauty which moves the stars.

Many other pilgrims walk with Dante in his search. They too have awakened in their thirties and forties to find their life without savor or purpose. What once showered meaning and nourished dreams is now shallow and empty. The plans of youth, now realized, are found lacking. Marriage has grown stale or failed altogether, the vocation has become only a job, and the possessions so eagerly sought after have not brought satisfaction.

They realize, too, that their crisis is not merely a private hell; it menaces and shakes the entire culture. Dante's world is threatened by political corruption, fierce civil wars, and the degeneration and collapse of the faith that had once given meaning and nourishment. His fellow travelers today sense the same overall chaos, but they will not surrender even though the sign over the portals of hell tells them to abandon all hope. They will to move out of the darkness; they dare to put down their masks and look into their very souls; and they believe that their cities and their culture can once more nourish and inspire rather than distort and destroy. They walk this pilgrimage with Dante, confident that there can be a future through the hell, through the current crisis, the sense of loss and lostness, the ennui, the rat race, the divorce, the career change.

Other knights who went forth upon their quest long ago and who prevailed over dragons, magic fires, and frightening obstructions form another group of pilgrims. Through their trials and tribulations they become heroic and now shine like gods themselves.

Among them is Beethoven, who won for music a power of expression never heard before and seldom since. But his heroic struggle was not only against the musical establishment of his day; this man whose name is synonymous with music was condemned never to hear much of what he created. Yet he fought the dragon deafness, and his lifelong struggle gives way in his later years not to defeat and bitterness but to a music so pure, serene, and secure in its mastery and strength that it could only signal spiritual triumph.

With Beethoven walk others who have been called, whether they have willed it or not, to become heroic. They no longer ride forth as did the knights of old to battle external dragons. For now the dragons are within, but nonetheless terrifying. Among these pilgrims journey people such as Carl Jung who know that the stories of heroes, far from being simply entertainments for a world come of age, can actually reveal the patterns and pathways of our own lives.

These pilgrims prepare themselves for their adventures much as did the Arthurian knights who jousted in the medieval courts. They are inspired by the stories of heroes as they themselves prepare to battle the dragons of deafness, sickness, defeat, humiliation. They train so that they might prevail over whatever obstacles litter their way. And they dream that they might come through, ready to enter the presence of the Grail, not embittered and defeated by what they have undergone, but serenely triumphant.

Other pilgrims have looked outward and been aroused by a world of injustice where some eat and waste while many starve to death, where a few enjoy freedom and even license while many are enslaved by politics, economics, prejudice, or simple ignorance. They have given their energy and life for the betterment of such a world.

Among them is Martin Luther King, Jr., who dared to stand up and call his blackness good and who seized dignity and freedom for himself and his people. He walks in a select company of men and women who have persevered with their vision and love uncontaminated by trials, setbacks, and defeats along the way. Martin Luther King did not lose heart nor surrender and resort to the violence that was often used against him and would finally assassinate him. He walked through ridicule, rage, and scorn but was not contaminated or destroyed by it.

With him walk others who would give their lives to the poor and the unwanted. They undertake the pilgrimage in search of a strength that will enable them to endure as did King. They search for a vision that might sustain their desire to better the human condition. They seek a dedication that might keep their vision pure and unsullied by bitterness and despair, that will provide them the power to keep going when giving up seems natural.

Still others have undertaken the quest in alienation from the majority in their society. They are different from the mainstream in faith, race, sexuality, or physical appearance. Yet they have in their own way gone in quest of wholeness and have often contributed to the very mainstream they were cut off from in life. They were condemned, or called, to go against the grain; only later was it seen that their solitary struggle provided light and guidance for the pilgrimage of others.

Among them is Gustav Mahler, the composer, a romantic forced to suffer and survive the death of the world he loved, a Jew in a world increasingly anti-Semitic, a convert to a church in which he could neither believe nor find nourishment. Yet Mahler, whose internal crises his fellows never did comprehend, has become a prophet for our own times. For though his agonies seemed to be limited to his own life, today he articulates the uncertainties, the upheavals, the dark faith, the despair for vast numbers. On the other hand, in his Second Symphony he has detailed a passage from death through resurrection that has shed light and provided hope and renewal for the Christian tradition from which he felt himself cut off.

In the same company, yet again alone, walks Simone Weil, who is now considered a seminal thinker for the Christian tradition. Yet in her lifetime she found herself unable to enter that tradition, although she felt a love for Jesus and his message and hungered desperately for the nourishment of his Eucharist. She chose instead to spend her life outside that community in a place where, as she put it, she would wait for God.

Scattered through the dark wood walk others cut off from their society for one reason or another. Because they feel the pain of alienation so deeply, they are forced to make a pilgrimage in search of healing, community, and peace. They walk alone, unsupported by others who, unknown even to each other, are nevertheless on the same pilgrimage.

The activity of pilgrimage is not restricted to the people of the West. The search for wholeness is a concern of the human animal in whatever culture or tradition. Indeed in the East the seekers and quests far surpass the West in variety.

Suffice it to point out Gautama, the Buddha who left his world of riches and power to travel in search of a way out of suffering. From his long meditation under the Bo tree he found the Noble Eightfold Path, which has served to guide millions in their own individual journeys.

Among this latter group of pilgrims we can see the infinite richness of the quest. For in addition to the Buddha there are the Bodhisattvas who speak of a path of compassion. There are those of the Hindu tradition who explore the infinite number of pathways through mind, body, spirit, politics, and nature. The Chinese offer a way of seeing and walking in harmony with the cosmos. The American Indian offers a variety of ways of seeing the different worlds that coexist in the same time and space.

But by far the largest group of pilgrims are those who may not even be dedicated to the quest. They are simply living their lives—living and acting according to their own insights. In the Middle Ages they were referred to as the ship of fools, but they were made immortal by that pilgrim Chaucer who recreated them in their wonderful uniqueness—warts, wits, and wisdom.

Among them we find a pardoner who traffics for profit in sacred things, the wife of Bath who revels in the richness of human flesh, the pious, the profane, the cultured, the vulgar. They live from day to day with dreams of riches or glory, eager to fill their pockets before their spirits, their stomachs before their hearts. Yet they too are on a pilgrimage—a holy pilgrimage at that—although some would say they are only along for the ride or the good company.

We wonder what will happen to these pilgrims when they have reached the martyr's shrine in Canterbury. Will they be transformed and brought into the peace and perfection for which the Grail serves as a symbol? Or will they return to their homes much as we see them now? Who is to know? For better or worse, for good or ill, for their transformation or merely their profit, for the holy quest or for the simple joy of good stories in delightful company, they too are on pilgrimage.

And what of us? Are we too on this pilgrimage? Have we felt kinship and communion with these groups of pilgrims? What has brought us to this quest? What do we hope to gain through making this journey? Take a few minutes now, put down this book and reflect upon what brings you to this point. We all have a history of whence we come and how we came to be here. What is that history? And now that you find yourself here with this illustrious company before the dark wood, what do you seek from this journey? What are your hopes? Your fears? What is your experience of the journey so far? (For you, like those pilgrims in Chaucer, have been on pilgrimage up to now even though you might not have been aware of it.) What do you hope to gain and achieve by entering this wood and beginning this quest?

A Path and a Guide

Our pilgrimage is created out of the individuality of our own unique lives; still, if we are not to journey entirely on our own (as some have done), we must now ask where we find both a map to provide us with knowledge of the terrain and a guide to provide assistance on our way. Indeed, this entire book is really concerned only with that one crucial question of the selection of a guide and a map for the quest. During this part of our pilgrimage, we shall explore what the pilgrimage is, investigate the guide and his map to find out whether we wish to entrust him with leading us, and set out on that pilgrimage itself.

Whom shall we choose as a guide? In the West the person who has served as guide for the majority has been Jesus of Nazareth. While it is true that he no longer serves many of us today, and some of us may believe that he can no longer serve us well, it still would seem reasonable to examine his qualifications. Then, if he appears to hold promise, we can begin our pilgrimage with him and test him further before we make any final commitment.

So let us look again at the different groups of pilgrims and what they are searching for. Then we can discover whether Jesus might possibly be able to serve as their guide.

Our first group was headed by Alice and Dorothy. These people wanted to journey in some way out of the present world and back to the kind of world they had glimpsed in their childhood. There are two statements of Jesus which indicate he might not be adverse to such a journey. One day as he is teaching, a group of children approach him. The disciples, knowing how children can disrupt a gathering, try to keep them away. But Jesus sees what is happening, and he asks the disciples to allow the children to come forward. He then tells the crowd that the kingdom of God—that special kingdom he came to tell about—belongs to the little children. And further, he says that unless people become like little children they cannot enter into that special kingdom. At another time when he is speaking with a Jewish teacher, he tells him that one must be born again to enter the kingdom. So it would seem that Jesus agrees with these pilgrims who seek something glimpsed in childhood; he, too, acknowledges a reality there that is missing to us adults.

Now Dante in our second group of pilgrims comes to Jesus for help in his midlife crisis, and his pilgrimage becomes one of rediscovering the Christian faith. But our fellow travelers with Dante might not be willing to do the same thing. After all, they say, Dante lived in a fully Christian world. But the Christian faith is no longer the center of our life; what could it possibly have to offer us?

However, when Dante began this pilgrimage, the Christian religion was certainly not the center of his life either. Nor was the Christian religion really powerful in his life. Indeed, it was in a period of decadence and decline. And although Dante was always a member of the Christian Church he goes on a pilgrimage not to become a better church member but simply to become a better human being.

If we decide to choose Jesus as a possible guide for our journey, we choose a guide who by the Christian church's own admission often has stood against that church in order to bring about a return to his original message. For it is the *good news of Jesus* that finally brings about many of the reforms that Dante himself comes to advocate. By choosing Jesus as a possible guide, we are choosing a man whose spirit has again and again brought renewal out of decadent and outworn structures and who has for two thousand years been the principle of change, revolution, and rebirth for our culture; even the Communist revolutions have their roots in the teaching of Jesus. In accepting him as a guide, we are choosing someone who has again and again brought people from darkness into light, from weakness into strength, from Dark Ages to Renaissance, from corruption to reformation. What would prevent him from doing the same in our life today?

Although we might not think of Jesus primarily in terms of heroism, he has often been cast in just that role, along with Orpheus, Siegfried, Saint George, and all the other heroes of legend. The early Christians often told the story of the death and resurrection of Jesus as a story of the battle with the dragon Satan. For them, the place of Golgotha where Jesus was crucified was actually the center of the

13

earth. The name Golgotha means *the skull,* and those Christians believed that the skull was that of Adam, the first man. Therefore the cross of Jesus was pitched at the navel of the world, and at this place, according to Greco-Roman myths, one could gain access to the underworld. So when Jesus died on the cross his spirit slid down the pole of the cross into the earth's bowels and into the domain of Satan. Armed with only his cross, which he now grasps like a sword, Jesus enters the dragon's lair and defeats him. Then through his victory he rescues and leads into paradise all those the dragon had captured since the foundation of the world.

This story has obvious prefigurings of the later Christian myth in which Saint George slays the dragon. But it echoes as well the story of the singer Orpheus, who risks the underworld in search of his beloved Eurydice. It also shares similar themes with the Teutonic Siegfried, who destroys a dragon and frees a maiden.

The traditional representation of Jesus as a delicate, meek soul is thus seen to be only one understanding of him. Although the exotic and fantastic details of this myth might strike us today as quaint, we can still see that Jesus might have something to teach concerning the serpentine obstacles that threaten our own life. And his response to those dragons might be closer to the heroic model than our Sunday School memories hint.

In the case of those heroic in the cause of justice and reform, there can be little quarrel with Jesus' credentials. His predecessors, the prophets of Israel, spent their lives and often their blood in opposing a political establishment that oppressed the poor and the powerless. Jesus continues that opposition. He criticizes the scribes and Pharisees for their indifference to the plight of the poor.

One of the greatest glories of the Christian religion has been its constant insistence upon works of charity and the general and overall improvement of the human condition. This religion is known not only for its great churches and cathedrals but for its hospitals, orphanages, schools, and leper colonies. The vision and strength to promote and keep faith with this vision is certainly to be found in Jesus.

But what of the alienated? Often they have been cast into this role by Christianity itself. We cannot overlook all those who were cast off from the Christian church of their day only to be reclaimed later and often canonized as models for future believers. When we consider Jesus himself, we see a man who shared the fate of the outcast. He was

14

a Jew, a member of a group scorned and ridiculed by the world of his day. Furthermore, he was rejected by his own people and put to death. One can only wonder, as did Dostoevski, what might have been his fate had he come into the presence of his own church's inquisitors. His fate as outcast provides him with authority to speak of alienation. In his own life those are the people he addressed; his constant companions are those tossed to the edges of Jewish society—the tax collectors and prostitutes.

For much of the time that Christianity has known about Buddhism, the assumption has been that the two religions are quite incompatible. After all, Christianity is theistic, and Buddhism often claims to be atheistic; Christianity speaks of the fulfillment of life in the kingdom, while Buddhism shows a way to the extinction of existence. But when we examine the two founders and their words, we begin to discover two teachers who agree and complement one another far more than the great difference in their cultures and times would lead us to expect. Here is the Buddha:

> "Look how he abused me and beat me, how he threw me down and robbed me." Live with such thoughts and you live in hate.

15

> "Look how he abused me and beat me, how he threw me down and robbed me." Abandon such thoughts, and live in love.

> In this world
> Hate never yet dispelled hate.
> Only love dispels hate.
> This is the law, ancient and inexhaustible.

Compare the words of Jesus:

> You have heard that it was said, "You shall love your neighbor and hate your enemy." But I say to you, Love your enemies and pray for those who persecute you, so that you may be sons of your Father who is in heaven; . . . For if you love those who love you, what reward have you? Do not even the tax collectors do the same? And if you salute

only your brethren, what more are you doing than others? Do not even the Gentiles do the same? You, therefore, must be perfect, as your heavenly Father is perfect.

Matthew 5:43-45
The Revised Standard Version

Of course Gautama and Jesus do not always say the same thing. But the differences between them seem less ultimate than the agreements. Today many of us have heard the call to spiritual growth from traditions such as Gautama's. We might also hear it closer to home, from out of our own heritage, in our own language, in harmony with our own culture: We might hear it from Jesus himself.

Finally, what has Jesus to say to those of us who have grown up with him at the center of our lives? We may already call ourselves Christians, but somehow we have the feeling we have not come into real contact with his power. Often in the course of Christian history, the good news of Jesus has become lost in the welter of doctrines, rituals, ethics, theologies of his church. We may have grown up within a Christian community and still not be sure just who Jesus is and what he teaches. We are now searching for richer, fuller lives. This figure of Jesus might be able to awaken us to a great pilgrimage of discovery.

We can begin this pilgrimage right now. Here is how the evangelist Mark introduces Jesus to the world:

And after that John was delivered up, Jesus came into Galilee, preaching the gospel of the Kingdom of God, and saying: The time is accomplished and the Kingdom of God is at hand. Repent and believe the gospel.

And passing by the sea of Galilee, he saw Simon and Andrew his brother casting nets into the sea (for they were fishermen).

And Jesus said to them: Come after me; and I will make you to become fishers of men. And immediately leaving their nets, they followed him.

And going on from thence a little farther, he saw James the son of Zebedee and John his brother, who also were mending their nets in the ship: and forthwith he called them. And leaving their father Zebedee in the ship with his hired men, they followed him.

Mark 1:14-20
Douay-Rheims Version

If in our imaginations we take up the invitation Jesus extends, we will explore with him what this kingdom of God is. We shall then explore what it means to repent so that we might enter that kingdom. At that point we will be able to decide more definitely whether, like Peter and his friends, we are willing to abandon our fishing in order to follow Jesus, because by that time also we will have caught a glimpse of where following Jesus will lead us.

That is our pilgrimage in this guide. But let us start at the very beginning. What is our starting point on this pilgrimage, our entrance, as it were, into the dark wood? We turn first to this present moment and place in our life. What brought us here? What are we seeking? What shall we take with us on our quest?

For the present all we need are this guide, some notebook paper, and perhaps the good company of friends. Later we shall also need a complete Bible and a loose-leaf notebook with dividers. (Help on selecting a Bible is available on page 100.)

PART ONE

The Point of Departure

In the beginning was the Word,
and the Word was with God,
and the Word was God.
He was in the beginning with God;
all things were made through him,
And without him was not anything
made that was made.
In him was life,
and the life was the light of men.
The light shines in the darkness,
and the darkness has not overcome it.

There was a man sent from God,
whose name was John.
He came for testimony,
to bear witness to the light,
that all might believe through him.
He was not the light,
but came to bear witness to the light.

The true light that enlightens every man
was coming into the world.
He was in the world,
and the world was made through him,
yet the world knew him not.
He came to his own home,
and his own people received him not.

But to all who received him,
who believed in his name,
he gave power to become children of God;
who were born, not of blood
nor of the will of the flesh
nor of the will of man,
but of God.

John 1:1-13
The Revised Standard Version

We shall be using the opening chapters of John's gospel as a guide for our present pilgrimage. One of the great early Christian teachers, Clement of Alexandria, said that he had become a Christian by being taught how to read the Scriptures. On our pilgrimage, we shall want to learn to read the Scriptures in such a way that we too might be able to follow Jesus, should we so choose. The catch to understanding what Clement meant lies in the word *read*, which in his mind must mean something different from our usual understanding of the word.

Now read once more the first paragraph of John's gospel. Certainly there are no obvious difficulties of understanding here. Each word is common and known to everyone. Nor are the words arranged in unusual formations; the sentences are quite simple and not at all obscure. Indeed, the entire passage is straightforward. If there is any difficulty at all, it lies with believing what John says to be true rather than in understanding what he says.

Yet Augustine, another early theologian, had the following to say about this same passage:

> "In the beginning was the Word, and the Word was with God, and the Word was God. The same was in the beginning with God. . . . " Who can fathom this? Who can imagine it? Who can conceive it? Who can contemplate it? Who can worthily meditate on it? No one!

As we listen to Augustine's questions and return to our gospel passage, something appears to be missing from our experience that was present to these early Christians. To us there seems no real difficulty in fathoming this passage. It does not seem too wild to imagine or conceive. And if we have trouble contemplating it or meditating upon it, it is because we might not know how to meditate.

This same idea occurs in other spiritual traditions as well. Here is how a young man who is learning from an Islamic teacher and holy man describes the same difficulty:

> Within only a few days, I realized that I was learning my Islam from the fuqara (teacher). That is not to say simply that I deepened my understanding of the Qur'an (the holy book) and the rites and the Sunna (community) and their company; it is to say that I learned how to live. I mean how to walk and how to sit and how to listen and when to be silent. I learned how to eat and how to refrain from food, how to wait and how to be still. Our Venerable Master had told us that in the stage we were at, there was no point in reading anything apart from the Qur'an. It was only as the days went by that the full meaning of the instruction became clear.

But Christianity and Islam are both religions which have books at their center—one the Bible, the other the *Qur'an*. It is thus natural that they should be preoccupied with reading; it is supremely important in these faiths to understand what one reads. But Buddhism, although it too has scriptures, does not center upon them as do Islam and Christianity. Yet when we turn to the Lord Buddha we hear:

> However many holy words you read,
> However many you speak
> What good will they do you
> If you do not act upon them? . . .

> Read as few words as you like
> And speak fewer.
> But act upon the law.

This is a kind of reading different from our society's. The Buddha tells us to read only those words we can act on; the rest is useless and just so much noise. For the Buddha, we read so that we can change our lives.

Our stores, libraries, and bookshelves are glutted with books that promise to change our lives. They may provide us with information; we may reach a new understanding of ourselves or our lives. Yet unless we find a way to act upon what they tell us, no change occurs.

These texts of John, the *Qur'an*, and *The Dhammapada* of the Buddha all are intended not only to supply information but also to change the texture of human existence. During the course of their history, they indeed have fulfilled that promise countless times. Here at the start of our own pilgrimage toward wholeness we will use John's book as our guide. But if it is to effect change in our lives we might need to read it in a different way than we are accustomed to reading.

EXPLORATION **1** **EXPLORING WHAT *READING* MIGHT MEAN**
time: ten to twenty minutes
materials: loose-leaf paper and pen

Before we begin to read John, let's take some time to explore what we have heard so far. Obviously if there is another way of reading, we will learn it only gradually.

We have been told by three different people that there is a way to read a book so that one's life is changed. Normally in our reading we would simply continue until we decided to put the book down. But let's pause right now and think about what we have read here.

In this exploration, we begin what we shall call our *journal work.* Later in our pilgrimage we will set up our journal and learn just how to use it in our explorations. But for now all you need is some notebook paper and a pen. Putting words down on paper helps us discover just what our thoughts and feelings are. The journal will also provide us with a record of our pilgrimage, a means of making the journey, and finally, a means of creating the real book we wish to read: that of our own quest for wholeness and growth.

Find a quiet comfortable place where you can write for the next twenty minutes or so. Title the page "Learning How to Read." Then in the margin of the first line, write the date.

• In this exploration we will explore three areas relating to reading. First let's explore just how you feel about the idea that there is a way of reading that will enable you to effect changes in your life. A simple answer may not be possible here, but that is not what we are looking for anyway. It is your thoughts and feelings that are important. So at this point we would like to explore just how you feel about this idea. What attracts you about it? Is there anything in it that makes you afraid? Do you tend to believe it, or do you have doubts that it could be so? Have you actually experienced this kind of reading before? Have you wanted such an experience? Take about five or ten minutes now to explore your thoughts and feelings; then write them down.

• Next, let's consider why the books we have read have not changed us. Why do you think they failed? Take a few minutes to explore your experience with these books. Write down your thoughts.

• Now consider those books that did change us. Perhaps some not only taught us new information but changed our thinking; others even changed our ways of acting. What was present in the process of reading in these instances that enabled the change to occur?

23

• Take another five to ten minutes to explore and write down your thoughts. If you already have a loose-leaf journal, keep your notes in it, or save them until you acquire a journal.

Over the next few days and weeks you may want to return to your notes as you discover further what this process of reading is all about. Encourage yourself to enter your discoveries into the journal. This journal, as we will eventually construct it, can be a powerful means of growth. But it can produce its results only if we work faithfully at it. It will be as useful to us as we are willing to make it.

2 READING JOHN'S GOSPEL
time: twenty minutes   materials: paper entitled
"Learning How to Read" from Exploration 1

Having considered that there might be a way of reading that could transform our life, we'll return to our passage from John. Here is part of the passage in a different translation:

> When all things began,
> the Word already was.
> The Word dwelt with God,
> and what God was,
> the Word was.
> The Word, then, was with God at the beginning,
> and through him all things came to be;
> no single thing was created without him.
> All that came to be was alive with his life,
> and that life was the light of men.
> The light shines on in the dark,
> and the darkness has never mastered it.

John 1:1-5
The New English Bible

24

● Let's read the passage again. This time read it more slowly than usual—out loud if possible. Is there a difference when you read it out loud? Is it different when you use your finger to underline what you are reading? The differences may be subtle, so we must be observant to appreciate them.

● Now let's enter deeper into the text. John starts with "In the beginning." What associations does that phrase bring to you? Do you think it signals something important?

Beginnings are important, for without them there can be nothing. If something is from the beginning, it will be a part of all that follows and grows out of it. So John is setting before us the keynote of his thought. What is great enough to have existed in the beginning, even *before* the beginning of everything?

• "In the beginning was the Word." It seems simple enough. But what is a word? How do words function in our lives? How important are they? What do words bring into our lives that would not be there without them? Reflect on these questions for a few minutes.

John speaks not of words but of *the Word*. So let's shift our focus to think of just one Word. This is a word like all the other words, but it is different as well. It stands behind all the other words; it is *the* Word. Allow the idea to be with you and reveal itself to you. What, really, is *the Word*?

Words bring the gift of meaning into our lives. Granted, life has meaning without our using words. But there is a fullness and richness of understanding and significance that simply would not exist without words and language. *The Word* then could represent the underlying meaning of everything, of all the world from the very beginning of its existence. John is saying that life and the universe are far from senseless, for there is a present at all times and from all time a meaning, a *Word*.

• That Word (or what provides everything with meaning) was not only *with* God, says John, but *is* God. Let's explore this idea to taste its fullness. John says that the Word is God. Now *God* is surely a charged word. It means many things to each of us. We might believe in or deny the existence of God. We may think of God as a Father or simply as a force behind the world. It is almost impossible to use the word *God* in a discussion without first clarifying just how each person understands it.

So let's first be aware of how the word *God* resonates within us: What are the associations, thoughts, and feelings it calls up within us? We need to be aware of our own thoughts and feelings about God as we read this passage; if we unconsciously permit them to color what we think we are reading, then we will not really be reading what John is saying.

To enter into John's thought, we'll take him exactly at his word. God is the Word. The Word is what brings meaning into human life. So John is saying that the source of meaning in human life, that which opens our life to meaning, is divine. Therefore, whatever we look to for meaning in our life is a part of God.

Thus, for John, the atheist would be a person who not only does not believe in God but does not believe that there is any real meaning in life. Of course, such a person would be willing to say that there is meaning; that there are thousands of meanings created out of human language and life: the meaning of traffic lights, the meaning of tears. But the atheist believes there is no *ultimate* reality apart from what human intelligence is able to establish or agree upon that stands behind life and the universe and gives it meaning.

On the other hand, following John's line of thought, any person seeking a fundamental meaning of life, as opposed to a conventional meaning agreed upon by some human group, is actually searching for God. Whatever meaning we find in our lives, therefore, John would call God. Thus to the extent that I find meaning in my work or in my family and am nurtured by this meaning, I have discovered God through my work and my family. This is not to say that I make either work or family God, but that the meaning I perceive shining through them is the presence of God in my life.

We will find many more names for God in the course of our search, but here, at the beginning, John has revealed a powerful name for God: God is *the Word*, the meaning in the world. So as we search for meaning in our lives and in our world, we are doing the same thing, at least in John's eyes, as others have done when they have claimed to be searching for God.

Perhaps we have difficulties with the whole notion of God; most modern people do. During the course of our journey we will explore those difficulties and hope to resolve them. Right now, all we need do to follow John's path is agree to the idea that meaning is truly important for us; that we are searching and hungering for meaning. If this is so, then John assures us that the search and our hunger for meaning are identical to what others have experienced as a search and hunger for God. Ask yourself whether you can agree to this idea. Do you see any problems with approaching your search in this way? Does it help you to look at your search in this way?

Let's be careful not to jump ahead of where we really are. At this point we are not dealing with whether there really is a God; we are not asking assent to the existence of some Word that gives meaning to everything that is. All we need do at this moment to continue our pilgrimage into John's gospel is agree that meaning is important in our search and development. Further, we need to allow John to use the traditional word *God* to describe a possible meaning that lies behind everything.

• John goes on to describe the Word further. Everything that exists owes its existence to the Word. Thus nothing exists that is ultimately meaningless. This does not guarantee that a human being can enter into the meaning of everything, but it does speak of a trust, a faith that nothing is without meaning.

Can we enter more powerfully into what John is saying? The New Testament in Modern English renders "In the beginning was the Word" as "In the beginning God expressed himself." That is, God spoke a Word which so expressed God and God's fullness that the Word itself *is* God. According to this idea, God creates all things through self expression. Through speaking the Word, God calls everything into being.

This image is much closer to an analogy than the previous translation revealed. When I speak a word it is certainly my word, but it is not me. But when God speaks a Word, when God expresses himself, then that Word, that expression, is itself God. The Word has within itself the fullness of God, God's being. The Word in turn calls everything into existence. It is by that Word that whatever exists exists. So all things exist by reason of the Word. Thus existence is "Worded"; existence and whatever exists are meaningful. There is a Word that calls everything into existence and sustains it in existence.

There are times in our lives when we are chilled by the fearful thought that whatever is happening to us is without meaning. It is simply senseless, chaotic, or if meaningful at all, it is so merely as a huge, cruel joke at our expense. But John trusts that whatever happens to us, whatever exists in this universe, is not without meaning.

How do you respond to this trust John offers us? Do you like it? Does it present problems for you? Are there difficulties in making such a trust your own? If so, try to articulate them. By relating to John's thoughts here, we can clarify our own thinking and feeling; we can give word to our own inner life. Keep in mind that at this moment in our journey, we are only looking at *the Word*, or *God*, as a possible source of trust.

• John goes on to say that in the Word was life. Here is a new, rich concept added to that of Word. Furthermore, the life which is the Word is the light that shines within human beings. So the Word is first of all life and secondly light. "In the Word was life." Let's carry John's thought further: The Word *is* life. We are now bringing the Word into sharper focus; the idea is becoming more concrete.

The life of the Word is the light of humanity. Where is the Word in my own life? John suggests that we locate the Word in that part of our life that we perceive as light. Obviously, our life is not entirely a thing of light. In our experience there are parts of our life that appear quite dark indeed. But there are also areas of our life that appear to shine out; there are times when our life takes on a shimmering, glowing quality.

Pause for a few minutes to discover and reexperience in memory those moments in your life when you were aware of this luminous quality. John will not persuade by argument. Rather, he speaks to us out of his own experience and asks us to come listen to him from out of our own experience. Our own experience will validate what he says. Can you remember times in your life that you could say are best characterized by the word *light*? In those light moments, can you see whether meaning was powerfully present? Were such light moments more meaning filled than the moments of darkness and confusion?

In those light-filled moments John sees the glimmerings of the Word that is life and light. If you have trouble with the metaphor of light, come at it from the opposite angle. Look for those times in your life when meaning is at the center, guiding and transforming your life. Then ask yourself whether in those times of meaning your life didn't seem transfused with light. We might not be able to put the meaning into words. Look for times of motivation, of understanding that is deeper than words can express. Are there times when you felt your life was being guided? Are there times when you felt your life unfolding almost without effort?

John expresses here a trust that, pervasive as the darkness may be in the world at large and in the life of the individual, the light will never be put out. Is this faith something that you can resonate to? Maybe you're not ready for it now. But at this point we want only to examine such a trust as a possible belief for us. Does such a trust appeal to you? If it does, why? Are there obstacles to accepting such a trust? Such obstacles could be anything from a vague, internal feeling to a very clear idea. Stay quietly with the idea of such a trust for a few moments, and allow yourself to interact with or simply be in the presence of this trust. In the silence, see whether your resonances and your resistances to such an idea become a little clearer.

• For the present we have completed our reading of this passage. You might want to return to it during your journey. For as we have seen, John does not so much communicate specific knowledge as share a vision. Thus our own goal in reading is not to extract what is there and so exhaust the passage. Rather, each reading can be a renewed entry into the vision, and each time we enter we bring with us a different aspect of our self, permitting it to come into the presence of the vision and be touched by it.

Eventually you might want to take a step beyond reading this passage or other Scripture. You might decide to memorize the text so that it becomes an intimate part of you. If you do, be aware of how the relationship between yourself and the text changes as a result of memorization. What new areas of the text are opened up and expanded for you? How are you changed by committing the text to memory?

• But for now we wish to conclude this exploration by once more reflecting on our reading process. Take out the paper you titled "Learning How to Read." In the margin enter today's date. Then spend a few minutes reflecting on the process we have just completed. How was the reading different from ordinary reading? What did you gain or lose by reading in this way? Did you experience obstacles to reading this way? How is what you learned through this kind of reading different from what you might have learned through your usual manner of reading? Do you see ways to deepen this experience of reading the next time you do it? Take a few minutes to jot down your reflections.

EXPLORATION **3** **GUIDED MEDITATION ON PARSIFAL**
time: twenty minutes

Although we have finished reading John 1:1-5, we shall continue to examine John's thoughts as we perform other explorations by which we can examine the place and importance of meaning. This exploration is a guided meditation. We shall be performing many such meditations on our pilgrimage. To do them, all we need is our imagination.

Unfortunately, in our culture imagination is not highly regarded, and so our imaginations may not be well developed. Our educational systems do not give imagination half the attention spent on perfecting our analytic and reasoning powers. So unless we happen to be particularly gifted in the arts, our imaginations are likely to be quite weak, not because they are poor or inadequate, but because they have been allowed to atrophy while other abilities were being culitvated. As we make our pilgrimage, we will attempt the use of imaginative meditations to discover a new vision of our world and a new way of "reading" our life. We might find these meditations difficult at first, but let's not be discouraged. If we return to these forms of meditations again and again in a spirit of enjoyment, we will find that with each attempt, we are strengthening our imaginative powers. Not only will each meditation be important in terms of what it can reveal to us at different stages of our journey, but the development of our imagination will enrich our total being.

Since our culture does not value the powers of the imagination as much as those of reason, we might believe that nothing of real significance could happen through imaginative play. If we don't really expect results from fantasy, such a belief easily turns into a self-fulfilling prophecy. Since we have entered into a spirit of exploration for our pilgrimage, let's guard against negative attitudes that actually prevent anything from happening. More positively, we should try to be alert to what we are thinking and feeling below the surface because such thoughts and feelings can be immensely important.

Our society's general dismissal of imagination's value may adversely influence our explorations in another way as well. Imagination is very different from the more familiar mental activity of reasoning. Therefore it will have a different feel to it. When the answer to a problem is arrived at, there is a feeling of certainty: "Eureka, I've found it!" We should not expect the same kind of feeling from our work with imagination. Real and well-remembered as imaginative experiences may be, they bear resemblance to a mirage or a dream when compared with the intellectual clarity and concreteness associated with the reasoning process. Especially at the beginning of our pilgrimage we might feel that the experience of imagination is weak. This is simply because we have not had enough practice. So let's accept the experience for what it is and enjoy whatever happens.

We are not likely to have that "Eureka" certainty after completing a meditation in which we have used the powers of imagination. We will probably not be sure whether the experience answers our inquiry or whether it is the right response at all. This feeling of uncertainty is part of imaginative thinking. Results here come in the forms of hints and wispy thought-forms rather than definitive pictures. But the perception and power of imagination is no weaker or less fit a tool because it has this element of uncertainty. With time, practice, and experience we shall enjoy this very quality as one of imagination's unique gifts.

There are a number of ways to do these guided meditations. If you are working alone, the easiest (though not the best way) would be to sit down with this guide and read through the exploration. Better still, record the meditation on a cassette. You can then enter into the meditation and allow the tape to guide you. Simply give yourself ample time for meditating as you record the meditation on tape. Finally, if you are working as a part of a group, choose someone to lead the meditation. Then rotate the leadership for the next meditation. As you gain experience leading others in a meditation, you will discover just how you can help people get the most out of the meditation.

Our meditation today will take about twenty minutes. We begin with a few moments of centering ourselves so that our minds are calm and collected, our bodies relaxed, at ease. This centering with which we begin all our meditations is as important as the actual meditation. It is itself meditation, and it makes possible the work of imagination that follows.

• We must first find a way to sit that will aid our meditation, a position that mades us comfortable but also keeps us attentive. This means that our spine should be straight but not rigid. Lying down to meditate makes it probable that relaxation will prevail over attention—we tend to fall asleep. But if we sit rigidly, we will not be receptive to the delicate feelings and thoughts of the meditation.

You might try sitting in a comfortable, cross-legged position on the floor. It isn't necessary to assume the full lotus posture, which many Easterners use for meditation, although centuries of practice have revealed this and the Zen posture of sitting in a kneeling position to be very good for meditation. The position you choose should be comfortable and easy for you to maintain for about twenty minutes.

If you choose to sit in a chair (this is probably the best position for most beginning Westerners), choose a hard chair with a straight back, and don't lean against the back of the chair. Instead, sit forward on the chair, supporting your back yourself. Experiment to find a position in which your back is both straight and relaxed. Sit with your feet flat on the floor and your hands resting on your knees. See if you can sit so that you do not have to continually concentrate on holding your back straight.

When you have found your position, shut your eyes and spend a few minutes observing your breathing. Follow you breath as it enters and leaves your body. Do not change it in any way; only be aware of it. Seek for a quiet, peaceful attentiveness. Do not strain to do this work, but do not let your mind wander around either. As you observe your breathing, you will notice that this simple act of attention can actually deepen your peace and calm.

Imagine that with each breath that enters your body a deeper feeling of peace and relaxation comes to you. As you notice any areas of tension in your body, imagine letting go of the tension as you exhale. The tension leaves you along with the breath. When you are centered and at peace in mind, feelings, and body, begin the exploration.

32

• Once again our exploratory story concerns the quest for the Holy Grail, the chalice from which Jesus and his disciples drank at the Last Supper. During the Middle Ages the story of the quest for the Grail was popular all over Europe (not only in Arthurian England) as a way of speaking about the spiritual search in which we ourselves are engaged. The Grail came to be a symbol both for that spiritual quest and for the gift of wholeness and fulfillment that the Grail would bestow upon any who were allowed into its presence.

Our story concerns a young knight, Parsifal, who eventually will not only discover the Grail but will become king over the knights who serve the Grail. Our story begins with a quite different king, the Fisher King, Parsifal's predecessor in the service of the Grail.

The Fisher King suffers from a mysterious wound in his side. It is similar to the wound Jesus received from the soldier's spear as he hung upon the cross. The wound in the Fisher King's side will not heal; it saps all his strength, ambition, and hope.

But not only is the king incapacitated; what is even more amazing, his entire kingdom suffers with him. The springs, fountains, and rivers throughout the kingdom cease to flow and eventually dry up. The river beds first become stagnant pools of water, then just masses of mud; then the mud dries and cracks, leaving only empty ditches. The trees, flowers, and plants wither and die throughout the kingdom. The animals are barren; even the king's subjects beget no more children. The decay, neglect, depression, and sickness go so far that the very buildings, castles, houses, and barns become rundown, crumble, and fall in ruins.

• Begin your meditation by imagining the process we have been describing. You come into the kingdom and observe what is happening. As you journey toward the castle of the king, you witness the barrenness. Allow your imagination to fill in the details. The springs and rivers are dried up; the vegetation withered and dead; the people listless and hopeless; even the buildings are in collapse. You feel the heavy weight of despair hanging over all.

The knights who serve the Grail and the Fisher King go forth on perilous journeys seeking a medicine that might heal the king's wound and rescue the kingdom, but all to no avail.

• Enter the story now by becoming one of those knights who serve the Holy Grail. Feel the frustration, the helplessness. You have ridden out into the world, and now you return with a new herb which you hope might bring some relief to the king. You enter the courtyard where the other knights are assembled.

There is a huge old oak tree in the center of the courtyard. It is barren of leaves and even the bark looks unhealthy. It too is dying. As you gaze at this oak, see it as a symbol of the sickness that pervades the entire kingdom.

Whenever a knight returns to court he first asks his comrades about the king's health; to do so is courtly etiquette. So you approach a group of knights and ask your question. They shake their heads: Nothing has changed in your absence. You hand over the herb to one of the king's pages, but you have no hope that it will work. Feel the heaviness and despair of living in this world.

• As you assume your place of waiting in the courtyard with the other knights and ladies, a new figure enters. It is a knight, but a rather peculiar one. He is very young and is obviously quite poor, for his armor is battered and rusty. He is awkward and clumsy, almost a ridiculous figure. Instead of making his way to the other knights to inquire concerning the king, this knight marches right through the courtyard and up to the porch where the king reclines on his bed. He asks the king, *"Where is the Grail?"*

Suddenly we see a wonderful thing unfolding before us. The king looks up at the young man; the king's face is now radiant. He rises from his bed, cured of his mysterious wound, a beautiful smile beaming from his face.

Suddenly life and health return to the old oak in the courtyard. How did it happen? What are you thinking and feeling as you see the transformation occur?

As you look about you, the entire world is renewed. The buildings are restored to their former beauty; the water in the fountain flows once again. As you observe these changes, ask yourself what it was in the young knight's question that could work such a marvel.

What does it mean to ask, "Where is the Grail?" If the Grail is able to bring wholeness and fulfillment to us, then is it enough just to ask the question concerning the Grail? Does merely asking that question (in our case the question of meaning) in itself change us? Can our life be renewed and changed just by turning our attention to our growth and development?

Let's consider the situation of the king and his knights. They lived in service to the Grail. But in their kingdom the Grail was forgotten because the king's illness and its remedy consumed everyone's time. Nevertheless, the true remedy was not far to seek at all; indeed, it existed all along right in their midst. Could the same be true in our own life? Could our search, which perhaps we believe will carry us far and wide, be really a search for something very close to home? Could it be a search for something we have simply forgotten or overlooked?

Allow these considerations to be with you as you now slowly journey forth from the castle and retrace your path away from the castle and through the kingdom. What does it mean to ask that question about the Grail? Can just the decision to ask that question about my life and its meaning create the same transformation in my own kingdom?

• As we leave this story, let's review what has happened here. How do we feel about what we have witnessed? Does it appeal to us? Do we find it difficult to believe? If so, why? What prevents us from believing the meaning of the story? How did our entering into this story help us examine the importance of meaning in our own life?

In those times when our own life has taken on new radiance, when we like the Fisher King have been renewed and cured, has there been renewed *meaning* as well? Can you say that renewal happened *because* meaning entered into your life at that time? Can you believe that meaning really has the power to renew and transform us? Or are you at least *drawn* to this belief? Do you *want* to believe it?

Most of the time we do not really consider the question of life's meaning. As a result, life seems monotonous, unfruitful, aimless; it is simply something that *happens* to us. But once we ask what life means—once we have come to see the importance of meaning, of wholeness, of fulfillment—transformation can occur. As with those knights of old, life for us becomes a quest, and meaning is already there; life takes on a shape and a purpose. In some sense, the Grail is already among us. Life is no longer routine, unfruitful, aimless. We have set off on an adventure, and our life has blossomed; the wasteland about us flowers into a lush garden.

EXPLORATION **4** **LIVING WITH AND WITHOUT MEANING**
time: five one-minute
periods a day for one week

New let's move our investigation into the present time and consider the place of meaning in our everyday existence. Our exploration is quite simple: During the next week we will observe the presence or absence of meaning in an ordinary day. Since our exploration will occupy only five one-minute periods each day, you may also want to work on the next exploration this week; it will complement this week's work.

• For the first three days we will explore the possibility and the experience of an absence of meaning in our lives. Just after you awaken each day, remind yourself of the exploration. If you are awakened by an alarm clock, associate the exploration with the alarm—an alarm to awaken us to the possibility of meaning in our life. We will explore for one minute, five times during the day. During the minute, continue to do whatever you are engaged in, but pretend that there is no meaning in it. As we do the exploration over the next three days, we will come to see the extent and the importance of meaning in our lives, and what our lives might be like with less meaning than is now present.

Remember that during the minute of the exploration you are to drain everything of all meaning. There is thus no meaning in words, thoughts, communication of any kind. Don't except anything in your world from this experiment; *everything* must be seen as meaningless. What would this minute be like? Of course, you should continue whatever you are doing at the time. If you are engaged in conversation, continue the conversation. In the experiment we are merely observing ourselves; we are stepping back and imagining what that moment would be like devoid of meaning.

• Before you retire for the night, spend a minute reflecting upon the day's explorations. What did you notice today? Did you observe a greater depth of meaning during the rest of the day because of the explorations? Take a piece of notebook paper, title the page "Observations on meaning and its absence," date each entry in the margin, and jot down your feelings and observations on the day's explorations.

36

• On the fourth, fifth, and sixth days we will continue the same format: five one-minute sessions each day. But instead of imagining an absence of meaning during our experimental time, we will explore the opposite situation. During these explorations, pretend that there is a wealth of meaning in whatever is happening. Continue to do whatever you were doing, but be aware of all the possibilities of meaning present—in words, conversations, signs, thoughts, gestures, symbols. If the minute does not appear to be filled with meaning for you, see whether you could imagine more meaning in it: What would happen if more meaning were present? At the end of each day, reflect on your explorations and jot down your reflections.

• On the seventh day we will conclude our exploration. Before, we either emptied or filled the moment with meaning. Now we simply want to observe the amount of meaning actually present to us in each minute. As you do your review at the end of this day, ask yourself just how much meaning was present in each minute and how important the meaning was for you.

If you like, continue this phase of the exploration for another week or so. Since we are seeking the importance of meaning for our lives, you might also consider whether you are *satisfied* with the place and importance of meaning in your life. Would you like more meaning or a different kind of meaning? What would your life be like with a deeper meaning? Finally, ask yourself whether this exploration has helped you become aware of and appeciative of the meaning already present and possible in your life.

5 READING OF TWO VISIONS OF LIFE
time: two twenty-minute sessions

This exploration may be done during the week you are carrying out Exploration 4. Now we are going to bring our exploration of meaning back to the Bible.

While we are continuing our exploration of meaning, we will also pursue our goal of learning how to read in a way that creates change. Each passage requires only a few minutes to read in the ordinary manner, but we will spend twenty minutes on each one. We are reading to explore the world of meaning and ultimately, to stimulate growth in our lives. We are not reading primarily to gain information, to absorb a *concept*. Rather we ourselves are seeking to be transformed. If that is our ultimate purpose, then *we* at least are as important to the reading process as is the book we read. Ordinary reading might be called a monologue: The book speaks, and we accept or reject. But in this different reading, we are engaged in a dialogue in which our response to the book is as important as what the book says.

In Western tradition, Scripture, or the Holy Book, is often believed to demand unquestioning acceptance. But this assumption is not quite true. The collection of books called Scripture can be seen quite easily as an ongoing dialogue between God and humanity. The picture of God that emerges from the Scriptures is not so much of a God who demands docility as a God willing to dialogue, to argue, to cajole, to commune. Dialogue does not necessarily involve agreement or assent, although it strives toward those ideals. It demands of both parties respect and a willingness to listen, but it does not impose servility upon one party. The name *Israel* (the human partner in the Judeo-Christian biblical dialogue) means "he who struggles against God and prevails." For it is in this deep struggle with God (or with meaning, as we are calling it) that our lives can open to new horizons.

When we read Scripture as a dialogue, we will need to bring everything we are into the dialogue, and we will expect to be met as fully from the other side. When read in this way, Scripture becomes not only a mirror in which we can truly see ourselves but also a means to enter a larger universe and a broader understanding of it and of ourselves.

Since we do not so much read as relate to Scripture, some disagreement is inevitable. The disagreement may be so serious that we must reject what is said, but this rejection is also a part of our tradition. Indeed, the whole history of Israel as well as of the Christian church can be seen as a struggle with, misunderstanding of, rejection of, and return to the vision of life revealed in these writings. But dialogue also includes the possibility of seeing things from new perspectives. It might change our own way of seeing the world and living in it. But dialogue cannot occur if we are only half present or if we allow the Scriptures to be only half present to us. Nor can anything happen if these two elements, ourselves and the Scriptures, do not risk interacting.

The dialogue then needs a scaffolding that will allow these conditions to be met. To begin, how can we be as present to this dialogue as possible? The techniques we are learning in our meditations can help us. We can use the first five minutes of our reading session to prepare ourselves for our reading. Sometimes, depending upon our own condition, it might take longer than five minutes; that's all right. But the preparation time is essential. If it is not done well, the reading will suffer.

The following paragraphs explain the seven-step process we will apply to our reading today and throughout our future explorations.

1. First, arrange an environment conducive to reading (or meditating). Are you comfortable, but able to remain alert? Have you sufficient light? Are you assured that you won't be interrupted? Are distracting noises at a minimum? When you have seen to all of this, sit down and close your eyes for a few minutes. Ask yourself if there is anything on your mind that might interfere with your reading process. Make a mental note to attend to these things after the session; then put them aside. For the remainder of the five minutes simply listen to your breath entering and leaving your body.

As the preparation period draws to a close, create a mood of receptivity. Suggest gently to yourself that you be open to whatever you might receive in this reading. Give yourself permission to enter into the process of reading wholeheartedly, and assure yourself that you will encounter there what your heart most desires.

2. Next, begin the actual reading. Since we are entering into a dialogue, someone must initiate it. We might come to our reading with a certain question or frame of mind. We may wish to grapple with a certain problem in our reading. So we can initiate the dialogue by allowing our question or our concern to form itself as fully as it can.

This process of initiating the dialogue involves more than merely phrasing a question such as "Is there a meaning to life?" This might indeed be our concern as we begin our reading today. But if we are to bring all of ourselves to this reading, we will be bringing more than this question. For example, how do you feel as you ask the question? Why did the question arise at this moment? Are there incidents or people who have contributed to the reality of this moment? What kind of response are you seeking from your reading today? With such questions we are setting up the dialogue in terms of what we are bringing to it and what we hope to receive from it.

But the Scriptures can also set up the dialogue. In this instance read through the passage you intend to work upon. Read it deliberately and slowly. If convenient, read it out loud. The Scriptures were originally intended to be oral literature, and most were proclaimed long before they assumed written form. When we reduce them to silent reading they lose much of their power. In the course of your reading explorations, observe the differences between what you read silently, what you read out loud, and what you hear proclaimed. (For you may also do this reading as part of a group. Then it becomes a different experience too, one closer to the original setting of the literature.) Teach yourself to notice the different kinds of reading; it is a step closer to the kind of reading we are seeking.

3. Read the passage through at least twice. Then take a few moments to reflect: What is the author trying to say? At this point we are not concerned with our own reactions. In true dialogue it is necessary first to listen to and understand each partner.

4. Now go back to the passage, but this time paraphrase the contents, using your own words, ideas, images, and stories. Then read it again, asking how closely your paraphrase retained the original sense and emphasis. Is there a shift in emphasis, a change in viewpoint? Are there other differences? This process should enable us to come closer to the original intention and thought.

What is at stake is not so much acquiring a body of information or teaching as coming into the presence of a wisdom, a way of understanding our life and world. Thus attitude, feeling, tone, emotional response are as important as ideas, concepts, and images. Do not limit yourself to an understanding of the head; an understanding of the heart and of the body is crucial as well.

This entire process has set the stage for the dialogue. How do we respond to what we have heard? Do we agree with it? Do certain elements give us pause, or even seem unacceptable? What about our emotional response? How does our own vision of the world differ from that of our partner in dialogue? Why? How are the two visions similar? What do you immediately relate to in what your partner says? Can you understand why these things appeal to you?

5. Focus now on your acceptance and your resistance. Can you come to a clearer, fuller picture of what they are? Suppose the passage speaks about an order to everything, and you find that unacceptable. Why do you resist such an idea? Mental reasons do not tell the whole story. Look for experiences in your own life that have taught you to think differently from your partner in dialogue. Perhaps you resist this element because accepting it would force you to reexamine other elements of your own world vision. What are those other elements? It is this kind of questioning that our dialogue with Scripture is designed to raise.

6. Conclude the reading process by summarizing your experience. Whether we agreed or disagreed with our partner in the dialogue is not the primary concern. Rather, the summary is more of an appreciation and bringing to consciousness of the process than a scoring of points. The process of reading is more crucial than what was read or said in response.

What happened in the process itself? Did we experience any movement? Did we feel ourselves opening? Closing down? Were we distracted? If so, when and how? Was it only an accidental occurrence, or was the distraction related to the reading? By becoming attentive to the process, we learn to become aware of the subtle movements of our own spirit.

7. Finally, close your eyes again and sit in silence for a moment. Be present to whatever is happening within you. This final moment of silence is like the process of digesting our food. In the silence we give ourselves time to assimilate what we have received through the ministry of words.

• Now let's put this process into practice. Our readings consist of two different Old Testament passages that focus on the presence of meaning in human existence. They are taken from Ecclesiastes and Ecclesiasticus, two biblical books that have similar names but are far removed from each other in spirit and outlook. (Ecclesiastes is found in the Old Testament; Ecclesiasticus is in the Old Testament of Catholic Bibles and in the Apocrypha [not always included] of other Bibles.)

Our first selection is from Ecclesiastes—a word derived from the Greek word for preacher. This particular preacher is an out-and-out pessimist. There is nothing new under the sun, according to him. His selection fits quite well into the first three days of Exploration 4. As you spend your twenty minutes with him today, try to enter his world. How does it strike you? How would it feel to see the world this way? What kind of life would this outlook lead you to live? How would you respond to the author from your own world view? Can you bring your own feelings about life and its meaning into a sharper focus through your dialogue with the preacher? As you read, it might be helpful to understand the preacher's use of the word *wisdom* as similar to our own use of *meaning*. (The ideas about wisdom in both these passages underlie the thought of John in the gospel passage we studied in Exploration 2.)

> I the Preacher was king over Israel in Jerusalem. And I gave my heart to seek and search out by wisdom concerning all things that are done under heaven: this sore travail hath God given to the sons of man to be exercised therewith. I have

seen all the works that are done under the sun; and, behold, all is vanity and vexation of spirit. That which is crooked cannot be made straight: and that which is wanting cannot be numbered. I communed with mine own heart, saying, Lo, I am come to great estate, and have gotten more wisdom than all that have been before me in Jerusalem: yea, my heart had great experience of wisdom and knowledge. And I gave my heart to know wisdom, and to know madness and folly: I perceived that this also is vexation of spirit. For in much wisdom is much grief: and he that increaseth knowledge increaseth sorrow.

I said in mine heart, Go to now, I will prove thee with mirth, therefore enjoy pleasure: and, behold, this also is vanity. I said of laughter, It is mad: and of mirth, What doeth it? I sought in mine heart to give myself unto wine, yet acquainting mine heart with wisdom; and to lay hold on folly, till I might see what was that good for the sons of men, which they should do under the heaven all the days of their life. I made me great works; I builded me houses; I planted me vineyards: I made me gardens and orchards, and I planted trees in them of all kind of fruits: I made me pools of water, to water therewith the wood that bringeth forth trees: I got me servants and maidens, and had servants born in my house; also I had great possessions of great and small cattle above all that were in Jerusalem before me: I gathered me also silver and gold, and the peculiar treasure of kings and of the provinces: I gat me men singers and women singers, and the delights of the sons of men, as musical instruments, and that of all sorts. So I was great, and increased more than all that were before me in Jerusalem: also my wisdom remained with me. And whatsoever mine eyes desired I kept not from them, I withheld not my heart from any joy; for my heart rejoiced in all my labour: and this was my portion of all my labour. Then I looked on all the works that my hands had wrought, and on the labour that I had laboured to do: and, behold, all was vanity and vexation of spirit, and there was no profit under the sun.

42

And I turned myself to behold wisdom, and madness, and folly: for what can the man do that cometh after the king? even that which hath been already done. Then I saw that wisdom excelleth folly, as far as light excelleth darkness. The wise man's eyes are in his head; but the fool walketh in darkness: and I myself perceived also that one event happeneth to them all. Then said I in my heart, As it happeneth to the fool, so it happeneth even to me; and why was I then more wise? Then said I in my heart, that this also is vanity. For there is no remembrance of the wise more than of the fool for ever; seeing that which now is in the days to come shall all be forgotten. And how dieth the wise man? as the fool. Therefore I hated life; because the work that is wrought under the sun is grievous unto me: for all is vanity and vexation of spirit.

Yea, I hated all my labour which I had taken under the sun: because I should leave it unto the man that shall be after me. And who knoweth whether he shall be a wise man or a fool? yet shall he have rule over all my labour wherein I have laboured, and wherein I have shewed myself wise under the sun. This is also vanity. Therefore I went about to cause my heart to despair of all the labour which I took under the sun. For there is a man whose labour is in wisdom, and in knowledge, and in equity; yet to a man that hath not laboured therein shall he leave it for his portion. This also is vanity and great evil. For what hath man of all his labour, and of the vexation of his heart, wherein he hath laboured under the sun? For all his days are sorrows, and his travail grief; yea, his heart taketh not rest in the night. This is also vanity.

There is nothing better for a man, than that he should eat and drink, and that he should make his soul enjoy good in his labour. This also I saw, that it was from the hand of God. For who can eat, or who else can hasten hereunto, more than I? For God giveth to a man that is good in his sight wisdom, and knowledge, and joy: but to the sinner he giveth travail, to gather and to heap up, that he may give to him that is good before God. This also is vanity and vexation of spirit.

Ecclesiastes 1:12-18, 2:1-26
The King James Version

● For our second reading we turn to a quite different author. The theme is the same as the preacher's, but the vantage point is quite different. Our reading comes from the book of Ecclesiasticus, which means the "Church Book." For in the early Church it was used to instruct new converts in morality and human life. It is also known as Sirach after its supposed author. Sirach sings many songs in honor of wisdom. But unlike the preacher, he is not pessimistic; everything does not tend only toward futility.

Read through the passage from Sirach, first only to grasp what the author is saying. Next use your imagination to paraphrase what the author is saying. You do not have to use words. You might paraphrase by using only visual images; imagine this same passage done as a silent film in your mind. Or you might want to dance the passage, paint it, mime it, sing it. The important aspect of paraphrasing is that it enables you to enter into the real spirit of what you have read, to enter into the dialogue-partner's skin.

After you have paraphrased, enter into dialogue with Sirach. How do you relate to his viewpoint, his attitude toward the world? Finally, bring back the preacher and create a trialogue among Sirach, the preacher, and yourself. How do each of you speak and address the others concerning the place of meaning and wisdom in the world?

44

Wisdom speaks her own praises,
in the midst of her people she glories
   in herself.
She opens her mouth in the assembly of
   the Most High,
she glories in herself in the presence
   of the Mighty One;
"I came forth from the mouth of the Most
   High,
and I covered the earth like a mist.
I had my tent in the heights,

and my throne in a pillar of cloud.
Alone I encircled the vault of the sky,
and I walked on the bottom of the deeps.
Over the waves of the sea and over the whole earth,
and over every people and nation I have
    held sway.
Among all these I searched for rest,
and looked to see in whose territory I
    might pitch camp.
Then the creator of all things instructed
    me,
and he who created me fixed a place
    for my tent.
He said, 'Pitch your tent in Jacob,
Make Israel your inheritance.'
From eternity, in the beginning, he
    created me,
and for eternity I shall remain.
I ministered before him in the holy
    tabernacle,
and thus was I established on Zion.
In the beloved city he has given me rest,
and in Jerusalem I wield my authority.
I have taken root in a privileged people,
in the Lord's property, in his inheritance.
I have grown tall as a cedar on Lebanon,
as a cypress on Mount Hermon;
I have grown tall as a palm in Engedi,
as the rose bushes of Jericho;
as a fine olive in the plain,
as a plane tree I have grown tall.
I have exhaled a perfume like cinnamon
    and acacia,
I have breathed out a scent like choice myrrh,
like galbanum, onycha and stacte,
like the smoke of incense in the tabernacle.
I have spread my branches like a terebinth,
and my branches are glorious and graceful.
I am like a vine putting out graceful shoots,

my blossoms bear the fruit of glory and wealth.
Approach me, you who desire me,
and take your fill of my fruits,
for memories of me are sweeter than honey,
inheriting me is sweeter than the honeycomb.
They who eat me will hunger for more,
they who drink me will thirst for more.
Whoever listens to me will never have to
   blush,
whoever acts as I dictate will never sin."

Ecclesiasticus 24:1-22
The Jerusalem Bible

•   You may continue this investigation, if you wish, by proceeding in the same fashion through other passages of these two books. Ecclesiastes is quite a short book and should provide no real difficulties. Ecclesiasticus is much longer. You might hunt around in it for what you want, or read through the book at your ordinary reading speed and when your come upon a passage that appeals to you, read it as you have learned to do here.

46

As you begin to read the Bible, try not to feel intimidated. True, it is a formidable book: over a thousand pages long; over a thousand years old; revered and argued over for centuries. It is enough to scare anyone away. But the Bible is first and foremost a book of the people, and perhaps the most read book in the Western world. It was not written for experts and scholars. It began as popular literature—tribal literature.

If you find yourself bogged down in a passage, move on to another. Not everything in this book is going to speak to us or be worthwhile to us all the time. If we meet something we do not understand or find difficult to relate to, let's accept that feeling and move on.

Reading Ecclesiastes may raise another difficulty. Many times it seems as though the author is being inconsistent. He appears to contradict himself; he changes his viewpoint; he says things not typical of his thought. But many of the biblical books have passed through various stages of editing before they assumed the form we are familiar with. Thus, there were other editors of Ecclesiastes after our original author, and some of these editors dialogued with the original author within the book itself; they tempered the original pessimism and seeming agnosticism with a more "orthodox" viewpoint. So discrepancies are not the fault of our author so much as traces of the hands through which the book has passed.

6 THE EXTENDED PRESENT AND ITS MEANING
time: thirty minutes
materials: notebook paper and pen

So far we have investigated the presence of meaning in human life in general and in the everyday moments of our own lives. Now we broaden our exploration as we examine the place of meaning at this particular period in our life. Does the same search for meaning that we found in the story of Parsifal in Exploration 3 manifest itself right now in our life? What nourishment and enlightenment do we receive from the meaning in our life at this time?

47

• On a sheet of notebook paper, write "My Extended Present," dating your entry in the margin. In this exploration we will be describing the movements and contents of the present period in our lives. This book has raised the question of meaning. And perhaps we ourselves are becoming conscious of and concerned about meaning.

We begin our exploration by marking off the boundaries of this present moment in our life. There have been other periods of our life when our overall questions, concerns, activities, people, and ideas were not the same as they are today. This current phase of our life is given shape by certain things that have happened to us or that we have done.

Can you see just when this current time in your life began? The beginning of this period might be easy for you to discover. It might be marked by some important event, some change in your life: a move to a new home, a transfer in your job, the beginning or the end of a significant relationship. Or the signs of the new beginning might be more subtle: a shift in outlook, a renewed commitment, depression, the change of a calendar year.

Take a look at this moment of your life. Then ask yourself when it might have begun. Right now you are dealing with certain events, people, and struggles. When do you think this period began? Perhaps it was preceded by certain events that gave it birth but are not really a part of it. List these conditions as instrumental in creating this period.

Now turn your attention to the actual contents of this period. Begin by simply listing the important components of your life at present. What are the important events and people now? What feelings are dominant in your life? What important physical conditions are you dealing with right now? (Consider external conditions, such as environment, and internal conditions, such as physical health. Consider also the place of work and leisure. Include everything of importance to you right now.)

• Now that you have a skeleton outline of your extended present, spend a few minutes reflecting on what you've written. Allow your memory to wander through the contents, savoring whatever each memory calls into presence.

Now sit back, relax, and close your eyes. We are going to seek an image from our unconscious that might help us appreciate the tenor of this present period more deeply. As you sit back and relax, allow the image to come to you. It is not necessary to grasp after it or to go hunting for it. Be open to whatever comes into your consciousness. Explore what arises and allow it to expand. What does the image say about your present life? How does it reveal the texture of this present period?

When you have received your image and allowed it to expand, open your eyes and write a full description of it on your paper. Title your paragraph "Image of My Present Life," and as you write, add any detail that presents itself to you. You may find that in writing the image expands and may even change. Allow it to do so. Follow the image wherever it leads you. The process of writing is important precisely because it can deepen our reflections.

• Now that we have a summary of our present life and an image of it, we can turn to the question of its meaning. Is this a period when you are particularly searching for meaning? In what areas of your life are you most concerned about meaning? Meaning can focus upon many different aspects: sexuality, vocation, philosophy, relationships, health. Where does meaning dwell in your present life?

• When you have completed your writing, read out loud, if possible, what you have written. If you have done this exercise with others, you might want to read it aloud to them. However, it isn't necessary to reveal the contents of your writing, and the possibility of revealing it to others shouldn't color what you write in the first place. The journal work you do is meant to help you come into contact with the deep currents of your life; an idea that it is meant to be shared could affect your writing. If you do decide to read your work aloud to others, the group should listen, but need not respond. It is enough to listen to one another's writing: it helps the reader by reading it out loud, and it aids the listeners by giving them a sense of how other lives are structured and of how others have performed the same explorations. As you read your work, jot down in the margins or at the end of your writing any feelings, thoughts, or reactions that result from the reading.

• Our reading of the first paragraph of John's gospel has led us to explore the importance of meaning both in human life generally and in our own life. Now we'll return to the gospel so that John may continue to direct these first steps of our pilgrimage.

> A man called John was sent by God as a witness to the light, so that any man who heard his testimony might believe in the light. This man was not himself the light: he was sent simply as a personal witness to that light.
>
> John 1:6-8
> *The New Testament in Modern English*

Use your new skills in reading to examine this passage. How does it continue and fill out the exploration of meaning that John has begun? Notice that John continues his theme of light, but now the focus shifts from the light itself to this man named John (not the gospel writer but John the Baptist). John is a witness to the light.

In our own pilgrimage we will continue to explore the theme of light and meaning by seeking meaning in our own lives. Through exploring the meaning, we will deepen our own understanding and appreciation of the place of meaning in our lives.

7 WITNESSES TO MEANING
time: thirty minutes
materials: notebook paper and pen

In our last exploration we explored the search for meaning in our present lives. Now we gaze backwards, looking for moments in our past that have shaped and defined your lives. Seen from our present vantage point, what has shaped your life, and what place has meaning occupied in it? Could these stages in your life's journey be like John the Baptist—pointers toward the meaning of your life? Do they reveal to you the meaning already present in your life?

• Sit down with your writing materials. Entitle this page "Stages of My Life's Journey" and date your entry. Then take a few minutes to relax and quiet your body and mind. Sit back in your chair; close your eyes. If any part of your body is tense, imagine that area relaxing as you exhale. If you find thoughts and concerns that might intrude on your exploration, acknowledge them and assure yourself that you will give them the attention they deserve after the exploration is completed.

With your eyes closed, allow your memory to wander through your past. What have been the two or three major moments in your life so far? Imagine your life as a suspension bridge. One end of the bridge is your birth; the present moment forms the other end; the landmark moments are the suspension pillars from which the bridge hangs.

• On your sheet of paper, number from 1 to 12 down the left-hand margin. We are going to look for about twelve of these suspension points, these landmarks in our own life's journey. We already know some of them. After number 1 write: "I was born on. . . ." Now think of the next dozen or so peak moments, turning points, periods of your life. It might take some time to sort them out. After number 2, write "and then. . . ." We are writing a brief outline of our own history. When we have finished, our outline might look something like this:

> and then I went to school
> and then I started my career as a doctor
> and then I met Bob and we were married

• When you have completed your list, read it over to yourself, out loud if possible. How does it sound? What are your reactions and feelings as you read it? Enter your reactions in the margin or at the end of the exercise.

• Now we can consider the importance of meaning in each of these periods. Can you remember what each of these periods meant to you at the time you were living it? Did some seem chaotic, meaningless? Were others tremendously significant and full of meaning? Next ask yourself what meaning each of these periods has for you from the vantage point of the present moment. Do some periods have a meaning and significance for you today that they did not originally have? Have periods that at the time seemed senseless taken on meaning from this later vantage point?

Now let's consider the overall place of meaning in our life. What periods were relatively meaningless? How did it feel to live through them? How do they differ from those periods that seemed significant and filled with meaning? Write a brief paragraph that describes the presence and absence of meaning in your life's journey. How important has meaning been throughout your life? How does a meaningful life differ from one in which meaning is lacking?

7a

**FURTHER EXPLORATIONS
OF WITNESSES TO MEANING (optional)
time: indefinite   materials: notebook paper and pen**

• If you wish to continue the explorations we began in Exploration 7, treat each period of your life in the same way we explored the extended present in Exploration 6. Describe each of these periods in detail. Who were the important people? What happened in your own life during this time? What were the dominant feelings and ideas? How did you think of your life during that time?

• Once your memory has resurrected the period, explore the period for the place and importance of meaning. How would it have been different if there were less meaning present, or more? Was there meaning present that escaped your notice at the time? How might you have become aware of it?

The reclamation of our own past is enjoyable. Try to keep this and all the other explorations we perform pleasant for yourself. For if our pilgrimage brings us pleasure, we will be that much more motivated to continue our journey.

EXPLORATION **8** **DEVELOPING OUR WITNESS**
time: ten minutes a day for one week

We have concluded all our explorations by turning our attention to the process of the exploration itself. This examination is not incidental to our quest, nor is it done to guarantee the correctness of the exploration. In this process of examination, we are developing the capacity to witness to what is happening on our pilgrimage.

The spiritual path is not straightforward and obviously marked. Spiritual movements do not manifest themselves in the same way as do those of the body or mind. For the most part, the spiritual is not open to direct observation; it must be approached by a circuitous route.

Much of our work on this pilgrimage will consist of learning to become aware of processes that ordinarily escape consciousness. For example, are you really aware of how you can move into a state of depression? Many of us would say that depression just happens. Yet we can only say so because we are not conscious of the subtle patterns that, without our knowledge, are capable of blowing us here and there into depression or fear or joy even against our conscious will.

We are engaged in a difficult task when we decide to bring our spiritual life into consciousness and to take a hand in directing its growth. It is not so much a problem of having adequate physical strength or a certain intellectual ability. Indeed, many of our explorations will appear ridiculously easy. We might read an exploration over and say that we already know what it is looking for.

But do we? Does our knowledge of the outcome arise from our own experience or is it proffered by our intellect, which tells us what we *should* experience, or from our world, which tells us what *it* believes we should experience? To a large extent our life is determined by intellect and opinion, and in many ways these are at variance with the reality of the spiritual dimension. So our knowledge of the spiritual journey must come from our own experience; we cannot afford to trust either knowledge or opinion.

The explorations are easy to perform, but it is not always so easy to observe what is happening in them. If we develop this capacity of witnessing, then, like John the Baptist, we could witness the coming of the light into our own life.

There are really two parts to each of our explorations. First we put ourselves into the situation: Does the world of the exploration speak to or appeal to us? Does it beckon us to a fuller and richer life? In these explorations we are testing the hypotheses of the spiritual path. For example: Is the spiritual life a life where meaning is supremely important? But the exploration is designed not only to test hypotheses. Equally important are our own lives and experiences. How do the explorations bring the workings of our own spirit into consciousness so that we can determine whether the hypotheses have anything to offer us for the living of our life? The explorations are designed to reveal the feelings and thoughts (mostly unconscious) that have patterned us and that create the world we live in. On our spiritual journey, we want to move behind those feelings and thoughts into a deeper and more satisfying experience of life. Thus in these explorations we are not only evaluating the hypotheses that the spiritual path provides; we are also evaluating the hypotheses on which we have been basing our lives. To do that, we need to develop a witness to the light—either a loving outside observer or at least a capacity to observe ourselves; otherwise we will continue in darkness.

First we wish to discover just what the exploration has revealed. In the course of the exploration, did we catch a glimpse of the light coming into our life? What did the exploration reveal about this spiritual pilgrimage we are on? What did it reveal about our own lives and our own thought processes?

It is important that we do not confuse the role of witness with that of judge. Our lives are filled with making judgments about ourselves and others, and we are tempted to carry the habit into this

53

work as well. We are always evaluating ourselves: I did this poorly; why can't I do it correctly? Judging may be useful in some areas, but it is of little value in the work of witnessing.

The witness does not evaluate; it is concerned with perceiving what is there—quite a task. The presence of the judge makes it more difficult for the witness to do its job; the judge will interfere constantly. For example, various thoughts come into your mind as you are meditating. The witness observes these thoughts as a part of the meditation. But then the judge steps in; he insists that these thoughts are distractions and must be banished from the meditation. Now the witness is likely to ignore these thoughts, dismissing them as irrelevant.

But the thoughts are not irrelevant. There is no such thing as distraction in our meditations. Those thoughts might be speaking to us, though indirectly. It is important, then, that we take notice of them. They are not an expected part of the exploration, but since they *are* part of the experience, it is important that we be aware of them and what they might be telling us. The presence of distracting thoughts is often a good indication that, at some level, our spirit is resisting the exploration.

We should also pay attention to the performance of the exploration. Were there ways in which the exploration could have been conducted so that it might provide clearer results? Could it be purified of chaff and nonessential materials that might bias the exploration? Here our judgment *can* aid us. If we feel that we have not really experienced the exploration correctly, the judge might encourage us to perform it again.

During this week we will use another exercise to develop our witness: our capacity to compassionately observe ourselves. Now instead of observing the process of an exploration, we will observe the process of our day.

This exercise will build the witness which is indispensable to our journey. It willl alert us to the real light which shines in the midst of our life. Witnessing only serves our living. So to practice our witnessing in the arena of our life is to engage in the real exploration and to enter into the real laboratory for which all the explorations are only a preparation and a practice. As John says, the real light, which enlightens everyone, is even now coming into the world.

Later on, the one who is the true Light arrived to shine on everyone coming into the world.

But although he made the world, the world didn't recognize him when he came.

Even in his own land and among his own people, the Jews, he was not accepted. Only a few would welcome him and receive him. But to all who received him, he gave the right to become children of God. All they needed to do was to trust him to save them. All those who believe this are reborn!—not a physical rebirth resulting from human passion or plan—but from the will of God.

John 1:9-13
The Living Bible

John is moving from the ideal world of the first part of his prologue into the real world in which we live. The first sign of conflict appears: The light came into the world, but the world did not recognize it. The Word has been rejected.

Every spirituality and every spiritual journey must recognize that human existence as we know it is not sufficient. Somehow or other we are exiled from what we truly desire, from what would fulfill us and give us true happiness. The insufficiency or resistance has various names: Buddhists call it *samsara*; Christians call it original sin. We may not want to look at this dark side of things; our age does not take to the idea of *sin*. We might prefer to shelve all negative ideas and simply proceed with the path of human development. But it simply is not possible. We must know why this path is so difficult, why the happiness we need is so far away and elusive.

Our exercise this week will let us witness the negative of our life as well as the happiness. We will practice this week's exercise for about ten minutes before going to bed at night. After this week you might want to continue it as a part of your daily spiritual practice. For the next week we'll practice it to observe its power in our lives.

• Do the exercise sitting up in a chair; if you do it lying down you are likely to fall asleep. As in most of these spiritual practices, we are aiming for a delicate balance between relaxation and alertness; if one element dominates at the expense of the other, the exercise is compromised.

Sit with your back straight but not rigid. Close your eyes and take some deep breaths. When you are relaxed and calm, begin the exercise.

• This exercise is a review of the events, thoughts, feelings, and moods of our day. We can begin with our waking up and work forward, or begin with the present moment and work backward. This is an exercise in witnessing; there is no evaluation or judgment. It is not the time to scold yourself for becoming angry with the children. If there was a scene with the children, review it dispassionately in as much detail as possible. What were your feelings? Were there times when you were carried away and not in control? What led up to the scene? (Consider both the incidents and your own emotions, feelings, and thoughts.)

Our capacity to witness depends on our capacity to perceive—to become aware of the entire complex of an event. Lay aside all thoughts of judgment and all resolutions to do better—they don't do much good. Demanding change from ourselves and beating ourselves for failure will accomplish nothing. The first step is only to witness. See if you can understand and appreciate just how such a situation was created. Can you see all the many threads that came together to weave this particular situation? It is only when we can discover how we do create these situations ourselves that we can begin to create new, more satisfying situations.

Use your imaginative powers to aid you in reviewing your day. Sounds, emotions, reactions, sights, tastes, feelings—bring them all into your experience now through your imagination.

EXPLORATION **9** OUR HUMAN CONDITION
time: twenty minutes

Before we can make progress on our journey, we must take a hard look at the human condition. During this week we shall each day explore a different facet of the human condition. By engaging in a week-long series of explorations here and at other points in our journey, we will be able to explore certain matters in depth. To explore the human condition, we must know our origins, because our origins tell us who and what we are. Once we know that, we will know far more about where we should go and how to get there.

By and large the story of Adam and Eve in the Garden of Eden has served as the basis in the West for understanding the human situation. So in this exploration, we will read that story to see just how it speaks of our existence. We do not come to this story for facts of human history or of science; we do not come to it for mere information about the first man and woman. Rather, we ask how it can help us to see and understand our present situation. In our exploration we will enter into the story and decide whether it speaks truth for us. That the story's science and history are primitive and outdated is irrelevant. The question is, is this image of human nature valid for us today?

• Before you read, prepare yourself by sitting down in a comfortable chair, closing your eyes, and focusing attention for a few moments on your breathing. Then take about twenty very deep breaths, inhaling as much breath as you can. Hold each breath a few seconds; then exhale as completely as possible. If you feel yourself becoming dizzy, stop and relax. After twenty breaths, allow your breathing to return to normal.

• When you feel relaxed and calm, begin the reading.

> At the time when the Lord God made the earth and the heavens—while as yet there was no field shrub on earth and no grass of the field had sprouted, for the Lord God had sent no rain upon the earth and there was no man to till the soil, but a stream was welling up out of the earth and was watering all the surface of the ground—the Lord God formed man out of the clay of the ground and blew into his nostrils the breath of life, and so man became a living being.
>
> Genesis 2:46-7
> *The New American Bible*

This description reveals the primitive time-setting of the story. The earth is conceived as a dusty barren plateau, for the earth was thought to be a huge slab of dirt that floated on top of a bowl filled with water.

Such an idea explains how the writer could describe the stream welling up out of the earth. When the water meets the earth, the result is mud, and out of this mud or clay God, like some great potter, creates human beings.

• Allow this primitive picture to form in your imagination; reconstruct the scene in as much detail as possible. Consider the images, sounds, and smells as well as the feelings, tones, and moods. What does this garden feel like? What is it like to be the man there?

> The Lord God then took the man and settled him in the garden of Eden, to cultivate and care for it. The Lord God gave man this order: "You are free to eat from any of the trees of the garden except the tree of the knowledge of good and bad. From that tree you shall not eat; the moment you eat from it you are surely doomed to die."
>
> The Lord God said: "It is not good for the man to be alone. I will make a suitable partner for him." So the Lord God formed out of the ground various wild animals and various birds of the air, and he brought them to the man to see what he would call them; whatever the man called each of them would be its name. The man gave names to all the cattle, all the birds of the air, and all the wild animals; but none proved to be the suitable partner for the man.
>
> So the Lord God cast a deep sleep on the man, and while he was asleep, he took out one of his ribs and closed up its place with flesh. The Lord God then built up into a woman the rib that he had taken from the man. When he brought her to the man, the man said: "This one, at last, is bone of my bones and flesh of my flesh; This one shall be called 'woman,' for out of 'her man' this one has been taken." That is why a man leaves his father and mother and clings to his wife, and the two of them become one body. The man and his wife were both naked, yet they felt no shame.
>
> Genesis 2:15-25
> *The New American Bible*

Even if the image of the creation of woman is not exactly on target in terms of the women's liberation movement today, there is no element of subjugation involved here, other than the fact that woman is created out of Adam and is named in terms of her relationship to "her man". In the passage as a whole, we can see similarities with other primitive creation myths.

Plato tells a similar story in his dialogue *The Symposium*. These stories wish to explain the way we are and help us find ourselves. They view the human situation with a great deal of insight, and from that insight the stories speculate on how the condition arose. For example, in Plato's story the insight into the human condition is an insight into the nature of the sexual urge. Realizing that we have a tremendous desire to couple with one another, a desire that even in the coupling never seems totally satisfied, Plato therefore conjectures that the original human being was a hermaphrodite: both male and female. Hence the fall involved a splitting of what originally had been one whole being into two parts, male and female. Thus our striving to couple is really a longing for that old state of wholeness which has been lost to us.

Plato's story is much more concerned with sexuality than is the story of Adam and Eve, which is often blamed for all the puritanism that follows in its wake.

There is no sexuality directly involved in the myth as we see it in Genesis. The fall occurs because the woman is influenced by the serpent. Later interpretations, based on the fact that Adam "knew" Eve (sexually) only after the fall give the story sexual overtones.

This common misreading of the Adam and Eve story is a good illustration for us as we read on our pilgrimage. The human temptation is to assume that one already knows what one is setting out to learn. Thus when we read a story that we have heard many times before, we tend to fill in what we think the story says rather than meet the story in its own territory.

Another failure to see the story in its own terms arises when the serpent is taken as the Devil. Such an interpretation is not at all a part of the original myth. The serpent is simply the serpent, although no less a sinister figure for that. And the poor serpent is chosen for this dishonorable role partly because the serpent was a powerful god for the fertility cults that existed side by side with Israel and continually tempted the Israelites to abandon their high monotheism for the more sensual rites of these serpent goddesses. Interpreting the serpent as the Devil discredits the cult by blaming the serpent for our original fall.

These misreadings of the Genesis account can warn us to be as careful as possible that we are truly reading what the author wrote rather than what we believe the author wrote. In your reading here and elsewhere try to be aware of the extent to which you are substituting you own ideas for those of the author. For if we are to journey along a spiritual path, and if it is a journey we need help with, then we must learn to see all the blindnesses we create for ourselves by believing (mostly subconsciously) that we already know what we are being told.

Now let's return to the story of Adam and Eve.

Now the serpent was the most cunning of all the animals that the Lord God had made. The serpent asked the woman, "Did God really tell you not to eat from any of the trees in the garden?" The woman answered the serpent: "We may eat of the fruit of the trees in the garden; it is only about the fruit of the tree in the middle of the garden that God said, 'You shall not eat it or even touch it, lest you die.' " But the serpent said to the woman: "You certainly will not die! No, God knows well that the moment you eat of it your eyes will be opened and you will be like gods who know what is good and what is bad." The woman saw that the tree was good for food, pleasing to the eyes, and desirable for gaining wisdom. So she took some of its fruit and ate it; and she also gave some to her husband who was with her, and he ate it. Then the eyes of both of them were opened, and they realized that they were naked; so they sewed fig leaves together and made loincloths for themselves.

When they heard the sound of the Lord God moving about in the garden at the breezy time of the day, the man and his wife hid themselves from the Lord God among the trees of the garden. The Lord God then called to the man and asked him, "Where are you?" He answered, "I heard you in the garden; but I was afraid, because I was naked, so I hid myself." Then he asked, "Who told you that you were naked? You have eaten, then, from the tree of which I had forbidden you to eat!" The man replied, "The woman whom you put here with me—she gave me fruit from the tree, and so I ate it." The Lord God then asked the woman, "Why did you do such a thing?" The woman answered, "The serpent tricked me into it, so I ate it."

Genesis 3:1-13
The New American Bible

We discover the truly primitive nature of our story in God's response to what Adam and Eve have done. "See! The man has become like one of us," he says. (Genesis 3:22) The serpent was apparently right; the fruit would make Adam and Eve as gods. And so it seems that the punishment inflicted on the pair is not so much to punish them for their forbidden action as to prevent them from seizing their godhood forever by eating of the tree of life. "He must not be allowed to stretch his hand out next and eat from the tree of life also," worries God. So Adam and Eve are expelled from the garden.

On the surface, this is quite a tragic story. It is intended to show why the human condition is so difficult, and that condition is spelled out in the curses God flings at Adam and Eve.

61

I will intensify the pangs of your childbearing;
  in pain shall you bring forth children.
Yet your urge shall be for your husband,
  and he shall be your master.
To the man he said:
  "Because you listened to your wife and
    ate from the tree of which I had forbidden you to eat,
  Cursed be the ground because of you!
    In toil shall you eat its yield
    and all the days of your life.
  Thorns and thistles shall it bring forth to you,
    as you eat of the plants of the field.
  By the sweat of your face
    shall you get bread to eat,
  Until you return to the ground,
    from which you were taken;
  For you are dirt,
    and to dirt you shall return."

Genesis 3:16-19
The New American Bible

To come to grips with this myth as a true myth of the human condition, it is not necessary that we accept the concrete details of the curse. What is of more concern is the central idea of a fall from grace, a plunge from the protected conditions of the garden into the present world.

Nor are we obliged to view the myth as primarily an account of human origins. The story has much more importance for us as a psychological narrative. It is not so much the story of our original ancestors as the story we ourselves have lived through in the course of our own human growth. It is on this psychological level that we will explore the story's ability to reveal the truth.

And, finally, we are not obliged to leave the story just as it is. We have seen how through the Christian tradition details of the story have been changed in order to fit into certain Christian understandings of sex and Satan. But the primary Christian reinterpretation of this story flows out of a part of the curse given to the serpent:

> I will put enmity between you and the woman,
> and between your offspring and hers;
> He will strike at your head,
> while you strike at his heel.

Genesis 3:15
The New American Bible

While this passage may have originally been no more than an encouragement to animosity and hostility toward the serpent (and by extension toward all fertility rites in which the serpent figures), the early Christians saw in it a forecast of the struggle between Jesus and evil, a struggle in which Jesus emerges victorious in our name. In the light of Jesus, then, this story became not an end in itself, but the first act in a glorious romance. Instead of the tragedy of human suffering, it now is seen as a necessary and wonderful preparation for the triumphant human pilgrimage toward holiness. "O happy fault!" sings the Christian church at the Easter Vigil. In other words, thank God that Adam ate the fruit of that tree.

For what would be our lot had Adam and Eve not partaken of the fruit? We would still be in that childlike garden, just half a step more evolved than the rest of the animal kingdom. Our fall from that dreamlike existence of Eden provides us with our real humanity. We would have remained children in Eden, for children are those who are ignorant of the difference between good and evil. Would we wish our own children to remain ignorant of this distinction? Would we want them to grow up with no conscience, no knowledge?

By eating the fruit, Adam and Eve took a giant step forward, even though suffering became their lot. For they left behind the smothering nursery of the garden and walked forth into the world as adults.

Each of us has taken this step in our own life. When we examine our lives in terms of this story, we can find that movement from the protected garden into the world. At some time, perhaps not traceable to any one event, we have fallen from the world of the child into that of the adult. And it is truly described as a fall, for we have indeed lost something important: the nursery and its comfort. Nor is it always obvious that we gain. Are the freeway and the supermarket and all the other hassles of adult existence an adequate compensation? The world is not safe. Mommy and Daddy are no longer here to protect us. Our wounds can no longer be healed with just a kiss. We cannot be put to dreamy sleep with a lullaby, although we may try to retreat into that dreamlike world with tranquilizers.

• To conclude today's reading, ask yourself whether you can begin to glimpse that fall in your own life. When and where did the world of childhood close to you and force you into the less secure and frightening world of adults? We will continue our explorations of this view of the human condition throughout the exercises in this week. But are you beginning to see the truth of the story we have read today?

XPLORATION **9a** THE WORLD OF INNOCENCE
time: ten to fifteen minutes

We have lost something through our fall from the garden. But when the myth is interpreted within the Christian context, we begin to see that something has been gained as well. To help us explore just what has been lost and gained, we will read four poems by the great English mystic, William Blake, during the four segments—9a through 9d—of this extended exploration. Blake composed two sets of lyrics called *Songs of Innocence* and *Songs of Experience*. The *Songs of Innocence* are those sung before our fall; the *Songs of Experience* are those sung in our world. Blake's geographical descriptions of garden and world become attitudes toward life.

Our first poem is one of the most famous *Songs of Innocence*, "The Lamb." That Blake is able to enter into this vision with such purity is his genius. There is no irony in the poem itself; any irony involved is external to the poem.

In our explorations, we will enter into the world of the poem. What would it be like to be this speaker? How does this person view his or her world? What is the world like to this person? In what kind of world does this person imagine himself or herself to be living?

We do not want to analyze the poem but to consider it as a gate or doorway into the world of innocence. Is there a way we can put the poem on, as if it were a pair of spectacles, so that we might see the world through its innocent eyes?

• We will treat the poem as a meditation. Sit comfortably but upright; close your eyes; for a few moments center yourself on your breathing; when you have established a mood of peace and calm, begin. Read through the poem a couple of times (aloud if possible) to become familiar with it. Then try to enter into it in any way you can. Visualize the scene. Allow the images to grow and develop in your imagination. You might want to draw or paint the scene.

The main difference between our meditative approach and literary analysis is that we are being passive to the poem, allowing it to reveal itself to us. Attacking the poem is not necessary; if we can be with it and are open in its presence, it will open itself to us.

THE LAMB

Little Lamb, who made thee?
Dost thou know who made thee?
Gave thee life, and bid thee feed
By the stream and o'er the mead;
Gave thee clothing of delight,
Softest clothing, wooly bright;

Gave thee such a tender voice,
Making all the vales rejoice?
Little Lamb, who made thee?
Dost thou know who made thee?

Little Lamb, I'll tell thee,
Little Lamb, I'll tell thee!
He is called by thy name,
For he calls himself a Lamb.
He is meek, and he is mild;
He became a little child.
I a child, and thou a lamb,
We are called by his name.
Little Lamb, God bless thee!
Little Lamb, God bless thee!

William Blake

Allow all the different elements in the poem to help you in this
meditation: the images, the way the speaker of the poem presents
ideas, the verse form. Who is this speaker? What does the poem sound
like—a nursery rhyme? How old is the speaker? Is he or she full of
wonder, or matter-of-fact? Would you call the speaker childlike?
Naive? Innocent? Do you have memories from your own life when you
saw the world as this person does?

• Once you have a good idea of the person in this poem and of his or
her world, why not initiate a dialogue between that person and
yourself? Use the model set forth in Exploration 5.

65

EXPLORATION 9b THE WORLD OF INNOCENCE (continued)
time: ten to fifteen minutes

In this segment of our extended exploration of the human condition we will continue to explore the world of innocence. If you are doing this exploration as a separate section, you should begin by preparing yourself for meditative reading as you did in Exploration 9a. (If you are reading this poem immediately after "The Lamb," there is no need to prepare yourself.)

The scene of the poem "Holy Thursday" is a procession of young children into St. Paul's church on the day Jesus celebrated the Last Supper with his disciples. The children are led by their schoolmasters. Again we want to enter into the vision, the particular viewpoint, of the poem's speaker. How does the speaker perceive this procession? Is it beautiful? How is the speaker innocent?

HOLY THURSDAY

66

'Twas on a Holy Thursday, their innocent
faces clean,
The children walking two and two in red
and blue and green,
Grey-headed beadles walked before,
with wands as white as snow,
Till into the high dome of Paul's they
like Thames' waters flow.

O what a multitude they seemed,
these flowers of London town!
Seated in companies they sit with
radiance all their own.
The hum of multitudes was there, but
multitudes of lambs,
Thousands of little boys and girls
raising their innocent hands.

Now like a mighty wind they raise to
heaven the voice of song,
Or like harmonious thunderings the
seats of Heaven among.

Beneath them sit the aged men, wise
guardians of the poor;
Then cherish pity, lest you drive
an angel from your door.

William Blake

• Do you catch any hints that the speaker's innocence is really a blindness to what is in front of him? For example, he or she speaks of the beadles' wands as "white as snow." The beadles (masters) use these wands to discipline the children; is the image "white as snow" really appropriate? Can you sense in this poem—written at the time of the Industrial Revolution, sweathouses, and orphanages—any feeling that the poem's vision is unreal or ignorant? If you choose to dialogue with the poem in order to experience it more fully, you might want to question the speaker about what is really happening in this scene. Is it really as serene and beautiful as he or she describes it?

EXPLORATION **9c** **THE WORLD OF EXPERIENCE**
time: ten to fifteen minutes

Perhaps you found that the world described in "Holy Thursday" was not quite real. In *Songs of Experience* the singers have fallen into our adult world, with all of its ills and sufferings. Among those songs is another also called "Holy Thursday." But now instead of seeing the beautiful children processing into the church, the poem's speaker realizes that these are the exploited children of the workhouses, and the poem becomes an outraged cry against such conditions. The scene is identical to the poem of innocence, but everything has changed, for the speaker is no longer innocent. He or she has experienced the world, knows right from wrong—knows they exist and what they are. He or she has tasted the forbidden fruit.

• If this is the first poem you are reading today, take a few minutes to prepare yourself to read. In reading the poem, consider how it compares with the vision of innocence. Is one way of seeing more realistic than the other? Is one more adequate? What does it mean to be more realistic? Which of the "Holy Thursday" poems seems closer to your own outlook?

HOLY THURSDAY

Is this a holy thing to see
    In a rich and fruitful land,—
Babes reduced to misery,
    Fed with cold and usurious hand?

Is that trembling cry a song?
    Can it be a song of joy?
And so many children poor?
    It is a land of poverty!

And their sun does never shine,
    And their fields are bleak and bare,
And their ways are filled with thorns—
    It is eternal winter there.

For where'er the sun does shine,
    And where'er the rain does fall,
Babe can never hunger there,
    Nor poverty the mind appall.

William Blake

68

• As part of your time with this poem, you might want to construct a trialogue between the speakers in the two poems and yourself. What would the first speaker say to the second? Are there advantages to remaining in the state of innocence? You might want to question both visions. Is it possible that there is a vision beyond that of experience, or are we stuck with this brutal vision of a corrupt world?

9d THE WORLD OF EXPERIENCE (continued)
time: ten to fifteen minutes

For our final vision of the world of experience we turn to what is perhaps Blake's most famous poem, "The Tiger." Before we look at the poem, let's take another look at our meditation. Are you being truly imaginative? Have you been content to sit, close your eyes, and imagine? Is that enough for you? Is it becoming a little dull? Why not try something different? After all, the content of our meditations is not the whole of what we are seeking. The spiritual path we are experimenting with sees our growth as an expansion of our imaginative powers. In a very real sense the modern saints of the Western path are the artists and creators, such as William Blake. If we would walk with them we must develop this fascinating visionary ability that we have witnessed in the poetry of Blake and the Bible.

Blake was once on a mountain at sunrise with a friend. Blake asked his friend what he saw.

"Well, I see the glorious sun rising to begin a new day," said the friend. "What do you see?"

Blake said, "I see a chorus of the heavenly host shouting, 'Glory to God in highest heaven.' "

It is that ability to see, to be a *seer*, that we want to develop on this pilgrimage. That ability will not only help us see the vision we long for; it is a part of the vision itself.

Blake was not only a poet; he was a painter as well. Each of our four songs was engraved on copper plates complete with Blake's own illustrations. Perhaps you would like to enter into the poem we are about to read by illustrating it as it lies in this book. It is not necessary that you be a great artist, only that you learn to enjoy the gift of seeing and imagining. It offers you an entire world—a chorus of angels singing the praise of God. This gift offers you the entire world, and it is available to us all.

"The Tiger" mirrors in the world of experience "The Lamb" in the world of innocence. Now that we know both good and evil, the vision of "The Lamb" appears quite limited. Indeed, Blake often describes the world of innocence as a great womb. Unless we leave it behind we cannot have life; we are never really born, for everything goes around in circles and nothing happens.

"The Tiger" holds more than simply another vision of experience, however. Blake is a master of irony, and the greatness of these songs is not only that they are able to capture these two visions of existence but that they carry Blake's own attitude toward these visions as well. For he does not identify himself with any of his speakers. Of course, he no longer shares the vision of innocence, but neither does he see himself limited by experience. The process of human life does not end with the fall from innocence into experience. The vision of experience is as limiting as that of innocence. But the limitations are harder to discern since we are still in the vision of experience. However, for Blake there is a vision beyond experience.

●　In our meditation we will enter into this world of experience once more. We will do as we have done in the previous meditations, but we will also search for the limitations to this vision so that we can see a little beyond what we are accustomed to seeing. Can you catch the irony of the poem? What kind of person would speak like this? Is this person very much removed from the speaker in "The Lamb"? Is there something of childishness in this poem as opposed to the childlikeness of "The Lamb"? What are the hints or longings in your own life for a vision beyond that of experienced adulthood?

70

THE TIGER

Tiger! Tiger! burning bright
In the forests of the night,
What immortal hand or eye
Could frame thy fearful symmetry?

In what distant deeps or skies
Burnt the fire of thine eyes?
On what wings dare he aspire?
What the hand dare seize the fire?

And what shoulder and what art
Could twist the sinews of thy heart?
And when thy heart began to beat,
What dread hand? and what dread feet?

What the hammer? what the chain?
In what furnace was thy brain?
What the anvil? what dread grasp
Dare its deadly terrors clasp!

When the stars threw down their spears,
And watered heaven with their tears,
Did he smile his work to see?
Did he who made the lamb make thee?

Tiger! Tiger! burning bright
In the forests of the night,
What immortal hand or eye
Dare frame thy fearful symmetry?

William Blake

9e OUR PERSONAL FALL INTO EXPERIENCE
time: one-half hour
materials: notebook paper and pen

Now we are going to test our hypothesis of a fall in our own life. In his *Confessions*, Augustine is intrigued by an incident from his adolescence. One night he and a group of teenage friends stole pears from an orchard. Years later the Christian Augustine sees in that action the depths of his sin. Why did I take those pears? he asks himself. We weren't hungry. We didn't relish the fruit, for they were not ripe and so not worth the theft. Besides, muses Augustine, I don't even like pears. Yet why did I enjoy this evil thing?

Augustine is thinking of his own evil actions. We are going to use his method of reflection in this experiment. However, we seek to discover not our own first sin but rather the sinful human situation (which Blake calls experience) that we fell into or inherited. For the Christian concept of original sin is not an action we do so much as a condition we find ourselves in. The fall includes moral actions, but it goes on to encompass the entire human situation: physical, emotional, moral, intellectual, spiritual.

• To begin the meditation, sit down, close your eyes, and center on your breathing. Then read through the following questions in order to set the tone for this exploration.

Was there a time in your life when you lived in a state of innocence? If you do not believe there was such a time, do you nevertheless have an attraction for this kind of world where everything is good? Where does this attraction come from? Can you pinpoint a time in your own life when you passed from innocence into experience? Look especially at incidents with your parents. Was there a time when you were disappointed to discover that they were not wholly good—when they had not been truthful, when they had hurt you? When did you first become aware of the existence of evil? Can you remember the first action you did that you knew to be evil? Can you remember a time when, like Augustine, you realized that you actually enjoyed doing evil?

• For the main work in today's exploration we will center upon just one segment of our world of experience in order to discover its history in our life and perhaps its part in our own fall from innocence. To do this we will use a simple technique. As you sit quietly for the next fifteen minutes, take an experience that especially concerns you and put it in the form of a statement to help you search your memory. For example, if you suffer from depression now, you might want to trace the history of the depression. So you would say "I learned how to feel depression . . . ." Repeat this phrase over and over throughout the meditation. Do not go searching for experiences; the phrase will help bring them into consciousness. When a memory comes up, enter into it and reexperience it in your meditation. How did you feel at the time? What was the full scene? When you have exhausted a memory, return to your phrase until another memory arises.

Here are examples of phrases that can help you recall experiences from your past. Do not, however, feel limited by these moods.

I learned how to feel depressed when . . .
I learned how to feel left out when . . .
I learned how to feel unfulfilled when . . .
I learned how to resent things when . . .
I learned how to feel inadequate when . . .
I learned how to be disillusioned when . . .
I learned how to be distrustful when . . .
I learned how to overeat when . . .
I learned how to feel lonely when . . .

I learned how to put myself down when . . .
I learned how to deny my feelings when . . .
I learned how to be afraid when . . .

• For the last five minutes of the exploration, write down the
memories you have recalled for eventual inclusion in your journal.
Describe your memories in the present tense to make them more vivid.
Date your entry and label it with the phrase you worked on today. You
might want to continue with this exploration by examining another
phrase some other time.

9f

SUMMING UP THE FALL
time: about one-half hour
materials: notebook paper, pen, and paper entitled
"Learning How to Read" from Exploration 1

Fear and fright are the overwhelming experiences of the fall from
innocence into experience. Adam and Eve are frightened because of
what they have done. They step from Eden into a frightening world:
He will have to draw food from a hostile earth; she will bear children
in pain; and they will both face death as the conclusion of their life.

Shame is a second experience of the fall. When Adam and Eve
come to know themselves, they recognize their nakedness, and,
ashamed, they put on clothes to cover themselves. Similarly our world
of experience is one of shame; we are often all too aware of our
inadequacies, failures, and betrayals.

But our present condition is also given over to a propensity to
dream. We dream of returning to that garden where everything was
good and we were well provided for. Not only do we dream; we wish.
"If only I could do that over again . . . ." "If only I had gone to
college . . . ." "If only I hadn't gone to college . . . ." "If only I had
married So-and-so instead of this clown . . . ." "If only I could return
to that place where things were simple, I was taken care of, and where
there were no real problems . . . ."

And we dream with our history as well. We become nostalgic about the good old days. We lament the decline in our civilization. We bemoan the fact that the young people are going to the dogs. From the perspective of the seventies we look back on the sixties as our time of innocence when we believed the New Frontier could restore the world. But the seventies brought Vietnam and Watergate, and the whole society was expelled from that naive vision we called the American Dream.

No matter how much we yearn and dream, there is no way back into the garden. In the original story, the way is blocked by an angel with a fiery sword. In our own lives, the way back is a way that would bring our own destruction. We revert to childhood only at the expense of sanity. If we tried to reenter the world of the sixties, we would either be poisoned with what we have learned in the world of experience or we would have to abandon the present world for a life alone in the woods. We can't go home again, and most of us know it. But knowing does not stop the yearning, the longing for something more than what we have now.

The basic knowledge needed to force us on to a pilgrimage is that our present existence, no matter how secure and comfortable, is nevertheless unsatisfactory. Only at this point are we open to what a spirituality offers. In Christianity the idea of our insufficiency has gone under the title of original sin; in Buddhism it forms the first noble truth. It is not a pretty truth. It offers no comfort; we challenge it, we resist it, we even deny it. But as Chesterton said, it is the one Christian dogma that is proclaimed loud and clear in each day's newspaper headlines.

The knowledge that our existence is unsatisfactory is only the beginning of the spiritual path. The Buddha teaches a way out of suffering; Jesus calls himself the way. But the way does not involve a return to that lost world of innocence; the garden of Eden is closed off to us. We do not know the path ahead; the road is dark and unsure. And we will resist the pilgrimage many times through fear and our longing for the womb.

John is quite clear: The darkness resists the light. When truth came to his own home, people not only did not recognize him or make room for him; they rejected him outright. This rejection is not the work of someone else; scapegoats have no place in a real spirituality. The rejection comes from ourselves. Perhaps we haven't experienced it yet, but the work of pilgrimage involves dealing with resistance and even rejection as a part of its very nature.

• Our exploration today is a summary of what we have experienced and learned so far in this extended exploration which began on page 56. Make your preparations as usual. Then when you are ready, reflect on the following questions and considerations. We are concerned in this exploration with the extent to which you are able to espouse the view of life revealed in the story of Adam and Eve.

How unsatisfactory do you find your existence now? Go beyond material or psychological comforts to the root of your existence. How much real and lasting happiness do you have? Leaving aside all considerations of history and science and human equality, what does the story of Adam and Eve presented in Exploration 9 reveal concerning your own experience of living in the worlds of innocence and experience? To what extent are you able to accept this story as a true description of human existence? It is not likely, at this point, that you will be able to embrace this passage's teaching totally; you will learn its full truth only as you travel along the path. But are you open to the possibility that such a teaching might be true? Have you experienced in your own life anything that offers you real happiness in this present state of experience? You may have found great happiness in loving another person, but is that happiness absolute? What about the possibility of loss? What about the elements of jealousy, anger, and hurt that are part of any human loving?

Many who are willing to acknowledge this existence as unsatisfactory still do not choose to leave it behind. Are you able to hope for another kind of existence? Or do you believe that this present existence, bad as it is, is all there is and that there is no sense searching for something else? How eager are you to find some other way of living? What would you be willing to pay for it?—not in money, but in other things such as relationships, emotions, pride. What if someone came along tomorrow with the promise that there is a way out of this present existence? Would you follow that person? Would you suspect that person? How much? What would you sacrifice if you thought he or she were right?

• Take about ten minutes to write up your conclusions regarding this story of Adam and Eve. Is the picture of human existence we have

75

found in this story and in Blake compelling for you? To what extent do you believe or hope to find a way out of this unsatisfactory existence into a more fulfilling one? Date your entry and title it "Reflections on Adam and Eve."

● To conclude, take about five minutes to reflect on your reading process throughout this extended exploration (9—9f). How have you improved your new reading skills? What has helped you to enter more deeply into the story? Write these observations on your paper titled "Learning How to Read" and date your entry.

EXPLORATION **10** **THE PROBLEM OF EVIL**
time: twenty minutes   materials: paper entitled "Learning How to Read" from Exploration 1

To speak about the fall into experience does not exhaust the great mystery of evil. And it is just that mystery of evil that Western tradition has confronted in seeking a path toward wholeness. There is a folktale common throughout most of the Middle East concerning Job, a wealthy and good man, who has both family and servants.

One day the heavenly prosecutor walks into God's court. God asks the prosecutor how things are going, and the prosecutor raises the case of Job. He seems to be a fine and upstanding man, says the prosecutor, look at him; he has everything he could want. What if all were taken away from him? Would he still be as good, religious, and thankful as now? God gives the prosecutor permission to carry out the experiment, and Job loses everything—family, farm, servants, even his health.

So far we have only a folktale. Moderns would consider this kind of God quite savage as he plays games with Job's life. But in the Old Testament this story is only a framework upon which to hang an exploration of the problem of evil and suffering.

In Job the question of evil is probed far more deeply than in the story of Adam and Eve. What about the very existence of evil? What are we to think of the chaotic and irrational experience of this evil, especially when we are trying to believe that there is meaning to this world and that meaning is the ground and core of the world? If Job were an evil man, there might be no problem in what happens to him; he would deserve what he gets. But Job is not evil; he is upright. Here is exactly the problem that arises when we try to make sense out of things; our search for meaning seems futile.

At the time Job was written, evil was thought to be a punishment for one's sins. Job's friends come to comfort him, saying there must be some hidden sin that has brought this punishment upon him. Job protests that he can find no sin in himself. He asks that his sin be revealed if he has sinned. He wants some meaning to what is happening to him. He does not ask that his suffering be lifted, only that he be enlightened. None of his friends can respond to Job's demand; all they can do is ask him to continue the search for his sin.

• Prepare for your reading as you have learned to do. When you are ready, enter into the spirit of Job's situation. Put on Job's condition. Picture yourself with everything you value lost to you. Use your own suffering to enter imaginatively into Job's situation. Then ask with Job the meaning of your suffering. Does meaningful suffering differ from senseless suffering? Can you understand how important it might be that there be a meaning to our suffering? To conclude this section of your reading, take the part of a friend of Job's. What can you say to him? You do not have to restrict yourself to the answers of his friends in the book.

> Oh, I am weary of life; I will speak out, come what may; my soul is too embittered for silence. I will protest against God's sentence, demand to know why his judgment is so cruel. Is it well done in thee to play the tyrant, to spurn me, the creature of thy own hands, to smile on the ill designs of the godless? Are those eyes of thine human after all; is thy sight, too, blinded, like the sight of men? Hast thou a mortal's span of life, a destiny brief as ours, that thou must search for faults in me, labour to convict me of wrong done, when thou knowest full well that I am innocent, knowest that I am in thy power beyond hope of rescue?
>
> It was thy hand that made me, no part of me but is thy fashioning; and wilt thou cast me aside all in a moment? Thou the craftsman, though of clay thy handiwork, and

must all be ground to dust again? Milk of thy milking, cheese of thy pressing, were flesh and skin that clothed me, bone and sinew that built up my frame; the life given by thee, by thee was spared; thy vigilance was all my safety. Only in thy heart the memory of this is stored, but I know thou hast not forgotten. And was it thy purpose to spare me for a little, if I sinned, but absolve me never? Woe to me, if I rebelled against thee! And if I remained innocent, what then? Why, I would be drowned in misery and despair till I could lift up my head no more! Or if I did, that were pride in me, to be hunted down as a lioness is hunted; thou wouldst devise fresh miracles of torment; wouldst bring fresh witnesses against me, redouble thy avenging strokes, array against me a new host of punishments.

Why didst thou ever take me from the womb; why could I not perish there, never to meet men's eyes; a being without being, carried from womb to tomb? Brief, brief is my span of days; for a little leave me to myself, to find some comfort in my misery. Soon I must go to a land whence there is no returning, a land of darkness, death's shadow over it; a land of gloomy night, where death's shadow lies over all, and no peace haunts it, only everlasting dread.

Job 10
Knox Translation

● Finally, God answers Job from the midst of a whirlwind. He refuses to respond to Job's demand for a reason; there is no need for the Creator to justify his ways to the creature. Instead we have a magnificent revelation of divine power, majesty, and awe. In the face of that revelation Job ceases his questioning and bows in acquiescence. We humans cannot demand an account from God, for the ways of God are far above our own.

As we read God's response, we are not seeking answers to our own and Job's questions, then. We are entering an experience. Listen from within Job's skin to this voice of God. Feel the immense power and distance. Is there comfort in these words? Is there any possible attitude except resignation? If God is meaning, as John says, then what does this Scripture say of our own search for meaning? What does it say of senseless, meaningless suffering? Could suffering be seen as resistance to the light?

Job listens to God, then bows his head and accepts. As you listen from within Job's skin, see what it feels like to bow your head and accept. How would you respond? Would you protest and refuse to give in? Would such action gain you anything? Lose you anything? Where does acceptance lead? What is your own attitude toward inexplicable suffering in your own life?

Who are you to question my wisdom
with your ignorant, empty words?
Stand up now like a man
and answer the questions I ask you.
Were you there when I made the world?
If you know so much, tell me about it.
Who decided how large it would be?
Who stretched the measuring line over it?
Do you know all the answers?
What holds up the pillars that support the earth?
Who laid the cornerstone of the world?
In the dawn of that day the stars sang together,
and the heavenly beings shouted for joy.
Who closed the gates to hold back the sea
when it burst from the womb of the earth?
It was I who covered the sea with clouds
and wrapped it in darkness.
I marked a boundary for the sea
and kept it behind bolted gates.
I told it, "So far and no farther!
Here your powerful waves must stop."
Job, have you ever in all your life
commanded a day to dawn?
Have you ordered the dawn to seize the earth
and shake the wicked from their hiding places?
Daylight makes the hills and valleys stand out
like the folds of a garment,
clear as the imprint of a seal on clay.
The light of day is too bright for the wicked

and restrains them from doing violence.
Stand up now like a man,
and answer my questions.
Are you trying to prove that I am unjust—
to put me in the wrong and yourself in the right?
Are you as strong as I am?
Can your voice thunder as loud as mine?
If so, stand up in your honor and pride;
clothe yourself with majesty and glory.
Look at those who are proud;
pour out your anger and humble them.
Yes, look at them and bring them down;
crush the wicked where they stand.
Bury them all in the ground;
bind them in the world of the dead.
Then I will be the first to praise you
and admit that you won the victory yourself.

Job 38:2-15, 40:7-14
The Good News Bible

80

In the Book of Job the Old Testament reaches its profoundest confrontation with senseless suffering. But this failure to deliver an answer makes Job, for all its depth, inadequate. Job is important to us for exploring the problem, but it can offer no way out.

As we continue our pilgrimage we shall be seeking for a more adequate response to this mystery. If the Book of Job is a setting forth of the human predicament at its most painful, then any spiritual path will need to address this predicament and offer a means of passing through.

The Book of Job shows the gulf, the chasm between us and any source of meaning. It throws light on the mystery of resistance to meaning that John speaks about. We might not recognize the true light because our hopes are nostalgically set toward that realm of innocence from which we fell. If the Word points our pilgrimage away from that place of safety and onward toward a still different realm, we might not recognize this pointing as a help nor receive it as a path. Also, to live in this world of senseless evil (or darkness, as John would say) means to be changed and corrupted by it. Being a part of this fallen world, we will resist and have trouble with anything that is not of our world.

• To conclude our reading today, ask yourself if in this exploration you have learned to read better. How do you feel that your reading is different from the way you read before the pilgrimage began? Jot down your thoughts on the sheet "Learning How to Read" and date your entry.

11 ADDRESSING MEANING
time: ten minutes

In the last part of our passage from John, we catch a glimpse of where our pilgrimage toward meaning is leading us. So far we have agreed with John that *meaning* is a possible interpretation of the word *God*. What people call God is whatever provides the center of meaning in their life. Our investigation has focused on meaning's presence and importance in human life. Now in the last sentence of the passage, which began this chapter, John implies that our relationship to meaning might be personal:

> But to all who received him [the Word], who believed in his name, he gave power to become children of God; who were born, not of blood nor of the will of the flesh nor of the will of man, but of God.
>
> John 1:12-13
> *The Revised Standard Version*

In our own quest we are not yet ready to accept or even to explore the possibility that there might be a personal relationship with meaning open to us. John only provides a preview of what we will eventually encounter on our journey. But right now we can enter into an experiment as if this were so. Aristotle once said that philosophy begins in wonder. The real philosophical quest is also a form of pilgrimage, and philosophy's evocation of wonder and awe, this growing love for wisdom or meaning, is characteristic of the spiritual journey also. Our

81

wonder and love lure us ever onward toward the Grail. Now we will complete our investigation of the place of meaning in our lives by giving expression to that wonder.

Today in our exploration we will use one of the prayers of Israel. These prayers are found in the Book of Psalms in the Old Testament. "Psalm" designates a prayer-song. The psalms are quite ancient, some over three thousand years old, and they manage to articulate the entire spectrum of human experience, including some experiences modern people find it difficult or inappropriate to voice. Since the psalms are so old and from a foreign culture, we at times find them quite strange. On the other hand, they provide access to the vision of life that gave birth to and has nourished our culture throughout its history.

The concept of prayer, which is conversation with God, implies for us at this stage of our journey that it is not only possible to dialogue about meaning as we have done in our reading of John, Ecclesiastes, Ecclesiasticus, and Job, but that we can dialogue with meaning itself. Eventually in our journey we will establish our own ongoing dialogue with meaning. At this point, however, we are only beginning to test the possibility of such a dialogue, and we will engage in our dialogue today through the medium of this psalm. We will use a particular prayer of a particular person, a method that has been approved as a valid channel and expression of prayer by both the Jewish and Christian spiritual traditions. This prayer will be our first lesson in dialogue. We will insert ourselves into the world and the outlook of this psalm; its sentiments, views, and words will become our own. We need not believe that these words are the only words, or that these ideas are the best ideas for today. Nor need we agree to everything the psalm says in order to pray it. Imagine the psalms as model conversations for the dialogue with meaning. We can then use these models for our dialogue, and we can learn from the models how to fashion dialogues from our own thoughts and words.

There is bound to be disagreement and struggle not only with these psalms but with many other circumstances we encounter along our pilgrimage. How shall we deal with these problems? Do we leave this pilgrimage when we encounter concepts we cannot wholeheartedly agree to? Or do we try to swallow them, pretend to agree to them, or even force agreement from ourselves?

An ancient story will give us the way of dealing with problems and disagreements on our quest.

And Jacob was left alone; and a man wrestled with him until
the breaking of the day. When the man saw that he did not
prevail against Jacob, he touched the hollow of his thigh;
and Jacob's thigh was put out of joint as he wrestled with
him. Then he said, "Let me go, for the day is breaking." But
Jacob said, "I will not let you go unless you bless me." And
he said to him, "What is your name?" And he said, "Jacob."
Then he said, "Your name shall no more be called Jacob,
but Israel, for you have striven with God and with men, and
have prevailed."

Genesis 32:24-28
The Revised Standard Version

The very name Israel means "he who strives with God and man and
prevails." So in this tradition and along this path, agreement is not the
absolute. The struggle to appropriate the truth, the dialogue, the
wrestling between God and humanity defines the path. Jacob wins
something from his fight, which according to tradition is not with a
man at all but with an angel or with God. Jacob will carry the dream
of a new people set apart and dedicated to God. But Jacob is also
wounded in his struggle. He is made lame by the angel, and he will
bear the limp as a sign of his struggle. Similarly, in our own pilgrimage
we too shall be changed and will bear the signs of our struggle. These
wounds, however, do not cripple us. We will wear them proudly as
proof of our growth and development.

83

As we journey on our pilgrimage, let's keep in mind this story of
the naming of Israel. Often we too will move forward only by struggle
with our tradition, with our guide, with God. Sometimes the struggle
may look like the death of us, but that is so only if we walk away from
it. For it is in the wrestling that we can also win life. We will discover
that what is gained and accepted easily is often not worth much. What
challenges us deeply and wounds us in the winning can transform us
with its power.

● Many of the psalms are poems of wonder at the beauty and
spendor of the world. Our psalm today is one of praise. Read through
the psalm several times to catch the idea of praise. What is the action
of praising? How does the psalmist praise? Can you taste something of
the feeling of praise?

As you pray the psalm, enter into this feeling of praise. Pray the psalm slowly and aloud if possible. As you come upon each image used to praise God, allow yourself to dwell with the image. Give the image over to your imagination so that the image can evoke in you the sense of thanksgiving and wonder it originally brought forth from the psalmist.

If during the course of your prayer you want to add something in your own words, feel free to do so. Give yourself the opportunity to pause and remain with an image, allowing it to expand and to carry you. If in your prayer you do not understand or relate to a certain phrase, simply move on to the next.

> Bless the Lord, my soul!
> Lord God, how great you are,
> clothed in majesty and glory,
> wrapped in light as in a robe!
>
> You stretch out the heavens like a tent.
> Above the rains you build your dwelling.
> You make the clouds your chariot,
> you walk on the wings of the wind,
> you make the winds your messengers
> and flashing fire your servants.
>
> You founded the earth on its base,
> to stand firm from age to age.
> You wrapped it with the ocean like a cloak:
> the waters stood higher than the mountains.
>
> At your threat they took to flight;
> at the voice of your thunder they fled.
> They rose over the mountains and flowed down
> to the place which you had appointed.
> You set limits they might not pass
> lest they return to cover the earth.
>
> You make springs gush forth in the valleys:
> they flow in between the hills.
> They give drink to all the beasts of the field;

the wild asses quench their thirst.
On their banks dwell the birds of heaven;
from the branches they sing their song.
From your dwelling you water the hills;
earth drinks its fill of your gift.

You make the grass grow for the cattle
and the plants to serve man's needs,
that he may bring forth bread from the earth
and wine to cheer man's heart;
oil to make his face shine
and bread to strengthen man's heart.

The trees of the Lord drink their fill,
the cedars he planted on Lebanon;
there the birds build their nests:
on the tree-top the stork has her home.
The goats find a home on the mountains
and rabbits hide in the rocks.

You made the moon to mark the months;
the sun knows the time for its setting.
When you spread the darkness it is night
and all the beasts of the forest creep forth.
The young lions roar for their prey
and ask their food from God.

At the rising of the sun they steal away
and go to rest in their dens.
Man goes forth to his work,
to labor till evening falls.

How many are your works, O Lord!
In wisdom you have made them all.
The earth is full of your riches.

There is the sea, vast and wide,
with its moving swarms past counting,

living things great and small.
The ships are moving there
and the monsters you made to play with.

All of these look to you
to give them their food in due season.
You give it, they gather it up:
you open your hand, they have their fill.

You hide your face, they are dismayed;
you take back your spirit, they die,
returning to the dust from which they came.
You send forth your spirit, they are created;
and you renew the face of the earth.

May the glory of the Lord last for ever!
May the Lord rejoice in his works!
He looks on the earth and it trembles;
the mountains send forth smoke at his touch.

I will sing to the Lord all my life,
make music to my God while I live.
May my thoughts be pleasing to him.
I find my joy in the Lord.
Let sinners vanish from the earth
and the wicked exist no more.

Bless the Lord, my soul.

Psalm 104 (103)
Grail Translation

• When you are ready to conclude this exploration, close your eyes
and rest a moment in quiet. Then summarize the psalm in your own
words, keeping it in the format of prayer to God.

• Now let's reflect on our prayer experience. How did it feel to pray
this psalm? What was difficult for you? What did you enjoy? Did the
psalm give you anything? A feeling? A viewpoint? An experience?

During the next week notice whether this prayer might have any
implication for your life as a whole and for the way you are living and

experiencing at different moments. Would the psalm and its attitude have something to bring into these moments of living? Would you like to bring the psalm's praise into the ordinary moments? Try to do this throughout the week. It is not necessary to read the psalm at these times (although you might). It is enough to recall the feelings of praise and then to allow yourself to give thanks from within whatever moment you find yourself.

PART TWO

Outfitting Ourselves for Pilgrimage

So far, we have examined our own journey to this time in our lives. We have examined the entrance into the dark wood, exploring the place and the importance of meaning for human life. Now we are almost ready to enter the wood and begin our spiritual journey. But before we do so, we will pause to outfit ourselves for this quest. The knights of old went on the quest with horse, armor, and spear. What do we need to take with us to make the journey successfully?

We are already acquainted with our three principal aids, but before setting out, we will take a closer look at our equipment and receive final instructions on how to use it in our quest. The first piece of equipment is the Bible. So in the first exploration of this chapter we shall examine a Bible and become acquainted with its different books and how to locate passages. (We have already read a number of passages from the Bible and have a good idea of how to read this book.) Next we will look at our writing and set up the journal which will be the book of our own personal pilgrimage. Finally we will look at the process of meditation we will be using throughout the pilgrimage.

12 EXPLORING THE CONTENTS OF THE BIBLE
time: one-half hour   materials: a complete Bible
(either a Catholic version or at least some version that
includes the books of the Apocrypha, if possible)

In Part One we read a number of Scripture passages that were printed in this guide. Now it is time to move out of the guide and into the Bible itself. During the course of our journey the Bible will be one of our primary sources and guides, so it is important that we become familiar with it.

The Bible might be a closed, unknown, and formidable book to you, but it need not be so. It was not written as a scholarly book but as a book of the people. Granted, it is quite old and comes from a culture very different from our own. But its vision still shines clearly and has illumined many lives throughout the centuries. In this exploration we will gain some overall view of its contents, so that we can continue to explore it and grow more familiar with it throughout our pilgrimage.

We begin our investigation by looking at the major divisions of the Christian Bible: the Old and New Testaments. The Old Testament occupies about the first two thirds of your Bible; the New Testament comprises the final third. Find these divisions now. If your Bible also includes a section called the Apocrypha, you will find it after either the Old or the New Testament. In Catholic Bibles the books of the Apocrypha are scattered throughout the Old Testament.

The Old Testament contains those writings considered sacred by the Jews of Jesus' time. The New Testament contains the writings by the early Christian community and is the specifically Christian part of the Bible. The Apocrypha fall chronologically between the time of the Old and New Testaments. Those books exist only in Greek or Latin translations; either the Hebrew original has been lost or the book may have been written in Greek. Jews and Protestants do not consider the Apocrypha as Sacred Scripture; Roman Catholics and Orthodox do.

• Turn now to the Old Testament. There were three basic divisions made at the time of Jesus. The first division, and for the Jew the holiest collection of Scriptures, is the Law. This comprises the first five books in your Bible:

Genesis—the legends of the world's beginnings and the stories of the patriarchs. (Among others, the stories of Adam and Eve and of Jacob's struggle with the man are found in Genesis.)

Exodus—the deliverance of the slaves from Egypt under Moses, their journey through the Red Sea, and the giving of the Law on Mount Sinai.

Leviticus—a book of ritual laws.

Numbers—the continuation of the journey through the desert toward the promised land, and the census of Israel (The book takes its name from the latter).

Deuteronomy—a second, later setting forth of the Law.

These books are known as the books of Moses although most modern scholars do not believe they were actually written by Moses. When Jesus refers to Moses or the Law he means these writings and what they represent.

The second division of the Old Testament is called the Prophets. Included are the writings and traditions of those prophets who brought the message of God to Israel. These prophets are grouped in your Bible as the last books of the Old Testament, beginning with Isaiah and ending with Malachi. But in Jesus' time this division also included those books that we would call historical because they continue Israel's history from the time of the entrance into the promised land (where the books of the Law end) through the conquest, the establishment of the monarchy, and the impending fall of Israel. In our present Bibles, these books are found from Joshua through II Kings, with the exception of Ruth. These books were known in Jesus' day as the earlier prophets to distinguish them from the later prophets who wrote. When Jesus refers to the prophets he is often speaking of all these books.

The third division is known as the Writings and includes whatever is left over. Here we find the book of Psalms as well as other poetry and wisdom literature such as Job. There are historical books which comprise a later segment of Israelite history as well as a retelling of the earlier history: Chronicles and Ezra-Nehemiah. Finally there are the five scrolls that were read on special Jewish feast days: Ruth, Song of Songs, Ecclesiastes, Lamentations, and Esther. The books of the Apocrypha, such as Ecclesiasticus, also fall into the category of Writings.

These books were originally written in Hebrew or one of its daughter languages such as Aramaic. Shortly before the current era the collection was translated into Greek by some Jewish scholars, for Hebrew at that time was a dead language, and Greek was the common literary tongue of Alexander's and later of the Roman Empire. The version produced by these Jewish scholars was called the Septuagint after the number of supposed translators, seventy. By the time of Jesus the Septuagint was the most familiar version of Scripture for the Jews scattered throughout the Greco-Roman world, since more Jews could read Greek than Hebrew. So the Septuagint became their adopted version of the Bible. It included all the books of the Old Testament and the Apocrypha as well as other books.

The first Christians were Greek-speaking, and they considered the Scriptures as what was contained in the Septuagint. But no one had as yet defined just what was or was not Sacred Scripture. The definition of Scripture was much more fluid than it is today. Certainly some books were much more important than others: the Law above all, the prophets, and certain Writings such as the Psalms. But Scripture was still only a loose collection of sacred writings which Jew and Christian alike used in prayer and study. When the New Testament referred to Scripture it meant precisely this Old Testament collection, for the New Testament writings had not yet formed a definite collection.

In the early Church, as in the synagogue from which it arose, the people would meet to read the Scriptures and meditate upon them. In addition other writings began to circulate through the scattered Christian communities. The letters from Paul were the first to so travel. Paul is the missionary who brought the good news of Jesus from the Jewish world of Palestine into the pagan world of Greece and Rome. When he went to a city, he would preach; as he gathered converts he would form them into communities. Once these new churches were established to the point where they could survive on their own, Paul would go elsewhere. However, he would keep in touch with them, and from time to time the local situation would call forth a letter from the apostle concerning difficulties and problems the community faced in understanding and living the way of Jesus. Cherished by the churches, these letters were read during the meetings and then circulated to sister churches as well. Eventually the letters were read at the services along with the Jewish Scriptures, and the Christians came to regard them as equal in importance to the Old Testament writings.

These letters are found in the New Testament from Romans through Jude. Their titles refer either to the addressee or to the person who supposedly wrote them. Paul's letters are first simply because of their importance. Scholars today generally agree that Romans through II Thessalonians and Philemon are actually written by Paul, although there are debates concerning even these. Timothy and Titus are called Pastoral letters because they are concerned with church structure and life; they are late in date and were written perhaps by a disciple of Paul. Hebrews is a Jewish-Christian sermon and not really a letter at all. James through Jude are called the Catholic letters because they are addressed to the Church at large rather than to any specific community.

Revelation or the Apocalypse is the last book of the New Testament. It is a book of fantastical imagery written during the early persecutions of Christians. In spite of the images, numbers, and visions, its simple message is one of comfort and hope to those suffering persecution: although there is suffering and calamity now, there is hope, for God will prevail in the end.

The final set of books forms the Christian equivalent of the Jewish Law—the Gospels. The word means *good news*, a term Jesus used for his preaching and which Christians in turn used to speak of the message of Jesus. There are four gospels. The fourth gospel, John, has served as our guide so far through this pilgrimage. The other three gospels—Matthew, Mark and Luke—are called the Synoptics because they share much of their content with one another; John on the other hand is usually unique in his material. Luke's gospel actually is in two parts. The gospel itself speaks of the good news in the preaching, life, death, and resurrection of Jesus, just as do Matthew and Mark. But Luke goes on in a second volume, the Acts of the Apostles, to recount how the good news continued in the early Christian Church. During the rest of our pilgrimage in this manual we shall be concentrating primarily on the three Synoptic gospels.

We have now concluded our survey of the books and sections of the Bible. As you can see, the Bible is not the work of any one person. It includes many kinds of writings and many opinions and ideas. Its unity comes not from anything internal to it, but rather from the community that has collected the various writings and determined that these writings and only these writings should be normative for the community's vision and experience. Thus when we come to read the Bible, we read it from within the tradition that created it. The Bible did not call into existence a Jewish or Christian community; rather, the Jewish and Christian communities created and set up the Bible as their scriptural norm. To read the Bible while ignoring the tradition that created it or even in opposition to the community that created it is to fail to realize its true purpose and its full significance.

The beginner's difficulties are not limited to the fact that the Bible is composed of various books and outlooks covering a period of over two thousand years. Even within a book by one author we cannot expect to find the same consistency or unity that we would expect from a modern book. The letters of Paul, for example, are not entirely Paul's creation. He quotes ancient hymns, prayers, and creeds in order to teach and correct his communities. Further, his letters passed through many early churches for years before finding the final version we have today. Thus in any one letter, there might be parts of other letters which were added to the original. Or parts of the original letter might have been lost and other material added to fill in the gap. Many things have happened to these books during the course of the journey from composition to the fixed type of our modern Bibles.

Finally, there is the simple fact that the Bible does not present one central doctrine. There are many different viewpoints, some of which seem in conflict with one another. We have witnessed this divergence already as we have studied and prayed a very orthodox psalm and read the book of Ecclesiastes, which some regard as a protest against Israelite orthodoxy. The diversity of opinions and outlooks might dismay and confuse us if we approach this collection expecting a party line. The diversity is one reason why it is necessary to read the Bible within the context of its community: the community can provide guidelines for understanding the books and their place in the overall tradition. For example, the Book of Ecclesiastes is simply not given the same importance in either Jewish or Christian tradition as the book of Psalms: it is seen as much more peripheral to the central tradition than the Psalms, which have been the basis for Jewish and Christian prayer. Seen from within, the tradition of the Bible becomes a way of understanding the whole of life and thought. It doesn't provide us with one definite teaching that must be followed. Instead it illuminates all the facets of human existence. There is a place here for all experience; nothing is excluded. The Scriptures can open our horizons and expand our understanding. They should not narrow our vision into a simplistic orthodoxy.

• Now that you are familiar with the general layout of the Bible, we will conclude this exploration by locating and reading some passages. Bible references are made by naming the book and then the chapter number and verse number. Thus Jonah 3:11 refers to the Book of Jonah, chapter 3, verse 11. Use the rest of your exploration time to look up and read these passages; they all speak of wisdom.

> John 1:1-12
> Jeremiah 17:5-11
> 1 Corinthians 2:6-16
> James 3:13-18
> Proverbs 8:22-36

EXPLORATION **12a** THE TRANSLATIONS OF THE BIBLE AND GUIDELINES FOR READING
time: one-half hour   materials: Bible

In Exploration 12 we traced the history of the Bible, but our story is far from finished. The early Christian church came to cherish the writings of the apostles equally with the Scriptures of Israel. But there was as yet no list of books or canon to state which writings were considered Sacred Scripture as opposed to those that were only to be held in veneration. Such a canon does not arise until some time into the Christian era.

Lists of New Testament books were drawn up at various times in the early church. The lists agree by and large as to contents. Only a few books, such as James or Revelation, are in question from list to list; there is never dispute concerning the gospels or the Pauline letters.

Within two hundred years, the Christian communities had agreed among themselves concerning a list of New Testament books. As far as the Old Testament was concerned, they simply continued to use the Septuagint.

Jerome's translation of the Scriptures into Latin, called the Vulgate, comprises the next major event in the Bible's history in the Western church. Jerome basically used the Septuagint for his translation of the Old Testament. But he had learned Hebrew in addition to Greek, and he compared the Septuagint to the Hebrew original. He noticed there were certain books in the Greek Septuagint that were no longer available in the Hebrew. Wondering whether these books should be put on the same footing as the rest, he finally decided to include them in the Vulgate but to label them Deutero-canonical, which means "second list," not quite on an equal footing with the first canon of Hebrew books. There were also a few books in the Septuagint that Jerome did not regard as scriptural; these he called apocryphal, but they are not the same books as the list of Apocrypha in today's Bibles. The Apocrypha in modern Bibles correspond to Jerome's Deutero-canonical books.

The matter is so confusing simply because the Christian church was not forced at this time to make a concrete decision concerning the Old Testament canon. It had a list of New Testament canon, but the Old Testament was still fluid; it wasn't as important to draw up a canon for it. About the same time as the New Testament canon was drawn up by the Church, the Jews drew up a canon for their Scriptures. The rule of thumb was that the book must still exist in Hebrew in order to be part of Scripture. Thus, the Jewish Scriptures do not include the Deutero-canonical or Apocryphal books.

The Reformation ushers in the next stage in the formation of the Western Bible. Luther, in his reaction against the Roman Catholic church, reinvestigated the list of Scriptural books. He followed the Jewish rule for the Old Testament, thus excluding what now began to be called the Apocrypha. Luther wanted to reexamine the canon of New Testament writings as well, but he was persuaded to let it stand. In reaction to Luther, the Roman church proclaimed Jerome's translation as the basic Scripture; thus, for the first time, the Deutero-canonical works were formally declared to be Sacred Scripture.

This confusing history explains the difference between Protestant and Catholic Bibles. The Orthodox Christians, on the other hand, simply followed the Septuagint for the Old Testament, leaving out a few books that were very late. Thus the Orthodox Bible has a few more books than even the Roman Catholic version.

These differences in what was regarded as Scripture were much more important in the past than they are today. In the current spirit of openness, Catholics concede that within the Old Testament itself the Deutero-canonical books are not as important or weighty as the others. No one today would consider II Maccabees as important as Exodus. On the other hand, Protestants have found these books valuable documents for that important period of Judaism between the end of the prophetic age and the coming of Jesus. This inter-testamental period is important for the history of Judaism, and it describes the Judaism of which Jesus was a part.

Now we shall narrow our history of the Bible down to the English-speaking world. Our history here begins before Luther's Reformation with John Wycliffe, the first English translator, who was regarded as a heretic for his troubles. But Wycliffe inaugurated the English Bible and began a great heritage of translation that profoundly influenced and shaped not only English literature but the English language itself.

The apex of English biblical translation is of course the great King James Version, also called the Authorized Version. It is a Protestant translation, done in the time of Shakespeare, and unsurpassed in its dignity and beauty. It has even been said that the King James Version is often more elegant and poetic than the original.

From today's vantage point the King James is somewhat inadequate in its scholarship; much has been learned in Scripture studies over the last four hundred years. This scholarship does not invalidate the King James; on the whole it is quite faithful to the heart of the biblical message. The changes modern scholarship would make are for the most part minor ones.

The changes the English language itself has undergone since the days of King James form a more telling argument against using the King James version today. For many today, Shakespeare's language sounds quite foreign, yet his is the same English as the Authorized Version. Enshrined as the Authorized Version is in our hearts, our language, and our heritage, we might want a translation that speaks more in our own idiom. Excerpts from each of these translations are included in our guide so that you can experience each firsthand. A passage from the King James Version is found on pages 41-44.

At about the time the King James Version was being made, the English Catholics undertook their own translation. The work was done in France because Catholics were outlawed in England. This version is generally referred to as the Douay-Rheims version, after the places where the translation occurred. On the whole, this version does not have the beauty, grandeur, or polish of the King James. It has been pretty well laid to rest by modern Catholic versions. A sample can be found on page 16.

The King James Version was revised in the 1950s in the light of the changing English language and modern scholarship. Called the Revised Standard Version, it retains the wording of the King James whenever that is consistent with the original texts or with what is comprehensible to a contemporary speaker of English. It is not a fresh translation, but a revision of an earlier translation. It preserves the beauty of the King James for our age while at the same time offering contemporary language and up-to-date scholarship. Excerpts from the Revised Standard Version can be found on pages 81 and 83. There have been other revisions of the King James as well, but none of them has the weight or popularity of the Revised Standard Version.

There are a number of modern translations, two of which rival the King James Version in terms of the number of churches involved. The English Churches (predominantly Protestant) commissioned what is called the New English Bible. At about the same time, the Catholic Church in the United States began to work on a translation that has since turned into an ecumenical effort involving many Protestant churches and scholars. This is called the New American Bible. Both these translations are sponsored by the national church bodies of their respective countries; neither is the work of one church or one individual. The differences between them are mostly a matter of style—the difference between American and British English. Samples of the New American Bible can be found on pages 58 and 60-61; an excerpt from the New English Bible is on page 24.

The Good News Bible and the Jerusalem Bible are two other modern translations that have achieved great popularity. The Good News Bible was commissioned by the American Bible Society, which wanted a translation into plain, simple English. The Good News Bible's concern is with clarity and simplicity. It tends to lose the elegance of the King James Version, but it is quite accurate and is often closer to the sound of the original writings than some of the more poetic translations. An excerpt appears on pages 79-80.

The Jerusalem Bible is an English translation based on a modern Catholic French translation produced at the Biblical School in Jerusalem. For the English version, the translators went back to the original languages rather than the French, but in points of interpretation they usually resorted to the decisions of the original French scholars. In its full editions this translation is very useful because of its full notes and introductions. The English translation also has great beauty. A sample from this Bible is found on pages 44-46.

Three Bibles that are not so much translations as paraphrases deserve mention. The oldest is the Ronald Knox translation, which is not used very much any more but is quite good in interpreting certain books such as the letters of Paul. Knox was an English convert to Catholicism in the early twentieth century before any of the modern Catholic translations had appeared. He translated the entire Bible from the Latin of Jerome. Of course, since his is a translation of a translation it is not always the most accurate version. But Knox had a superb gift of expression, and he could often bring to light ideas that are difficult to grasp and obscure in other translations. A sample of his work is found on pages 77-78.

Being over a thousand years old, the Scriptures are often not easy for us to comprehend. A paraphrase is sometimes more helpful for a beginner than a completely faithful translation. Of course the reader should bear in mind that there is always the chance he or she is reading the paraphraser's idea of what the original said rather than what the original actually said. But many people have claimed to understand Scripture for the first time in a paraphrased version. There is a beautiful paraphrase by J. B. Phillips called the New Testament in Modern English. Phillips has also paraphrased the four major prophets, but he has not gone on to complete the Old Testament. A sample of Phillips is found on page 49.

The most popular paraphrase today is called the Living Bible. Like the Phillips, it is very helpful. Simply keep in mind that these last three are not and do not claim to be translations. They might choose one understanding of a phrase or passage over another perfectly legitimate understanding. Ultimately they should not and are not meant to replace the originals or the translations. But they prove an invaluable aid in approaching the Scriptures without the need for many footnotes and other aids. A passage from the Living Bible occurs on page 55.

The last translation we shall consider is a very limited one: the Grail translation of the Book of Psalms. The psalms are originally poetry to be sung; yet many modern translations, although they might retain a feel for the poetry, are not designed for singing. The Grail version is the translation of the Psalms favored by the Catholic bishops of America and the British Isles for praying the psalms in worship services. You might want to have this little book as a prayer book for your own psalm praying. A sample can be found on pages 84-86. The psalms are designed to be sung to the chants composed by a modern French scholar, Gelineau; directions for singing are included in the book.

To conclude this exploration, take your own Bible and look up some of the passages we have read in the course of our pilgrimage. Compare your translation with some of the translations we have used. Some of our passages are quite short and cannot give you a real feel for the quality of a translation, but by comparing the different versions you can see what is involved in creating a translation. If you are looking for a Bible to buy, you can look up the different excerpts and decide which version would be most helpful for you. They are all adequate for our pilgrimage. Whichever version you decide to use for your own is really a matter of your own taste and needs.

EXPLORATION **13** **SETTING UP THE PILGRIMAGE JOURNAL**
time: twenty minutes
materials: loose-leaf notebook, five dividers, and paper

The journal is the second tool of our pilgrimage. In this exploration we will set up the journal and put into it the written work we have already done.

- Label the first section of your journal "Life Diary." This section is similar to a daily diary or log. Here you can place any observations concerning your day, feelings about the pilgrimage, reflections on your life from day to day. We are concerned with present time here—the movement of our life from day to day. There are no specific directions about your writing in this section; it is up to you to keep as complete or as fragmentary a record as you want of your journey. There may be times when you want to write in the journal every day; other times, weeks may go by without your writing in it.

The Life Diary is designed to allow us to see the movements of our pilgrimage. For there will be times when we believe that nothing is happening or has happened to us. This diary provides a record of the movements of our spirit, and if we do use it, it gives an objective picture of the high and low points of our quest.

The writing in Exploration 6, in which you described the extended present in your life, should be placed in this section of your diary. You might take a few moments to read over this material and jot down any new elements in this present moment that suggest themselves to you, dating any new entries.

- Entitle the second section of the journal "Life Experience." Here we will record any work we do on our past life. In this section place the material from Exploration 7, Exploration 7a if you have done it, and Exploration 9e. We will use this second section of our journal to explore our life and our experience. Thus we can test the teachings along this path we are travelling to see whether we wish to give them credence.

- Label the third section of your journal "Prayer Diary." Here we will record briefly the process of our exploration in prayer. For example, when we engaged in the dialogue in Job, at the end of our Exploration 10, we might have turned to this section and described any insights we gained, any difficulties we encountered, any observations we might wish to record concerning the exploration. This section then becomes a log of our prayer life just as the Life Diary is a record of our life's journey. From now on, at the end of each of our explorations we will give directions for recording the exploration in this section. You may also want to record other spiritual practices you engage in.

- Let's call the fourth section of the journal "Prayer Experience." In several of our explorations we will use writing as we enter into the meditation; that writing and dialogue will be entered into this section of the journal. In the Prayer Diary, the writing will be about the process of prayer. In this section we are using the journal as a part of the prayer process. The writing from exploration 9f, about Adam and Eve and that story's significance for your own experience, should be entered into this section.

● Title the fifth and final section of the journal the "Process Log." Here we will record our experiences of the pilgrimage process itself. In this section you should enter your writings entitled "Learning How to Read" from Explorations 1, 9f, and 10. As you make your pilgrimage, record here any insights or observations you have concerning the way of growth on which you are embarked. You will want to continue your observations on how to read. You will enter here any insights about how to meditate, how to work in the journal, how to live during the day. This section will eventually become your own textbook for spiritual growth.

● Now that you have set up your journal, take the rest of the time to write in the Process Log section just how you plan to use this journal on your pilgrimage. What would you hope from the journal? How do you want to use the journal? What part would you like to see the journal play in your development? You might do this in the form of a letter to your journal.

EXPLORATION # 13a
GUIDELINES FOR USING THE JOURNAL
time: twenty minutes
materials: journal

Today we will look at a few basic qualities of good journal work. First, it is important that you date each of your entries; this will make it possible for you to correlate work in different sections.

Whenever possible in your writing, use the present tense. In the Life Experience section, where we will be writing about our past, using the present tense will make the material more vivid for us and easier to recreate.

The journal is a record of your *whole* life, so you should be as holistic as possible about what you choose to include in it. There should be no censorship working here at all. No one should be allowed to read your journal, and you should never write in the journal expecting that someone else will read it. If at a certain time you choose to read from your journal to others, that is another question, but it can be decided later.

The journal is a record of your experiences, your fears, your hopes; it can contain events that happen to you as well as your dreams and fantasies. Whatever is a part of you should be included in your journal. The more complete a picture it shows, the more help the journal will be on your pilgrimage.

Since imagination forms a great part of your work on this pilgrimage, the journal should be a place where you can allow your imagination to roam and stretch. If you write poetry or draw, you can enter this work in the Prayer Experience section. Fantasies can be entered there as well. As you do this work, try to do it with imagination to keep the journey from becoming heavy and boring; the opening of your imagination itself is a main object of the quest.

In your journal writing, try to avoid tendencies to analyze. The journal is a place to enter all kinds of data from your life, your imagination, your explorations. However, it is not the place to analyze your life or the explorations. For example, if a certain exploration was difficult for you to do, or if you felt a certain resistance to it, simply record this in your Prayer Diary. Then you might also say that you were tired, or include any other facts that you think might be appropriate. But do not jump to the conclusion that because you were tired the exploration was difficult. We are using our journal to expand our consciousness. But analysis is always an attempt to understand everything by what we already know. It is a dead end to new knowledge most of the time. We will become more perceptive and knowledgeable if we can just learn to observe situations rather than analyze them.

Finally, in your journal work, try to avoid judgments. Our lives are full of judgments: This was a bad day, or this was a great day. Instead of judging or analyzing, just describe as fully as possible. For instance, if you had a bad day, instead of saying this, see if you can describe the day. "I am tired. I didn't get enough sleep last night. There are too many things to do. I am constantly being interrupted in my work." Such a description says much more about the day than any judgments you can pronounce upon it. And again be holistic. True, it might have been a hard day, but in your description do not censor out the good elements. If you do, your journal account will be biased and much less helpful.

• For the rest of the twenty minutes turn to the Life Diary section of your journal and to Exploration 8 in this guide. In that exploration we reviewed our day. Today do the exploration again, but now instead of just remembering, use the writing process to help you recreate your day. Follow these five principles: Write in the present, be all-inclusive, be imaginative (draw your day if you want), avoid analysis, and avoid judgment.

EXPLORATION **14** MEDITATION, FIRST PHASE:
LETTING GO OF THE WORLD
time: twenty minutes

We have already experienced a number of meditations on our journey. At this point we are going to set up a format that will enable us to gain the most from our meditation experiences. Today we will explore the first phase—our passage from our ordinary world into the realm of meditation.

At times, we have trouble entering into meditation because of where we have come from or because of where we see ourselves going after the exploration. At those times we might realize the need for a transition from ordinary life into the meditation. But the transition is important any time we choose to meditate.

On this pilgrimage our experimental meditations will last anywhere from twenty minutes to a half hour. Of this time we will spend about five to ten minutes in this first phase. As Westerners we might feel that since this is only the preparational period, it is not the core of the meditation and therefore not important. We might then treat it lightly or skip it altogether in our hurry to get to the meat of our work; but it itself is a kind of meditation, differing from the other kinds only in form.

• During the first few minutes we will perform a version of the daily review we learned in Exploration 8. Think about where you have just come from. In what ways have you brought your world and its concerns here with you into this meditation? If you were figuring out the checkbook, your mind may be filled with figures and confusions. Acknowledge whatever concerns are present in your mind, whether it be old business or future planning. Assure yourself that you will give everything your attention after the meditation and ask that it let you be for now. Then quickly review your day. Imagine you are watching a film of that day. See each scene flash before you on the screen, but watch with some detachment. You are begining to let go of the ordinary world and to enter into the quiet realm of meditation.

• At the conclusion of your review (or, if you are doing the meditation in the morning, of your preview) ask yourself what you are experiencing as you are about to enter into meditation. How does your body feel? Is it tired? Is it filled with nervous energy? Are you relaxed? Tense? Are you caught by powerful emotions? Is there anger, fear, impatience?

If you are anxious and nervous, some deep, calm breathing can help you find relaxation and calm. If you are filled with anger, beating on a pillow with your hands and fists will discharge the rage. Screaming and yelling will also help. If you feel fatigued, raise your energy level with some vigorous breathing or by jumping up and down in place. At first it might be difficult to know what to do for yourself, but a little experimentation and observation will help you. Begin to read yourself. You will learn to read yourself better with practice. Right now it is sufficient to begin this practice. Respond to what your body and emotions are telling you. Take the next five minutes to ten minutes to work through the body and bring yourself to a quiet in which you can meditate. We work here in the body because it is the easiest, quickest way to achieve the peace we seek.

• There are a number of physical disciplines that can provide us with body movements to bring us from the world into meditation. Yoga, Tai Chi, Kum Nye and others are really systems of movement meditation. The feeling we seek is calm and peaceful. We do not want to exhaust ourselves or raise our nervous energy. We will explain some movement meditations before some of the explorations so that you can try them. (Wear loose clothing for all of your meditations if possible. Remove all belts, watches, jewelry, wallets—anything that will restrict your movement or make you uncomfortable while sitting.)

Here is a movement sequence from Hatha Yoga that relaxes the body through a gentle stretching. In all these movement meditations, it is important to have a quite different attitude from that typical in Western sport and calisthenics. You should not strain doing any of these exercises. A gentle stretching is the most you should ever push for. There is also no place for competition, either against others or against your own past performances. As in all meditation, the object is to be present to what is happening at this moment. Be aware of feelings, tensions, loosenings in your own body. As we do these movement exercises we are already leaving behind the outside world as we turn inward and place our attention on our present experience. Thus these exercises need to be done with total awareness. If you find your mind wandering, or if the movements become automatic for you, you have lost the meditative dimension and the exercise has become useless.

• Now let us perform the Salutation to the Sun.

Stand up with your feet about two feet apart. Bend your knees slightly; your knees should never lock. Close your eyes. Relax all over. Take a couple of deep, relaxing breaths.

As you slowly inhale, raise your arms until your palms join and your arms are stretched out over your head. Exhale, and keeping the palms joined, lower your arms so that the second and third fingers touch your chin. You will then look as if you are praying. Inhaling, lock your two thumbs together, turn the palms outward, and stretch your arms up toward the ceiling, keeping the thumbs locked together. Continue to stretch your arms until you are bending backward. Hold this position for a moment, keeping your eyes on your thumbs at all times.

Exhaling, bend the whole body forward so that the head comes close to or actually touches your knees. Do not strain. Keep the knees unlocked. Rest your hands palms down on the floor, to either side of your feet. The fingertips and the toes should be on an imaginary straight line. Keep the knees as straight as possible, but if you have to, you may bend them in order to rest the palms on the floor.

Inhaling, stretch your right leg back as far as possible and let the right knee drop to the floor. Now look up at the ceiling and as far back as possible. Feel the stretch along the entire length of the body.

Exhaling, stretch the left leg back so that it joins the right. Both feet are now resting on the toes. Push up into a position where only the toes and palms touch the floor. Your body should now form a triangle with the floor, your buttocks at the high point. Keep the body relatively straight. Stretch the calf muscles by lowering your heels as close to the floor as possible.

Inhaling, lower first the knees, then the chin, and finally the chest to the floor. The body is now touching the floor only with the toes, the palms, and these three points. Your stomach should still be slightly off the floor. This position flows naturally out of the previous posture provided you do not move either your hands or your toes once you place them in the previous postures.

Holding your breath, push youself up into the cobra pose: Pushing up with the palms first, lift your head and continue lifting and stretching each vertebra all down the neck and back. Look as far up and back with your eyes as possible; they will act as a lever for you. Feel this stretch in your neck and all down the upper spine. Do not lift your navel off the floor; this decreases the stretch. Throughout the posture, your legs and feet should remain touching.

Exhaling, push your body again into the triangle, buttocks in the air, toes and palms on the floor. In this position check your neck for tension; your head should simply hang between your arms loosely.

Inhaling, bring the right foot forward to its former position between your palms. The left knee now sinks to the floor. Stretch the spine by looking up at the ceiling and backward.

Exhaling, bring the left leg forward to join the right.

Inhaling, slowly straighten up to a standing position, join the palms together again in the prayer gesture over your head, bend slightly backward, feeling the stretch, and then gently lower the hands, touching your forehead, mouth, and chest on the way down. Finally let your arms fall gently to your sides. Remain standing quietly with your eyes closed for a moment, aware of anything you are sensing or feeling.

Practice this movement several more times. Eventually it will flow naturally for you. In doing this movement, as well as any other movement exercise, it is important first of all to stretch your body gently to release tension and create the relaxation you are seeking.

Secondly it is important to preserve awareness or be a witness throughout the exercise. Be conscious of whatever feelings, sensations, and thoughts arise during the exercise. Do not judge them, do not ignore them, do not become involved in them. Simply observe them.

EXPLORATION **14a** MEDITATION, SECOND PHASE: DEEPENING
time: twenty minutes

In this exploration we will add the second stage to the meditation process. After we have left our ordinary cares and concerns behind us we look within and spend some time allowing the quiet and peace to deepen within us. We move down into the core of our being so that our meditation can engage our deepest self. This second stage of meditation, like the first, is a valid form of meditation in itself. Should you decide to use meditation as an aid to your pilgrimage and as a part of your daily life in addition to the explorations we perform in this guide, you can do the first and second stages of meditation together as a whole.

• Take the first ten minutes to repeat yesterday's exploration. Remember, this first phase is a transition. Be aware of where you are coming from, and be conscious of the movement from the world into your meditational consciousness. Perform the Salutation to the Sun about three times. Pause at the end each time and taste what is happening in your body, your emotions, your mind, your spirit. Do this entire phase with a spirit of lightness, calm, joy, delight, happiness. Really enjoy the gentle stretching and the letting go. This wonderful feeling is exactly what you have embarked upon your pilgrimage to find. Learn to recognize it in these moments. Discover that you can allow it to expand and become more powerful. Believe that you can bring it into other moments of your life as well. As you become more proficient, if there is ever a feeling of boredom or routine, it is a signal that you are not in contact with the present. If you are present to this movement, you can be in the presence of this wonderful bliss.

- When you have completed the first phase, select a sitting posture for your meditation. The traditional postures, such as the lotus or half-lotus used in yoga or the kneeling posture of Zen, are best because they maximize stability and minimize movement for the duration of the meditation. Unfortunately, many of us are not flexible enough to use these postures beneficially. If your joints are flexible, you might try one of these postures, but again, do not strain. The object is to find a posture in which you can sit quietly for about twenty minutes. Most of us will feel most comfortable in a chair. The chair should be hard and straight-backed; easy chairs and other heavily cushioned chairs will not do. Sit forward on the chair, both feet on the floor, and support your back by yourself rather than by leaning against the back of the chair.

The meditation posture, like the meditation itself, should be somewhere between relaxation and alertness. The posture then must be relatively comfortable for you, and there should be no strain in holding it. On the other hand, the posture should keep you attentive. With a little experimentation you will find the best posture for yourself.

When you have found and assumed your meditation posture, turn your attention inward. In the past we have done this by concentrating on our breathing. Now we will learn a new technique called the mantra. A mantra is a word or phrase used in meditation to deepen and calm the mind. Our mantra is an Aramaic word, *Maranatha,* that means "Come, Lord," and became one of the earliest Christian prayers. The *a* sounds are pronounced as in *father* with a secondary accent on the first syllable and the main accent on the last syllable. The meaning of mantras is secondary. Their primary quality is their ability to deepen meditation and bring a sense of peace and calm to the mind.

- Say the mantra over to yourself out loud until you become familiar with it. Pick a comfortable tone, take a breath, and chant the mantra on that tone. As you chant, allow your voice and throat to be open and full. Chant from your chest rather than from the throat. Chant loud enough that you can feel the gentle vibrations from the sound. Allow the sound to give you a massage. Let the chant resonate deep within you. As you chant, keep your mind on the chant; it will keep thoughts from entering your mind and distracting you. Until you have had experience with the mantra, it would be good for you to chant it out loud. But if you are in a place where chanting is not feasible, you can allow the mantra to repeat itself silently in your mind. Continue chanting the mantra for ten minutes. When you finish, sit quietly in silence for a few moments and feel the effects of the chant.

This form of relaxation and the mantra can be used for daily meditation. You may also chant the mantra, either aloud or silently, at different times during the day, such as when you are driving or standing in line. Used in this way, the mantra brings us to deeper levels of peace and silence, and it can create that inner peace in the rest of our day.

EXPLORATION **14b** MEDITATION, THIRD PHASE: ENTERING THE STORY
time: twenty-five minutes
materials: Bible (Luke 1:26–38; 1:46–55) and Journal (Prayer Diary)

• Today we add the third stage to our meditation. To begin, find the passage in the Bible that we are going to meditate on today, and now put the Bible where it will be convenient for you when you are ready to use it. Then spend five to ten minutes in phase one of your meditation.

In this meditation we should not limit ourselves to clock time, which is always simply an estimate. If you need more time for phase one, take that time even if it means not having time to do phase three today. If the time available for meditation is limited and you need more time to do the first phase, spend your time on the first two phases. This practice will help you learn how to relax, and the time spent relaxing is valuable in its own right. Do not rush the meditations; they cannot be forced. Take your time. The present moment is the important moment for you; receive what it has to give you. If you need the time to relax, take it. The meditation story can wait until another day when you have time to explore it.

● For the next five minutes, chant your mantra. Be with the chant and the mantra. If you find yourself distracted, try not to judge yourself or berate or condemn your mind. Be very gentle but quite firm; simply return your mind to the mantra and continue your meditation. The mantra will take us below thought. Thoughts distract us and keep us on the surface of consciousness. But when we seek to go beyond thought, we seek greater and greater awareness. Practice this awareness without thoughts now.

● Our purpose in the third phase of meditation is to encounter the story. What does the world of this story reveal to us? And secondly, how do I respond to the story from my experience? We are setting up a dialogue with the story. By entering into its world, we test that world and discover whether we wish to seek the world in this way.

The stories we will experiment with on our pilgrimage are quite special. (They lend themselves to the kind of reading and meditation we are doing.) At each encounter, the story reveals only what we are ready for and capable of learning at this time. But we can enter into dialogue with these stories again and again. The story does not change from time to time, but what we bring to the story differs as we progress along our spiritual path. So the stories open up for us on deeper and deeper levels.

Imagination is the key element in this phase of the meditation. It enables us to enter the world of the stories. We have already begun to develop this capacity, and as we continue our journey we will become more confident in our power of imagination. If we find ourselves falling into routine or if we find our meditations becoming dull and lifeless, we may not be using our imaginative powers as fully as possible; imagination offers a limitless world of possibilities.

There are a number of ways you can perform these meditations. Doing them in the company of others is best. There you have the support of the group and can share your insights and feelings with the group, enriching on another's experimentation. In a group setting choose a meditation leader each time. That person then leads the others through the story. When the meditation is completed and you have taken some time in quiet, share the experiences of the meditation. What have other people discovered on this same pilgrimage?

If you meditate alone, read through the entire meditation before you begin phase one. In this way you will know the general movement of the exploration, and you can guide yourself accordingly. If you have a cassette recorder, you can record the meditation and then allow the tape to guide you through the exploration. Leave blank spaces on the tape to allow you to enter into the exploration when you play it back or if your recorder has a pause control, you can simply start and stop the tape as you want during the meditation. Of course, you can also read the meditation as you are doing the exploration. With a little practice, you can learn to do this without interrupting your silence and meditative mood.

• Now let's enter into our meditation. The story of the Annunciation tells how Mary found that she was to be the mother of the Savior for whom all Israel waited. Israel's constant dreaming for over a thousand years is about to be fulfilled. She is the handmaid of the Lord who lives in the hope of a Savior.

To begin the meditation, reflect on your own dreams and hopes for this pilgrimage. What would fulfill your own dreams concerning this quest we have begun? What are your hopes concerning a teacher or guide for this spiritual journey? What kind of help would you like to receive on this quest?

• Now take your Bible and read the story of the Annunciation in Luke 1:26–38. Read it over slowly, perhaps twice. Read it as though you had never heard it before.

• When you read it, recreate it in your imagination. Perhaps you want to spend some time drawing the scene in the Prayer Experience section of your journal. The Annunciation has been a favorite theme of Christian artists throughout the centuries. How do you envision the encounter between the maid and the angelic messenger?

In our meditation we leave analysis behind. Our purpose is simply to be with the story, to enter into it, and to allow it to interact with us and reveal itself to us. Allow the scene to become present: Notice the background, what Mary is wearing, how she looks. Let your imagination supply all the details of color, texture, sounds, smells, touch, and feeling. Now picture the angel. Questions such as whether angels really exist do not concern us here. In these meditations we can accept anything we can imagine; allow your limits of what you consider real to expand accordingly. Let the story have the time and room to expand for you.

• Now pass over into Mary in this story. Put on her experience. As Mary, how do you react as you see the angel and hear the words? At any time you feel the need, return to the Scriptural account for help in putting on the story. Can you imagine how Mary reacts in her body to the presence of the angel? Does she express her surprise or fear in gestures? Repeat those gestures in your own body and observe what feelings they call up in you.

How does the angel make its presence known to you? How do you react to the news that you will be the mother of the Savior? Are you confused? After all, you are not even married. Are you afraid?

In the story Mary bows her head in obedience and says, "Let it be done to me according to your will." Bow your head and say these words in imitation of Mary. Can you taste some of the peace, the humility, the hope that is a part of this surrender?

• Mary understands the angel's message in terms of the traditions of Israel. She dreams of liberation for her people, salvation from tyranny and oppression. As part of your own meditation, pray Mary's prayer in Luke 1:46–55; it will help you gain insight into her own and Israel's hope for a savior. Can you see what kind of savior Israel was hoping for? What part do these hopes for political freedom and social justice play in your own dreams for yourself? Do your hopes and dreams for a better life include a desire for a better life for those around you? Is there any real difference between our dreams for a better way of living for ourselves and for our society and world at large? Aren't they one and the same? Would you be satisfied living in a world where others not only lacked what you had, but lacked even the bare necessities of food and shelter?

113

• As you finish your meditation, come back slowly to yourself. Spend a moment in quiet. Then open your eyes and review your meditation for a moment. What was revealed to you in this experiment? What is your response to the story—feelings, experiences, thoughts?

• Review your experience of meditation today, examining the process rather than the contents. Were you bothered by distractions? Did the meditation move easily? Was it enjoyable? Did you feel any resistance? Where? In the Prayer Diary of your journal now write a few sentences to briefly describe the meditation.

This procedure can be used for all the meditations on our pilgrimage. The entire process usually takes about twenty-five minutes, seldom more than a half hour unless you choose otherwise (drawing a picture would take more time) or unless you need more time for phase one. The first two phases are also an excellent way to prepare for biblical reading or for journal work and they can also form a complete meditation in themselves.

During our pilgrimage we will use many stories for meditation. Indeed this process will now become our primary way of entering into Scripture. We will reserve for special occasions the method of reading we have begun to learn. Of course, you can continue to read the Scriptures on your own, using the guidelines and skills we have been practicing to set off on your own journey of discovery.

In addition to the stories we explore together on our pilgrimage, you may choose other stories for meditation, using this process: Enter into the story imaginatively through one or more of the characters and look at this story world from the viewpoint of its characters. As you travel further in this guide, you will continue to develop the skills that make this process easy and rewarding. Meditation will become a wonderful means of enrichment, horizon expansion, and sheer entertainment.

PART THREE

Jesus and His Kingdom

So far our journey has been a close look at where we are in our present life and a glance backward at our whole life as a pilgrimage toward wholeness. Last week we continued our quest by outfitting ourselves for the journey. Over the next few weeks you might want to acquire other equipment to help you on your quest. If you have enjoyed drawing in the earlier experiments, you might want to acquire some paints or crayons to help you explore the story world we will be entering in our exploration. In this section we will meet our guide and teacher for this pilgrimage. Teachers are important on this journey because finding the way alone is difficult. And since this teacher is so important, it will be helpful if you have a picture of him. At one point we will use the picture for meditation. If you don't want to draw a picture, begin looking for one. We suggest you get an icon of Jesus. The icon is considered holy because it allows the light of the person to shine through. You can find icons today in many religious book and gift stores.

But enough of preparations. Let's begin this part of our quest. Here we stand before the dark wood. Where shall we enter? Once again let us turn to John the Evangelist for direction.

15

READING JOHN
time: twenty-five minutes
materials: Bible (John 1:14-18) and Journal (Prayer Diary)

● Prepare for your reading by doing the first two phases of meditation explained in Explorations 14 and 14a. When you are ready, read the passage from John. Use all of your reading skills to enter into the passage and understand what John is communicating.

The new movement in this passage is that the Word, the meaning, actually becomes enfleshed in one human being. The meaning at the center of the universe clothed itself in a human life and lived as we live. This is a startling idea. For if it is true, then our search for meaning is no longer simply a search for some vision or philosophy by which we might find true life. Rather our search becomes the seeking of that individual who, as John says, is the Word itself. In this section, as we encounter Jesus we should continually ask ourselves whether the Word—the meaning of all existence—is enfleshed in this man.

Jesus is hardly an unknown entity in most of our lives. Perhaps we already consider ourselves his followers. We are Christians. We have agreed with John that Jesus is the Word incarnate. But our very familiarity and commitment to Jesus might pose problems for us on our pilgrimage. On this journey, we have seen how easily reading, hearing, and learning can be merely a process of reading, hearing, and learning what we already know or what we think we are going to learn. True learning is learning of something we do not know or that we have forgotten; for true learning to occur we must open ourselves to the other, be it a book, an idea, or a person. And we must receive that book, idea, or person first on its own terms; we must try to understand it as other before we can assimilate what it gives us.

But what if we feel, as most of us rightly do, that we already know Jesus? We have already heard his words and listened to his stories. We have either accepted him as our Savior and call ourselves Christians, or we have rejected him and sought elsewhere. Does he have anything to teach us?

Consider your own experience with Jesus. Has he nourished you in the past? Perhaps you feel he could give you more than he has. Are you willing to reexamine his teachings with an open mind in the hope that he might provide more nourishment? Can you set aside what you think you know about Jesus, at least during our pilgrimage, so that you can imaginatively encounter him anew? It is not necessary that we discard our past beliefs, only that we be aware of them and not let them stand in our way. Christian beliefs about Jesus are the flowering of the whole experience of Jesus. Our pilgrimage now will lead us toward those same beliefs, but we want to experience each step along the way. We will encounter Jesus just as his first disciples did. For us he will be a teacher and a man of power. And we will allow him to guide us. Along the way we will decide whether we do indeed want him as our guide for the rest of the journey. We will test him and his teachings to see if they do respond to our desires in undertaking this quest.

If we have seemingly rejected Jesus before, are we willing to enter into this experiment and test him as our teacher? Many who believe they have rejected Jesus have really rejected the Christian church. Many realize this and call themselves followers of Jesus but not Christians. Have you rejected Jesus as a teacher because you have experienced him firsthand, or have you simply rejected a secondhand picture of him? Would you be willing to give the man himself an opportunity to present his vision? And are you willing during this time to set aside your own beliefs and nonbeliefs concerning him and his followers? All the explorations ask is that you listen to this teacher and test what he has to offer.

117

• Take a few minutes to reflect on your own personal history with Jesus or his church. What do you believe about him? What can't you believe? Whatever your beliefs, do you feel you can risk an exploration with him in the hope he might have a response to your quest for wholeness? How much of a chance are you willing to give him? Are you willing to risk changing your present conceptions about him in this exploration? How open would you be to believing about Jesus only what you experience on this pilgrimage? If you are a believer, would you be willing to risk your current feelings about Jesus as the Savior? If you do not believe in Jesus, would you be willing to risk coming to believe in him as Savior? In either case, how open are you to learning what this word *Savior* means?

• In our investigation in this section, we will concentrate on three of John's ideas set forth in this passage. John speaks of beholding the glory of Jesus. What is this glory? What does glory mean for you?

What would you expect to see were you to behold glory? We must find out the meaning and the reality behind this word if we are to understand John here. So our first task in confronting Jesus is to see whether we can behold in him anything we might call glorious.

John reveals another important image for God in this passage. He calls God *Father*. So far we have used the images of meaning, word, light, and life for God. But what are the implications of saying he is *Father*? Think about what differences it might make for you if you could consider the meaning you seek as a Father. How is that different from seeing meaning as some great cosmic principle? We will explore Jesus' vision of God as Father to discover its relevance and import for us.

In this passage, John uses two other words that we will explore further: *grace* and *truth*. He talks of the Law coming through Moses but *grace* and *truth* coming through Jesus. What is grace? Or for that matter, what is truth as it is spoken of here? And once again there is an implied opposition or conflict: Moses is of the Law but Jesus is grace and truth. We have seen that conflict in the tension between the light and the darkness, and in the rejection of the light by his own. We will have to explore that tension and conflict in the message and person of Jesus.

One translation of this passage speaks of Jesus as the one "who is nearest to the Father's heart." Other translations speak of him as in closest intimacy with the Father. Jesus' revelation then will be a revelation of knowledge of the heart, rather than just a knowledge of the head. Learning to read the heart—our own heart and the heart of God—is a part of our own pilgrimage. We will seek a way for heart to speak to heart.

As another step on that journey let us conclude by reflecting on how our reading today was a reading from the heart. Was it a reading that arose from your own hopes and aspirations? How might your reading be more from your heart and less from your head? What things prevent your reading from being from your heart? What might aid you in learning to read from your heart?

• As you conclude your reading, jot down your experiences in your Prayer Diary. Briefly describe your thoughts during the reading and add any pertinent matter on the process of reading. If you have gained any new insights into the art of reading, enter them in the appropriate page of your Process Log.

16

THE KINGDOM OF GOD

time: twenty minutes   materials: Bible (Mark 1:14-15) and Journal (Prayer Experience)

We need some central idea that we can use to gain a quick appreciation of Jesus and his message. We find such an idea in the first words of Jesus in the gospels of Matthew, Mark, and Luke.

• Read those words now in Mark's gospel, which is considered the first gospel to be written down. Matthew is even terser than Mark, and he quotes the same words: "Repent, for the kingdom of Heaven is upon you!" Being of Jewish origin, Matthew uses *Heaven* as a euphemism for *God*, for a Jew does not use the holy name.

• In the fourth part of our pilgrimage, we will explore the meaning of repentance. But now let's consider the second part of Jesus' statement: the kingdom of God is at hand. Just what is this kingdom of God? Where is it? What is it like? And what does it mean to say it is at hand?

119

What associations do these words have for us? If we were raised in the Christian tradition, we must have heard them before. Do we think we know their meaning, or does it elude us?

If we are not acquainted with the Christian tradition, these words still have many associations and meanings for us: They are familiar English words; we are familiar with them individually in many other contexts. We must have some idea what they refer to.

• Prepare for meditation as usual. But since this is not a detailed meditation, you can dispense with the physical preparation unless you feel particularly in need of it. Just focus on your breathing for a few moments and spend some time with the mantra.

• Put that phrase *kingdom of God* at the center of your thoughts. As you focus on this phrase, allow it to call forth associations. For example, the idea of *king* may arise. As an association comes into consciousness, reflect on it for a moment and then return your attention to *kingdom of God* and await the next association to arise. The next idea may be *political*; reflect on it a moment and return to the original. Your associations may be words, ideas, smells, touches, whole scenes.

Try not to censor; be receptive to whatever comes up even if it might not seem to have much in common with your key phrase. Continue this process for about fifteen minutes.

• Now turn to the Prayer Diary in your journal and write a brief description of your experience. What understandings do you already have of this "kingdom of God"? During the course of our exploration, keep in mind these understandings. Try not to let them color what you hear Jesus saying. They might be what he too has in mind, or they might not be. Nevertheless, they form your own side of the dialogue about the kingdom now, even if they do not fit in with Jesus' idea.

EXPLORATION **16a**
THE KINGDOM OF GOD
time: twenty minutes   materials: Bible
(Luke 4:14-22) and Journal (Prayer Diary)

Luke describes the inauguration of Jesus' ministry differently from Mark and Matthew. As he often does, he tells a beautiful story that throws further light on the kingdom of God.

• Prepare as usual for meditation. When you are ready, read Luke's passage several times and then close your eyes. Imagine the scene. You are present in the synagogue. Notice the other people around you. What do they look like? You are at the Sabbath service. Sense the atmosphere of prayer, solemnity, and holiness.

A young man gets up and walks to the front of the synagogue. One of the old men hands him a scroll. He bows to the scroll and kisses it. He is unrolling it. Listen to the words as he reads. Read those words of the prophet Isaiah over and over to yourself now. Give them time to speak to you. What are they saying? How do you understand them? How do you relate to them? Do they fill you with hope? Do they move you? Would you like to see such things happen? How does this description of the kingdom of God relate to your own ideas in the previous meditation? Do you feel that Isaiah's words are describing the kingdom of God?

The young man rolls up the scroll and gives it back to the old man. All eyes are on this young man. What will he say? There is a thrill of expectation. Now you hear the words "Today in your very hearing this text has come true" (The New English Bible). How do these words strike you? What do you feel would be necessary for the man's statement to be believed? Do you believe the man? If so, what makes you believe? Is it something you've seen here, or is it simply because you're used to believing him? See if you can lay aside any previous belief. What within this story might lead you to believe this man? What keeps you from believing him? Is there anything here that draws you toward belief? What hinders you from believing the man?

• When you have completed the meditation, add in the Prayer Diary of your journal any of your observations about the kingdom of God or about the meditation process.

EXPLORATION   **17** ENCOUNTER WITH ZACCHAEUS
time: twenty-five minutes   materials: Bible (Luke 19:1-10)
and Journal (Prayer Diary)

Now that we have found a focus—the kingdom of God—for our examination of Jesus, we are ready for our first face-to-face meeting with him. For this exploration we will learn another relaxation exercise during phase one of the meditation. This exercise, from Hatha Yoga, is one of the easiest and most important of the yoga asanas, or postures. Although it is called the corpse pose it is not at all gruesome and is quite enjoyable. It should be done lying down, but if that is not possible, you can practice in a chair. The key to this exercise lies in creating and expanding feelings of relaxation by applying tension and relaxation to various areas of the body.

• Lie on your back on the floor and make yourself as comfortable as possible. Your feet should be about half a foot to a foot apart, your arms resting about the same distance from your sides. Take a few deep breaths, and as the air leaves your body, imagine yourself sinking into relaxation.

Begin with the feet. Inhale and lift your left leg about six inches off the floor. Tense the muscles of leg and foot. Put as much tension into the leg as you can, all the while holding the breath. Then quickly expel the breath, drop your leg to the floor, and release all the tension. Exhale forcefully during this exercise: Allow your breath to rush out, and at the same time feel the tension and pressure fall away. Now do the same routine with the right leg.

Next move up to the buttocks. Inhale and tense the buttocks. Hold the breath and the tension a minute, then release both and relax.

Now we move on to the hands and arms. Leaving the left hand on the floor, stretch the fingers as far apart from one another as possible. Feel the stretch. Now inhale, make a fist, and raise the left arm about six inches off the floor. Create as much tension as possible in the arm and hand. Hold your breath and the tension a moment, then let go. Try to release the tension all at once, dropping the arm to the floor as if it were dead weight. Repeat this action with the right arm.

Now take a deep breath and push the air way down into your stomach and gut. Push it as far as it will go. Your abdomen should be distended. Hold your breath a moment and then exhale it forcefully.

Inhale again, but this time keep the breath in the chest area. Expand the chest and rib cage as much as you can. When you have filled your chest, see if you can take in just a little more air. Increase the stretch and the tension. Now let go. From now on, breathe gently; we will not be using the breath to create tension in the rest of this exercise.

Turn your attention to your shoulders; notice any tension. Bring the shoulders up from the floor as though you were trying to bring the shoulder blades together. Relax them. Now raise your shoulders toward your ears and then relax them.

Many of us carry much of our tension in the neck area, so it is very important to spend time relaxing the neck. Slowly roll your head from side to side. Stretch throughout this exercise but do not strain. As you roll your head, imagine the tension oozing from your neck and falling to the floor. Do this roll three or four times until you feel relaxed.

The face is another great repository of tension. This exercise may show you just how tense your body is. As you continue to practice the exercise, you will experience deeper and deeper relaxation, and you will also become more attuned to stress and tension in your body. Recognizing tension is the first step toward control.

We will do two stretches in the facial area. First bring the entire face inward toward your nose. Push the lips up toward the nose; bring the eyes and brows down toward the nose; pucker your cheeks and suck them in toward the nose. Hold this stretch a moment, then relax. The second stretch works in the opposite direction: Pull the entire face away from the center. Open your mouth and stick out your tongue as far as you can; feel the stretch in the lips, jaw, and tongue. Open your eyes as wide as you can. Stretch all the skin back from the center of your face and toward the sides. Hold the stretch for a moment and then relax. Now once more pull the face in toward the nose. If you feel the need, you may repeat any of these stretches until you feel the tension decrease in that area.

• When you are sufficiently relaxed, move into phase two of the meditation. Begin phase two by reading through the story of Zacchaeus.

• In our meditation, we'll enter into this story as deeply as we can. First we will assume the role of one of the townspeople. Experience the excitement around Jesus' intended visit to your town. What have you heard about this man and his teachings? You want to see him in person. What would you hope to experience when you see him?

123

You are now crowded in the street with all your friends and neighbors as Jesus approaches. Feel the excitement and anticipation in the crowd. Here he is coming down the street. If you jump up and down, you can see him over the heads of the people in front of you. But then he stops. He calls up into a tree. He singles out worthless, shifty old Zacchaeus. He wants to stay with him—the dregs of the earth. Imagine Zacchaeus as the person you have least respect and regard for. See Jesus talking with that person and inviting himself to stay with him. How would you feel? Allow that feeling to expand so that you can taste it in its fullness.

• Now pass over into the experience of Zacchaeus. What is it like to be an outcast in this town? You have felt people snub you, look down on you; children make fun of you. On the other hand, you are very rich. You try to convince yourself that your wealth makes everything all right. Put on Zacchaeus' experience now. He's not a very kind, outgoing man. He is shy and small. He's used to being the brunt of jokes. Feel what it is like to be this crabbed human being.

Zacchaeus too wants to see this great teacher. Go through his experience as he waits with the crowd and then decides to climb a tree. What makes you decide to climb the tree? Do you want to get a better view? Do you want to be unnoticed? Do you want to be able to see this Jesus up close without him seeing you?

You are now sitting up in the tree. You see Jesus approach. He stops in front of your tree and looks up—right at you. Then he speaks your name, tells you to come down because he wants to stay with you tonight. Go through this experience now; allow each progression in the action to expand so that you can explore your feelings and thoughts.

You hear the townspeople muttering about you. Can you ignore it? How does it sound in the face of what Jesus has just offered you? Something very big is happening to Zacchaeus now. Can you enter into and imagine what this change is like for him? Speak the words Zacchaeus speaks to Jesus: "Here and now, Sir, I give half my possessions to charity; and if I have cheated anyone, I am ready to repay him four times over" (The New English Bible). How does it feel to say and believe those words? How does this experience differ from Zacchaeus' experience before he encountered Jesus?

• Now reenter the story as yourself, but put yourself in Zacchaeus' place. If you had a chance to see Jesus, what would your expectations be? What do you want from Jesus now? What would you like to see him say or do? Now Jesus calls you out of your tree and tells you he will stay with you. How do you feel? Can you feel something of that change in Zacchaeus from closed to open, from misery to joy, from stinginess to generosity?

Zacchaeus gives up half his wealth. What physical things would you give up in a similar situation? What psychological things would you be willing to give up—your pride, anger, sense of security, sense of superiority, fear, shyness, power over others? What would Jesus' openness to you allow you to part with freely? And can you gain any sense of the joy that allows Zacchaeus to do what he does? Have you ever experienced such a liberating moment in your own life? Can you imagine what it would be like?

• Jesus tells Zacchaeus and the crowd, "Salvation has come to this house today!" (The New English Bible). What do you think he means here? What does salvation mean for Zacchaeus in terms of the way he will live from now on? Do you feel in the story any moral demand that

Zacchaeus be generous? Or rather does Zacchaeus' new generosity simply flow from the transformation that has taken place within him? Do you suspect that Zacchaeus has passed over into the kingdom? What would that imply about life in the kingdom? What does the story of Zacchaeus say about the kingdom?

Now what does the word *salvation* promise you? Be as concrete as possible: What do you want to be saved from? If that sounds too negative, ask what you want from Jesus. What specifically do you hope he might offer you? Would you like to become generous like Zacchaeus? What would you like?

• When you have completed your meditation, write a summary of it in the Prayer Diary of your journal.

EXPLORATION

17a

TO BE KNOWN BY JESUS
time: thirty minutes
materials: Journal (Life Experience)

We have discovered that Zacchaeus is in much the same position that we are in. He does not know Jesus, but he has heard about him and is curious. He wants a closer look at Jesus. Jesus discovers him, ferrets him out, and changes his life. We have learned that to enter Jesus' presence one runs the risk of being known through and through. In this exploration we will explore just how well we are known and how we feel about being known as Zacchaeus was known to Jesus.

• Prepare for this exploration by spending five minutes with the mantra, unless you feel a need for further relaxation.

• As we take Zacchaeus' place in the tree, Jesus calls us by name. He knows us. But what does he know? And what are our feelings about being known? On a blank page in the Life Experience section of your journal draw a large circle almost the size of the page. Within that large circle draw five concentrically smaller circles. Label the largest circle "public," the next "acquaintances," the next "friends," then "intimates," and finally "private." In the center draw a dot and call it "the unknown I."

This schema shows the different layers of ourselves we show to various groups and individuals. Take ten to fifteen minutes now to fill in the schema with things about yourself that you feel comfortable revealing to each group. What do you reveal about yourself to the world at large? How are you known there? Write down here your profession, your family status, and any other things that are public knowledge about you. Then next consider how you are known by your acquaintances. What further things about yourself would you reveal to friends? To intimates? Fill in as much of the circle as you can.

•   When you come to the last circle, "the unknown I," you cannot fill it in because it is unknown even to you. But you do have hints concerning this unknown layer. You have hopes, dreams, and fears that hint at your real self. On another page, put the title "the unknown I" and list any hints, hopes, or fears you have concerning this mysterious part of you. In your original diagram the unknown I was just a dot. But now on the second page consider just how big you feel that unknown I is. How large is it in your actual life? Is it tiny, or great? How well do you think you really know yourself? How much do you want to learn concerning what is really in the unknown I circle? Draw a circle to represent the size of your unknown self.

•   What might it be like to be known in each of these successive circles by Jesus? What might it be like to have this man penetrate through all my layers and know completely the "I" in each one? Are there things we would like him to know about us? Are there things we are afraid of his knowing? Are there elements of joy, shame, fear, or anger in being known? As Zacchaeus became known to Jesus, he was transformed from the tax collector and miser his neighbors knew into a very generous person who gave away half his possessions. Do you suspect that anything in your own being might change by being known?

•   To conclude your meditation, write a paragraph on the theme "What it might mean for Jesus to know me." Put it in the Life Experience section of your journal.

While our original intention was to investigate Jesus and his message to discover whether we wish to take him as our teacher and guide, we have seen in this exploration that an investigation into Jesus and his kingdom is likely to involve an investigation into ourselves as well. Jesus does not leave the kingdom on a level where it can be objectively and dispassionately studied. Rather he transports people into that kingdom.

Our attempt to see Jesus and examine the kingdom has revealed to us the possibility that we in turn might be known to Jesus in a very deep, startling way. Encountering Jesus may lead to encountering ourselves at depths we have not dreamed possible. For who would have dreamed that Zacchaeus the tax collector would be capable of giving away half his wealth? No one, least of all Zacchaeus himself. Yet this new generosity was indeed the generosity of Zacchaeus. No one asks him for it; no one requests it of him. It flows forth from that unknown depth of Zacchaeus and reveals its beauty to all the world. Could this be a clue to the kingdom: The kingdom is where all the hidden beauty within each of us can finally be revealed?

In our meditation we might have experienced fear at the thought of being known by Jesus. It is frightening to be known; it is even frightening to know ourselves; we keep much repressed. But look at Zacchaeus' experience of being known. It is neither fearful nor shameful, but liberating and joyous. Zacchaeus has no qualms or second thoughts about being known. He is freed by this knowledge. Beforehand he may have been quite terrified of the prospect; he may have been hurt by being known by other people. He was estranged from his neighbors and did not want to be known by them. But he has no hesitation when Jesus asks to come to his house. He does not hesitate to give up half his wealth. At least for Zacchaeus, and by implication for us all, the kingdom involves being known by Jesus, and that knowledge leads to liberation and joy.

18

THE PRODIGAL FARMER
time: twenty-five minutes
materials: Bible (Matthew 13:4-9)

● When you have prepared as usual for the meditation, read the parable in your Bible. Jesus often uses parables to teach us about the kingdom. We can see each of the parables of the kingdom as a vision of what life is like in the kingdom. Thus the parable becomes a little world, a microcosm, by which we can come to know and experience the kingdom.

Unfortunately, some of the parables are difficult for us today. Some have been misunderstood and perhaps changed as they passed from Jesus through the communities and finally into the hands of the gospel writer. Still other parables cause us difficulty today because situations depicted are no longer familiar to us and may seem quite exotic.

Our present parable is a case in point. Most of us do not know the first thing about farming, and so the parable loses its impact for us. Seed is expensive, and no one purposely wastes the seed as this farmer does. A normal farmer would carefully prepare his land for the seed. And when he plants the seed he would place each seed where he believed it had a good chance to grow and bear fruit.

● Spend a few moments now acting like a normal farmer. In your meditation, carefully prepare your land and then plant your seeds.

● Now pass over into this story that Jesus says resembles the kingdom of God. Envision the story in all its details. Allow your imagination free play. What does the land look like? Feel the heat of the sun. Is there a breeze blowing? Are there any trees around? What does the farmer look like? Is he old, or young?

Watch him scatter the seed to the wind. Compare him with the farmer who planted each seed carefully. How is he different? Would you say he is more carefree? Would you call him reckless or wasteful?

Watch where the seed falls. See it try to grow on the rocky ground. See the birds eat the seed on the footpath. See it choked among the thistles. But finally witness the hundredfold harvest that manages to survive and come to fruit. Imagine the field overflowing with grain.

• Now return to the field you sowed as a normal farmer. Your seed comes up as well. But is it as abundant as that of the prodigal farmer? Your seed grows in neat rows, but some of it doesn't grow; there are bare patches. Strangely, the other farmer's field is chock full of grain. You can hardly walk through it, it is so full.

• What does this story tell you concerning the kingdom of God? Jesus speaks of a wonderfully generous farmer who throws his precious seed to the wind. Much of the seed is lost, but the harvest of the seed that took root is tremendous. Our image of the kingdom from this story is that it is generous and prodigal. Does such generosity appeal to you? Have you experienced in your own life generosity and prodigality that give you some hope that Jesus might be right when he describes the kingdom in this way?

Would you want to live in such a world? What does this rich and overabundant life imply for you? Do you have any inkling that this world Jesus describes might be the way reality truly is? Or do you think the story is just a nice dream? Do you have any idea where you might find such a generous and abundantly caring place?

18a THE PRODIGAL FARMER (continued)
time: thirty minutes
materials: Journal (Prayer Experience)
and crayons or water colors (optional)

Today we will approach the same story we meditated on in Exploration 18 from a different angle. We will enter into dialogue with the story by translating it into a different artistic medium.

• Prepare for this exploration by doing the first and second phases of meditation.

• We have heard this story from Jesus as an example of what the kingdom of God is like. In response we will translate the essence of this parable into another medium. This will put us in touch with this story on a different level.

You may choose, for example, to draw or paint the story. It is not necessary that you have great artistic talent or training. The important aim is to enter deeply into the story through whatever artistic process you choose. We are using the creative process to expand our imagination.

• If you wish to work in the medium of words, try translating the essence of the story into, for example, a haiku poem. The haiku is a simple form of three lines. Usually the first line has seven syllables, the second and third lines five syllables each. This short, compact structure forces us to distill the essence of this parable down to seventeen syllables. We are not seeking an aphorism—a moral or a philosophic statement; we are seeking a poem that points in the same direction as the story. The poem may or may not use the imagery of the story. In this meditation we are going behind the imagery and behind any explanations to capture this experience of the kingdom of God.

In most of our explorations the process is almost more important than the contents. So here our finished product is not so important to us and to our pilgrimage as is the struggle between the parable and the artistic form we choose. It is through the struggle that we come to know the kingdom, and through the struggle we are transformed, just as Jacob becomes Israel in his struggle with the angel. The limits of this experiment are those of your own imagination. You can paint the story, make it a haiku, dance it, sing it, or mime it (the latter is great fun for a group to do). But whatever you do, enter into it fully and struggle with its vision of life.

EXPLORATION **18b** THE PRODIGAL FARMER (continued)
time: twenty-five minutes
materials: Journal (Prayer Diary)

• Prepare for the exploration by doing the first two phases of meditation.

Today we are going to enter once more into this parable. Now, however, we will do what the disciples often did to Jesus' stories: Use the story as an allegory of our life. You may see in Matthew 13:18-23 how Matthew's community allegorized the present parable. It would be best, however, if you didn't read this allegory until after the present exercise. We do not want it to limit your interpretation.

The beauty of Jesus' parables is their ability to communicate on many different levels and about many concerns. No simple explanation can set forth the parable's meaning. Otherwise Jesus could have forestalled much confusion by simply giving the explanation. Since the kingdom of God is so different from the world we know, it is only possible to point toward it by means of these parables. Each parable can say something to us, can address our own concerns and needs. Like all artistic creations, the parable then comes alive and can relate to us wherever we might be.

● First, imagine an ordinary farmer carefully planting the seed. When that image is established through your imagination, enter into Jesus' story by putting on the role of his farmer. Imagine that the seed is your own life. It can stand for the individual moments of your life and your whole lifetime. It can stand for your talents, your creativity, your ability to love and care for people. Like all seed, it is precious. Often we feel that we do not have enough: We aren't talented enough, we don't have enough time, we don't have enough love to go around. Have you ever felt this way? Enter into that experience now. Feeling this way, you are likely to plant your seed as does the careful farmer. You want that seed to take root and bear fruit. You can't afford to waste it.

131

● But instead, take the seed and cast it to the wind as the farmer in Jesus' story does. Cast the seeds of your life to the wind. What might it mean for you to live this way? Would you be afraid? Would you regret and fret about what you were doing? In your meditation, cast out all these inhibiting feelings. Within the shelter of this meditation you can experiment with what this kind of life would be like. Let this prodigality seduce you. What might it have to show you about living?

● How would you act differently if you could live this way, casting your seeds to the wind with confidence that you will reap a hundredfold? If you lived this way, would you be totally in charge? Would you have to relinquish some of the control you now wield? Would you also have to give up worrying? If you worry now, think about how your worry might be multiplied out of all proportion if you lived this way.

See the seeds that get eaten by the birds. Are there moments or seeds of your life that you feel have met the same fate? Use your imagination and memory. Are there any things or relationships in your life that have burst into flower very quickly, but then died for want of roots? Look at the elements of your life in terms of the fate of each of these seeds.

But now look at the hundredfold yield your prodigality has brought you. Have you ever experienced anything like this? Can you believe that this might happen if you could come to see your life and its chances with the eyes of this prodigal farmer? The world says that if you act this way, you are stupid and wasteful. The kingdom says that if you act this way, you reap a hundredfold. Which would you like to believe? Does anything in your experience lead you to think the world might be wrong and the kingdom right? Since we are firmly imbedded in the world, it should be easier to see the world as right and the kingdom as wrong. But can you at least imagine this other way of living? Do you dare trust your seeds to the wind? Do you dare trust this story of Jesus as a story about things as they really are?

• Spend the last five minutes or so summarizing your experiences over the three sections of this exploration. What have you learned about the kingdom? What makes you lean toward believing Jesus? What argues against him? Finally, describe your meditation process in this exploration. Enter your summary in the Prayer Diary of your journal.

EXPLORATION **19** BLIND BARTIMAEUS
time: twenty-five mintues
materials: Bible (Mark 10:46-52)
and Journal (Prayer Diary)

Today we will learn a new technique to help us relax in phase one of our meditation.

• First, review your day; then do the new relaxation technique. This exercise is helpful not when we are tense all over, but when we are excited and need to calm down. Begin by scanning your body. If you notice tension in any area, tense the area and hold your breath. Then relax the area as you release your breath.

The face and head usually carry much of our tension and worry. Yawning helps to release that facial and neck tension. For the next few minutes, engage in some conscious yawning to help you relax. Just begin to yawn. But really yawn. Feel the stretch all through your jaw, face, and neck. Yawn wider than you ever have before. Quickly the contrived yawns will give rise to real yawns; we are very susceptible to yawning. Unfortunately, most of the time we try to stifle them. But now give in to the yawn completely. Luxuriate in it. Let the yawning continue until you feel the relaxation flowing throughout your face and neck and out into the rest of your body. You won't yawn to death. When the tension is gone, the yawning will stop and you will feel quite relaxed and at ease.

• Now read the story of Bartimaeus in Mark and then follow as we enter the story. Recreate the scene of the story: the sights, sounds, smells, feelings, touches, thoughts, emotions, motions. Enter it as fully as possible. Enter first as yourself. You have already encountered Jesus once; here is another opportunity. What do you anticipate learning from him in this encounter? Allow your anticipation and excitement to grow.

• Begin to walk down the street to where Jesus is supposed to pass. As you walk, allow the sights and sounds to be present to you. What do you feel as you approach this meeting? What does your anticipation taste like? Speak about your expectations to an imaginary friend who is going to see Jesus with you. Perhaps you hope he will answer your questions. Perhaps you are afraid to meet this mysterious man again; he might challenge you. Whatever you are feeling as you walk, be aware of it and savor it.

You notice that there are many people walking in the same direction as you are. What kind of people are they? Do you recognize anyone? Feel the mood of the crowd and allow its excitement to add to your own. There is much expectation in the air. Get caught up in the feeling as you walk with these people.

You arrive at the corner where he will pass by. Quite a crowd is there already; the sidewalk is packed. There is some gentle pushing and shoving as people try to get a better spot. Jesus is due any moment.

Take in the scene around you: the people, the stores, the kind of day it is. Allow the details of your surroundings to make themselves present to you.

There is much noise and excitement all around you. A beggar has been standing near you. You try to stay away from him because he reeks of urine. He wears a tattered grey coat and a little cap. He is blind and carries a small cup which he shoves in front of people to beg for money. Now he shoves it in front of you and shakes it. What do you do? Do you give him some money? Do you ignore him? He is very pushy and aggressive, even mean. How do you feel about him? If you give him some money, what are your real reasons? Do you do it to help him out? Or do you just hope that he will go away?

There is a surge in the crowd. You assume Jesus has made his appearance about a block away. He must be moving down the street toward you. You strain to catch sight of him.

Now he is in sight. What does he look like? Your anticipation is rising higher and higher. Just as he approaches your section of the street, something happens. That blind beggar has squeezed through to the street and begins shouting, "Jesus, have pity on me! Jesus, have pity on me!" He screams it out at the top of his voice again and again. His voice is harsh and mean. He is very angry. He is used to making a nuisance of himself, so he continues to yell with a voice that reminds you of chalk on a chalkboard. How do you react?

The crowd tries to quiet him, but without success. He's sitting just a few feet from you. There is no way you can ignore him. What are your feelings? How does this man fit in with your own idea of what should happen at this encounter with Jesus? This may be your only chance to see Jesus. If, like most of the others, you want to keep the beggar quiet, do it now. What do you do or say to him?

The man will not be quiet. Jesus has obviously heard him by now. Jesus gathers his disciples in a circle and talks to them. The circle breaks and the disciples approach the beggar. They say something to him and then lead him back toward Jesus. What are you thinking? Are you frustrated? Confused? Expectant?

Now the crowd is very quiet. The beggar stands before Jesus. Jesus asks, "What do you want?" The beggar yells back, "I want to see." Jesus reaches out and touches the man's head. The beggar starts to leap and jump around. "I can see, I can see," he yells. The crowd goes wild, and you hear cries of "Miracle! Miracle!" Do you believe what you saw?

What if the beggar wasn't really blind? Do you think he might be a plant to make Jesus look good and win over the crowd? It certainly makes a good show. If you are skeptical, allow your skepticism to surface. You turn to someone near you and ask about the beggar. "Oh, he's been around here forever," you are told. "Everybody knows old blind Bart." How do you respond to this news? Now do you believe what you have seen?

Perhaps it's a psychosomatic illness—the man believed he was blind, and so he could not see. Jesus was able to destroy the block, and now he sees. But there was nothing physically wrong with his eyes. It's simply the power of mind over matter. How does this explanation strike you?

• Focus on your feelings about this healing. Do you notice any resistance? Are you searching for ways to explain away the healing? Does it help you to believe it is only psychological? Do you believe the man's eyes are physically healed and restored? Allow your resistance to surface. Don't fight or block it. Rather, observe it. Become familiar with it. How does it feel?

19a

BLIND BARTIMAEUS (continued)
time: twenty-five minutes

• Prepare again for meditation (unless you are simply continuing from the previous session).

• Pass over into the role of the blind beggar Bartimaeus. Imagine yourself blind from birth. Imagine your life without sight. You have never seen anything. You live in a world of darkness. You beg for a living. You are an outcast from society. Your hardships have made you bitter and angry. Put yourself into this role through feelings, thoughts, and imagined experiences.

You've heard that Jesus is coming to town. Some say he works miracles. As Bartimaeus, how do you feel about Jesus' coming? Are your expectations different from when you played yourself?

• Now begin your walk down to the street where Jesus is supposed to appear. Go with your blindness, your begging cup, your cane, your rage, your hopes. You take the same route everyday to go begging. You reek of urine. You are used to having people avoid you; you hear them make room for you. They pretend not to see you. But you're no longer afraid to make a nuisance of yourself. If you don't, you'll be totally ignored, and you'll die blind.

As you walk along, imagine one of your typical days. You wake up in your hovel or in the gutter. What do you do for breakfast? Then you walk down the street and spend ten hours begging. Feel the darkness, the frustration, the boredom, the fear. Now you are going to see this miracle worker. What do you hope from him?

136

You arrive at the corner where he will pass by. You feel the push of the crowd around you. There is a noise at the other end of the street. You know he's coming. Here's your chance. Push your way through the crowd now. You don't care what people think; you've got to get to the street. Suddenly the crowd clears and you feel yourself in the open. Yell out now, "Jesus, have pity on me!" Yell it in your imagination. If you can do so, yell it out loud. Really yell. Yell it out of your blackness. This is your only chance. Make sure he hears you. The people are trying to keep you quiet. How do you respond to them? Yell again with everything you have. You have to make Jesus hear you if you really want to see.

Now you feel hands on you. They are leading you out into the street. The voices around you are soft and kind. Let them lead you. What are you experiencing now?

You are standing in the middle of the street. The crowd is all around and not too friendly. But there is another presence here. You hear a voice, "What do you want?" What does that voice sound like? Have you heard it before? Now tell the voice you want to see. You feel hands on top of your head. What do they feel like? What is happening to you?

Now the first light hits your eyes. For the first time in your life you see. At first, it is just light, and it hurts. You don't know what it is because you've never experienced it before. Now your eyes begin to focus. There is a face in front of you—the face of Jesus. It's your first sight. Take time to look closely at that face. What does Jesus look like?

Your joy and excitement overflow. Your body shakes. You are dancing in the street, yelling at the top of your lungs, "I can see! I can see!" Enter into that ecstasy now.

• Now look at the begging cup in your hand. You've carried it practically all your life. It's been your salvation. But now that you can see, you can no longer hold on to this cup, you can no longer hold on to your begging, to your poverty, to your anger, to being a nuisance. You can't hold on to anything from your past. You have started a new way of living right now. So take that begging cup as the sign of your old life—and of all its pains and insecurities—and let it fall from your hand. Give it up.

Now look into your future. How will you live? You need a job. You can't depend on charity anymore. As you follow Jesus, be aware of all these feelings: the joy of seeing, freedom from your past, your anticipation, hope, and fear for the future. You may not fully realize it yet, but your life is totally transformed. Feel the difference between the person who walked onto this street and the person who is leaving it now.

• Now let's pass over once more into the role of a spectator in the crowd. You now realize what is involved in that blind man's healing. As you walk away from this encounter, ask: Knowing what is involved, do I want to be healed? Would I want to see? Knowing what changes it might make in my life, how would I feel about being touched by Jesus?

19b

AREAS OF BLINDNESS
time: fifteen minutes
materials: Journal (Life Experience)

In our meditation in Exploration 19a, we have witnessed what happens when the light enters into a human life. We may have difficulty with this story. We are not accustomed to miracles. We have been taught to doubt. Our science has made great advances because it dared doubt unquestionable wisdom and tradition. Whether we like it or not, we are people more open to doubt than to belief.

But doubt is not necessarily a bad thing. It prevents an easy seduction into cozy beliefs. On our pilgrimage it can foster our growth. For as we come to know our doubt, we will be able to discern between doubt that prevents us from being taken in and doubt that narrows our horizon and hinders our development.

In our meditation, as we passed over from bystander to beggar we sidestepped the issue of doubt and explored the texture of the miracle itself. We discovered that the miracle is more than a demonstration of supernatural powers; it effected a profound change in the blind man's life.

We can look at this miracle and the other miracles of Jesus not so much as shows of supernatural power but as signs and windows into the kingdom of God which Jesus proclaims. The miracle then becomes a parable in the flesh. In the miracle the reality of the kingdom erupts into the world. If we see miracles in this way, whether they happened or not is not the greatest question. The real question is what they mean, what they say about this kingdom. Here again we go back to our original idea that meaning is our most important concern.

If for the time being we can suspend our questions about the reality of the miracles and instead investigate their meaning, we can continue our search for the kingdom of God. When we have reached a decision concerning the reality of the kingdom of God—Is this kingdom that Jesus announces a reality, and is it the way we wish to live?—then at the same time we will have decided concerning the reality of the miracles that proclaim that kingdom.

When we look at this story now, we see two different realities presented. One is the world, in which Bartimaeus is blind, angry, crippled, and dysfunctional. The other is the miracle; by means of the miracle, Bartimaeus is transported into the kingdom, and his life undergoes a profound change. We begin to see that blindness in this story represents every kind of blindness and by extension symbolizes the fallen human condition. The blind man is actually fortunate; he knows his condition and is eager to leave it behind. What about us? Are there ways in which we too are blind and need to be made whole?

- Sit down with your journal, close your eyes, and spend a few minutes with your mantra. Then allow Bartimaeus to appear once more before you. Study him and his handicap. Put yourself once more in his place. Can you discover your own form of blindness? In what areas of your own life are you blind? Where are you desperate for the light to enter? These may be relationships where you are stumbling and groping. Your own blindness may be a feeling of depression that overwhelms and cripples you. Your blindness may be a bad self-image: You see yourself as ugly, inadequate, clumsy, or stupid. This self-image you carry around is projected onto others and handicaps you. Explore the areas of your blindness and write your findings in the Life Experience section of your journal.

20

THE GOOD SAMARITAN
time: twenty-five minutes
materials: Bible (Luke 10:30-35)

In the stories of Zacchaeus, the prodigal farmer, and Bartimaeus we have seen a care and concern that we might suspect plays a key role in the kingdom of God. Let's continue our pilgrimage by exploring this element of care and concern. What is it like? Where does it come from?

The parable of the Good Samaritan has a different context in Luke from the way we shall use it. In Luke, Jesus tells the story in response to the question "Who is my neighbor?" We are instead asking, "What is the kingdom like?" But Jesus does not tell the parables only to respond to a certain question. Each parable is a world unto itself; it can respond to a wealth of questions. It responds not by being a simple narrow answer but by opening a door into another world, another way of living. In the gospels themselves we can see the same parable in different contexts: Mark may use it one way in one situation; Matthew or Luke may use it in a totally different way. The question we bring is merely our entrance into the parable; it does not begin to exhaust the parable or its world. That is why we can return to these same parables again and again throughout our pilgrimage, and each time we return, the parable might have something new to show us.

• Today we will learn a new relaxation technique for the first phase of meditation. First take a moment to review your day. Then prepare for the relaxation by lying down in a comfortable position. Now do some deep breathing. It is not necessary to breathe quickly; it is only important to breathe as deeply as possible. Inhale and exhale as much air as you can. Continue to breathe deeply for about thirty breaths. If you feel a tingling in parts of your body, it is nothing to worry about. If you feel a cramp, do not panic; simply move that part of your body and stop breathing deeply. During the deep breathing, keep your attention focused on yourself; imagine yourself going deeper and deeper into relaxation. When you have completed the thirty breaths, remain quiet until any sensations have subsided. If you need to relax more, begin another series of deep breaths. Once you are sufficiently relaxed, begin the meditation; phase two should not be necessary today.

• Now read the parable in your Bible. Enter the story first by assuming the role of the victim. Imagine you are walking on a downtown street in your city late at night. Take a few moments to construct the scene in your imagination. All of a sudden some thugs jump you, knock you down, beat you up, and steal your money. You can move over this part quickly by imagining they knock you out immediately. All you need imagine is the confusion and sudden violence.

You return to consciousness; you hurt all over. You are lying in the gutter, and you cannot move. Imagine your helplessness, your fear, your confusion, your need to be helped. You need not stay in your body now. Leave it there in the gutter so that you can be an invisible witness to what is happening.

Your body lies there for a long time. Finally you see a nurse coming down the street. There is a hospital nearby; the shift must be changing. Your hopes begin to rise. Here comes help. What do you hope the nurse might do for you? You can't call out because you can't speak. You are condemned to silence, but you can hope.

However, the nurse crosses the street and will not pass by you. How do you feel now? Do you suspect that the nurse saw you and is avoiding you? Be in tune with whatever feelings arise.

Now a priest or a minister comes walking down the street. What feelings do you experience? What do you hope for from this minister? But the minister is in a hurry and does not even see you. What do you feel now? The street is once more empty; two people who live to help others have not helped you. Do you still cling to your hope? Where can you expect to receive help now?

More time passes. Move deeper into the situation of the victim. You have been here for quite a while. You don't know how badly hurt you are, but you are in pain and can't move. What fears, anger, confusion, despair, hope do you experience?

Now another person is coming down the street. You would never expect this kind of person to be any help to you. Create this person now in your imagination. Do not model the person on any of your personal enemies. Rather, what type of person would you least expect to offer help? It might be a beggar, a streetperson, any undesirable type—we all have our own prejudices. Search out the last kind of person in the world you would expect to help you. Now imagine that person walking toward you. What can you hope for?

The person sees you and approaches. Are you afraid? Perhaps he or she will hurt you even more; perhaps you will be killed. How do you feel now?

The person comes up and stoops over you. He or she cleans off your blood with a handkerchief and examines you to find out where you are hurt. Then the person gently picks you up and takes you up the street to a hotel. In your meditation now be a passive recipient of all this care and attention. You are not able to speak; you are totally helpless. How do you feel about this person who is helping and saving you?

• Now come out of the story and into your own life. What care and concern have you needed in your own life? Do not limit yourself to physical care. Was that care available to you? Who provided it? Has it been sufficient for you to grow and blossom? Sufficient to bring you to real happiness and fullness of life?

Have you ever experienced care from an unexpected source, as in this story? Is it possible that you have not experienced care because you were looking in the expected places and were not open to the care offered you from unexpected sources? Is it possible you missed or did not recognize care offered to you?

EXPLORATION **20a**
THE GOOD SAMARITAN (continued)
time: twenty-five minutes
materials: Journal (Prayer Diary)

- If you are not continuing from the previous exploration, prepare for this meditation as usual.

- This time we will enter the thinking of the three people who walk by the victim; this will help us explore their worlds. Begin by reconstructing the scene. What time of night is it? What buildings are there? What is the weather like? Where is the victim lying?

- Enter the story now as the nurse. Put yourself into the nurse's life. What has your day been like? Where are you going now? How do you feel as you walk along this street late at night? Now catch a glimpse of the person lying in the gutter. You stop and hesitate for a moment. Then you cross the street and walk by on the other side. What did you feel as you saw the victim? Why did you as a nurse not go to the person's aid? Use your own feelings and experiences to create the nurse's world. How does the nurse feel about avoiding the victim? Feelings of guilt? Shame? Fear of becoming involved? Is it too much bother? Is the nurse exhausted? Is there a fear that this might be a trap?

- Pass over now into the person of the minister. Again take some time to enter into this person's skin. What are your concerns? Where have you been? Where are you headed? You see the victim. You pretend to be preoccupied and rush by without seeing the victim. Why do you avoid the situation? How do you as a minister feel about what you are doing? Do you justify what you have done? Do you absolve yourself of responsibility? Do you feel guilty?

• Take some time to explore this world of the nurse and the minister. They are two different people, yet they respond to the situation in the same way. Do they do it for the same reason? Do they feel the same way? What is it like to live in their kind of world? How much does it resemble the world you live in? Can you imagine yourself acting like this nurse or minister? Be honest.

• Now pass over into the person of the Samaritan. Use the person you imagined in the last experiment—the least likely to help. Now enter into and become that person. What do you do for a living? What are you doing on the street now? You see the victim lying in the gutter. You go over to the person, stoop down, and wipe the blood away. You check for injuries and take the victim to the hotel about a block away.

How does it feel to act this way? What do you experience—compassion, fear, incompetence, anxiety, joy, love? Why is the Samaritan willing to help when the nurse and minister were not? What is different about this third person? Is it a matter of innate kindness? A sense of duty and obligation? An absence of fear? A freedom from obligation? It is certainly not that he or she is better than you are—you probably saw to that when you created this Samaritan. What makes the difference?

• We might say that the nurse and the minister are living in the world while the Samaritan lives in the kingdom. Can you imagine a way of seeing things that would free you to be of help to the victim? Obviously, the world of the nurse and of the minister does not allow them to help the victim no matter how much they might consider it their duty or obligation. Yet the Samaritan is able to help even though we would not expect him or her to live up to the obligations and sense of duty that good, respectable citizens have. For a few minutes, see if you can somehow imagine what this different way of seeing might be like. It is not an easy task, and we are only beginning our exploration. Any adequate response must come from deep within us. It may be necessary to return to this meditation many times during the course of our pilgrimage to experience its deep meaning.

•   When you have finished, describe the contents and the process of these meditations in your Prayer Diary.

21 **EXPLORING THE KINGDOM**
time: thirty minutes
materials: Journal (Prayer Experience)

We have completed a number of experiments designed to allow us to investigate Jesus' idea of the kingdom of God. Let's take some time now to review what we have experienced and learned.

•   In the initial encounter with Jesus in the synagogue, we heard the words of the prophet Isaiah (Luke 4:14-22). Those words describe the kingdom of God. Go back and review those words. Jesus said that today those words were fulfilled. In the light of your experiences with Jesus, how do you respond to his statement now? In what ways have you seen those words fulfilled? What do you think this process of fulfillment means? Can you understand the words of Isaiah in a broader context than you did before? For example, when Isaiah says that the blind see, do you have a broader understanding of what that might mean than you did originally? What is that broader understanding?

We then encountered Jesus in the person of Zacchaeus (Luke 19:1-10). Like Zacchaeus, we wanted to investigate Jesus. But we found that the kingdom cannot be investigated with pure objectivity. We will be drawn into that kingdom, and we might be known and transformed by the process. What did you learn concerning the kingdom in this experiment? The kingdom here is not a dead thing but a very dynamic and transforming entity. What are your feelings in the light of this discovery?

In the parable of the prodigal farmer (Matthew 13:4-9), we saw an image of the kingdom as a place of overflowing, joyous, generous abundance. In contrast, the way planting is done in the world is seen as miserly, stingy, parsimonious, fearful. The kingdom overflows with opportunity for growth. The parable says that life is not just a few chances that we must be lucky enough to open ourselves to, but that life is an overabundance of time, talent, and opportunity. It suggests we can achieve this vision of life by being like the prodigal farmer.

In our encounter with Bartimaeus (Mark 10:46-52), we discovered the reality of healing in the kingdom. We also came to realize that we, like Bartimaeus, might need healing. For even if we are not physically blind, still our vision of the world, our way of perceiving the world, is blind. We saw in the miracle how a change in vision results in a healing and a transformation of one's life. We can be transformed from cripples into full, responsible human beings.

In our encounter with the good Samaritan, we explored the kind of care and concern and healing Jesus says is part of the kingdom. We found that healing comes from unexpected places. The kingdom might be right in our midst, but our accustomed ways of thinking blind us to its presence. And we explored the differences in the visions of the nurse, the minister, and the Samaritan.

• All these explorations have spoken to us about the kingdom of God. What picture of that kingdom is beginning to emerge? Take about ten minutes to explore what you have experienced about this kingdom. Write your observations in the Prayer Experience section of your journal.

• Now spend a few moments in quiet with the mantra. When you are quiet and calm, create your own parable of the kingdom as you have come to see it. You can write your own parable, compose a poem, paint a picture, compose a melody, or even dance the parable. Do something that involves you in the creative process, for within the depths of your imagination these seeds of the kingdom are already taking root. Today nourish them a little; allow them to grow. Enjoy yourself.

22

THE GOD OF THE KINGDOM
time: twenty-five minutes   materials: Bible
(Matthew 13:44-46 and Psalm 45)

Our exploration of the kingdom of God has led us to find there the characteristics of care, concern, and generosity. These characteristics are considered common to people, but not to things. From this, we might suspect that Jesus' kingdom is person-centered. During the next week we will investigate how Jesus sees God and will explore just what the personal nature of the kingdom is. Thus far in our pilgrimage, we have understood the word *God* as referring to the center of meaning in our life. God is the Word, the Light, the Life. What more does Jesus have to teach us concerning this God?

• Prepare as usual for your meditation. When you are ready, read the two parables from Matthew's gospel.

• Now picture the scene of the first parable. What does the field look like? What are you doing in the field today? How do you discover the treasure? Are you looking for it, or are you there in the field for some other purpose? How do you feel when you discover it? Is there joy? Unbelief? Is there any fear you may be discovered? Explore your feelings.

Hide the treasure again. Run off to your home and prepare to sell everything you own in order to buy the field. How do you feel as you go around disposing of your property? Are you worried that someone else might beat you to the treasure? Do you have any hesitation selling the little you own in order to buy this field with a treasure that will make you richer than you have ever been? Do you sell your possessions grudgingly, or do you sell them happily and joyfully?

Take your money and buy the field. Now you own it. How do you feel?

• Take a look at your own experience. Is there anything in your life that resembles the kind of experience described in the parable? Is there anything for which you would happily give up all you have? The love of a certain person? A certain moment of peace and fulfillment? The look in a person's face? For a few minutes, use this parable to help you discover moments in your own life that were close to the kingdom—times that you would have given all to keep with you forever.

• At first, the second parable might seem identical to the first. The overall structure of the plot is the same except that a fine pearl seems to take the place of the buried treasure. But in the buried-treasure story, the kingdom of God is the buried treasure. In this story, the kingdom of God is the merchant in search of fine pearls. To enter into this story we must become the pearl of great price. It might be a little pull on our imaginative powers, but let's become that pearl. Here we sit in our oyster shells. We can do nothing but we are worth all the money in the world to that pearl merchant who finds us. He discovers us and runs off to sell everything he has so that he can possess us.

How easily can you imagine this story as a story about you? Can you imagine yourself as this pearl? It may be hard to imagine yourself as an inanimate object, but our question doesn't concern this so much as it does imagining yourself as of great price. What about you would be valuable enough for the merchant to sell all he has in order to possess you? Have you ever felt this valuable? Has the merchant made a mistake about you? Would you find it easier to believe in the great value in other people but not in yourself?

147

• Take a few minutes to list those characteristics that might make the merchant want to possess you. If you feel any resistance to this process, examine the resistance: What does it tell you about your image of yourself? As you make your list, do you think you're exaggerating? Do you feel you're lying? How do you feel being a pearl of great price?

• Have there been any times in your life when you have felt valued like this pearl? Have there been instances when someone has seen your beauty and worth in a way that you have never seen it? What were these times like? What did you experience when your beauty was valued? Reflect back now to the story where Jesus calls to Zacchaeus. Might you say that when Jesus knows Zacchaeus, Zacchaeus becomes the pearl of great price? Are both of these stories—of Zacchaeus and of the pearl—describing the same reality?

We have seen in these two parables of the hidden treasure and the pearl the dual dynamic of the kingdom. We are searching for the kingdom because we hope it will bring us fulfillment and happiness.

But the kingdom is equally eager to find us. Already we can feel the strain on the images. Kingdoms do not search. If this kingdom does indeed seek us out, it acts much more like a person than a thing.

• To conclude our meditation today, we will pray a psalm originally composed to celebrate a royal wedding. But like the parables, the psalms transcend their original contexts. In the Christian tradition the king in this psalm is often understood to be Jesus and the daughter to be the Christian or the Church. Today let's pray the psalm in two different ways to fit our parables.

First imagine that you are the person searching for buried treasure, seeking the kingdom. Take the first nine verses of this psalm and imagine the king as the kingdom. Allow the imagery of this great king to be your imagery of the kingdom. Can you enter into this song of praise? If the battle imagery disturbs you, ignore it. Concentrate instead on the beauty of the king, the imagery of the holy anointing and of the royal wedding.

• As you move into the second half of the psalm, enter again into the second parable. You are now the daughter being joined to the king in marriage. The song now concerns your own beauty. See if you can believe what the song says about you. You are the pearl of great price.

EXPLORATION **22a** THE SHEPHERD AND THE SHEEP
time: twenty-five minutes
materials: Bible (Matthew 18:12-14,
Ezekiel 34, and Psalm 23)

• Prepare for today's meditation and reading as usual. Then read Jesus' parable of the lost sheep in Matthew. Take a few minutes to imagine this parable. It is not necessary to enter into it by assuming a role. Simply allow the scene to make itself vivid in your imagination and then allow the parable to play itself for you. What thoughts and feelings are generated by this parable? What does the parable say about the kingdom? Is this parable of an even more personal nature than the parable of the pearl? Can you see even more vividly here the seriousness of the kingdom's search for you? How does this make you feel?

• Jesus built upon a great tradition when he created this parable, so if we wish to understand the way Jesus experiences God, we must return to his tradition. The prophet Ezekiel lived at a disastrous time in Israel's history. He foresaw the imminent end of Israel, and he traced its downfall to the social and religious corruption rampant in his time. By using the imagery of the shepherds, he attempts to warn first the rulers, then the people themselves, of the impending doom. In this passage we catch another great characteristic of God in this tradition: God is the defender of the poor and the downtrodden rather than of the rich and mighty. We saw this theme in Mary's prayer after the Annunciation. Read through this passage of Ezekiel to deepen your experience of Jesus' God. Feel especially the great care and concern of God for the poor. Feel also the love of the shepherd for the sheep, especially in verses 11-16.

• To conclude our meditation today, we will pray one of the most beloved of the psalms, which speaks also of the good shepherd. Allow the imagery of this psalm to come alive for you. Feel the shepherd's and the host's care and concern. Explore what it is like to have the Lord for a shepherd and a host. Do these images offer you comfort? Solace? If you made such a prayer your own prayer, would your vision of the world be transformed so that it would be more like the kingdom?

22b

THE RELEASE OF PRISONERS
time: twenty-five minutes
materials: Bible (Deuteronomy 26:5-9,
Exodus 13:17–14:31, and Psalm 114)

Jesus has a name for God which he uses over a hundred times throughout the gospels: Father. He did not invent this name. It had developed over the course of Israel's two-thousand-year history with this God. Since he is speaking primarily to Jews, Jesus in his teaching presumes this common heritage, so it would help us if we could explore this tradition in our pilgrimage.

For the Israelite there is one primary event that brought into existence the people called Israel and that defines Israel as a nation. That event is the exodus from Egypt and the migration to the promised land. In this event—the deliverance of a group of slaves from Egypt, their passage through the wilderness and eventual establishment in what became the nation of Israel—the Jewish people recognized their God and came to know him.

• Prepare as usual for meditation. Then read the passage from Deuteronomy. These words summarize the way that an Israelite would identify himself or herself. They speak of the passage from a nomadic existence through slavery in Egypt and deliverance from the Pharaoh under the leadership of Moses and Yahweh. Use this brief summary as a way of entering into this great story.

• The full story of the Exodus—including the birth and growth of Moses, the plagues of Egypt necessary to change Pharaoh's heart, and the giving of the Law on the top of Mount Sinai—occupies the entire first part of the Book of Exodus. You might want to read the entire narrative, which is cast in the form of an epic (similar in many ways to the Iliad, the epic of the Greek peoples). For this reading experiment, we have chosen only the central episode in the Israelite epic: the leaving of Egypt and the crossing of the Red Sea.

This story has passed through many generations of storytellers who have embellished it and magnified the wonders. For example, many Scripture scholars today do not believe that the Red Sea was the body of water in question. They speculate that it was the Reed Sea and that the parting of the waters might have been a giant wind that blew back the shallow waters and enabled the slaves to walk through. The Egyptians, being in chariots, however, became stuck in the mud and could not overtake the slaves.

There is no question, however, that the more exalted myth that we read in the book of Exodus is a very good story. That a group of slaves did manage to escape Egypt and flee into the wilderness, eventually to conquer the present territory of Israel, is an established fact. The great mythic embellishments simply contribute to a rousing story, and we can accept them and enjoy them as such. Read the

Exodus account of how Moses and the people passed through the Red Sea with God's help. Through his act of liberating these people and establishing them in the promised land, they discover this God and he becomes their Father.

● To conclude our reading today, we will pray one of the psalms that remembers this great event. Imagine yourself as a member of Israel. You give thanks to God who has shown himself to your people, who has rescued you from the bondage of slavery and made you a great people. What are your feelings of thanksgiving and gratitude as you enter into this prayer?

22c

GOD THE LOVER
time: twenty-five minutes
materials: Bible (Hosea 1-2 and Psalm 123)

The story of Israel's relationship with its God can be understood in terms of a love affair, and the prophets often spoke of it in just this way. Unfortunately, it was a very rocky marriage. From God's viewpoint, Israel was constantly unfaithful. When Yahweh led the group of slaves out of Egypt, He brought them into the wilderness and there entered into an agreement, or covenant, with them. The core of this covenant was the establishment of a people who would live according to the precepts of the Ten Commandments. In God's eyes, this people was rescued from slavery in order to become a vanguard of human evolution. His people would live honestly, justly—would be holy as their God was holy. But Israel never lives up to this covenant. Social injustices run rampant; his people fail to remain faithful to Yahweh. Through the prophets, Yahweh attempts to call Israel back to those honeymoon days when he rescued them and provided them with the covenant that would create his kingdom among them.

The prophets use the image of marriage to explain God's relationship to his people. Our reading today creates a vivid experience of what God felt. He demands that the prophet Hosea marry a whore.

The whore of course is unfaithful, and when Hosea suffers, God tells him that this is the same suffering that he feels in the face of Israel's infidelity. Thus Hosea lives out God's experiences in his own life.

● Prepare as usual for your reading. Then read the account of Hosea's marriage and what it reveals to him concerning God and Israel. Hosea is one of the great tragic figures in human history. But go beyond Hosea. What does his suffering tell you about this God? How does Hosea's experience speak to you of this God of Jesus? What does it reveal concerning him?

The image of the divine marriage is developed by other prophets as well. And Jesus himself uses it, for in a number of parables he describes the kingdom of God as a wedding feast. He goes so far as to refer to himself as the bridegroom. The idea of God's love reaches its climax when the evangelist John sums up the entire revelation of Jesus in terms of God's love: "For God so loved the world that he gave his only begotten Son, that whosoever believeth in him should not perish but have everlasting life" (John 3:16, King James Version).

● Let's conclude today's reading by praying one of the great laments of Israel—Psalm 123. There was always a faithful remnant that stood by the covenant and kept alive Israel's love for God. As you pray this psalm, enter into its spirit. Can you make its humility and love your own?

EXPLORATION **22d** THE SECOND EXODUS
time: twenty-five minutes   materials: Bible
(Isaiah 43:1-21, 55:1-13 and Psalm 121)

● Prepare for the reading as usual. How is your reading proceeding? Are you using the techniques of paraphrase and dialogue? Is your reading deep and a real encounter, or just a gathering of information? How might you deepen your reading further?

In today's reading we pass to a later time of Israel's history. The catastrophe foreseen by Hosea and the other prophets has struck. Israel has been destroyed by Babylon and her leaders have been taken to Babylon as captives, to prevent any insurrections. But now Babylon itself has fallen to Cyrus the Persian. Cyrus organizes his empire by setting up a series of semi-independent states that owe their ultimate allegiance to him. He frees Israel. Thus Israel becomes a nation once more. A new prophet brings this good news to the people. We do not know the prophet's name; his message is contained in the later part of the book of Isaiah, so he is often referred to as Second Isaiah.

As you read this prophet's words of consolation, enter into God's concern for the poor, the powerless, the hungry. We have seen the themes of liberation and social justice prominent throughout our exploration of the kingdom of God in the last few days. These themes are presumed by Jesus. He presumes the idea of the Law that was given to Moses on Sinai to provide a way of life. He presumes the thirst for justice toward the poor and oppressed that finds voice in the prophets of Israel. He presumes the great compassion of God that finds expression in the visions of Second Isaiah. As we examine Jesus' heritage, we gain a deeper and richer image of both God and Jesus' idea of a kingdom.

- Read the two prophecies from Second Isaiah now. ·

- Our psalm for today continues the hopeful themes of Second Isaiah. It was originally prayed by pilgrims who were making their way to Jerusalem, which was built upon Mount Sion. It speaks of the protection of the Lord. Can you enter into this feeling and make it your own today? What is it like to have this consolation, this trust in the protection of the Lord?

22e

GOD OUR FATHER
time: twenty-five minutes
materials: Bible (Isaiah 63:7—64:12)
and Journal (Prayer Experience)

Israel after the Exile never regained anything like its original glory. It was now continually under the rule of one of the empires. Nor did the kings or the people of Israel come back to the glorious vision of the kingdom promulgated in the Law and advocated by the prophets. The last part of the Book of Isaiah contains the writings of yet another prophet (Third Isaiah) who lives in this time after the restoration. He pleads with God to redeem his people. He reminds God of his Fatherhood.

• In today's preparation, use only the mantra. The reading today should occupy only about five to ten minutes so you will have time to work in the journal. Now read this Third Isaiah as a final example of Israel's experience of God and his kingdom.

• Turn to your journal now; in the Prayer Experience section where you described the kingdom of God in Exploration 16, add what you have experienced in this week's reading about both God and his kingdom. How have you experienced God as liberator, friend of the poor, lover, and Father? How have you experienced the kingdom as it is envisioned throughout Israel's history?

• In conclusion today, we pray a psalm that describes the true servant of the Lord. Although *Father* is the name of God in the Old Testament and especially in Jesus' teaching, the imagery used to describe God is often quite feminine, such as in this beautiful psalm. The name Father does not refer to sex at all: It designates the parental caring and guiding love of God for his people. The imagery of God as mother is even more pronounced in Isaiah 66:7-13, where God is described as a woman giving birth.

154

EXPLORATION **22f** PRAYING TO OUR FATHER
time: twenty-five minutes
materials: Bible (Luke: 11:5-13)
and Journal (Prayer Experience and Prayer Diary)

Now that we have experienced God as a loving Father, we can turn to Jesus as Jesus' disciples did and ask him to teach us to pray. Throughout this pilgrimage we have used prayer in its broadest definition—as whatever opens us more fully to ourselves, our world, and

God. There are many different forms of prayer: among them, the silent prayer of meditation, the dialogue prayer of our reading of Scripture, the prayer of our guided meditations. Now we are ready to speak with our Father in our own words.

• To prepare for this experience of prayer, read carefully what Jesus teaches his disciples in Luke.

• For the next ten minutes or so, ask your Father for what you desire. Spend a moment before prayer putting yourself into the proper condition for prayer, just as you do for meditation. You might use your mantra to center you. Then open your heart before your Father. Ask him for what you need, for what you want. Give him thanks for what he has done already in your life and your pilgrimage. Your words need not be the poetry of the psalms; they need only be the words or even stammerings of your heart.

• Using the journal to help us pray often helps as we are beginning. If you choose, write out your prayer today in the Prayer Experience section.

• After you have opened your heart to your Father in prayer, enter into the second part of prayer: Listen to what your Father says to you. "Be still and know that I am God," the old saying tells us. We have spoken; now it is his turn. Wait in silence, without expectations; if you already know what he will say it is not a true dialogue. Wait in openness, and you will become aware of the response.

• Conclude your prayer with a final response to God. You might thank him and ask for his continued guidance on your pilgrimage. Then write a brief summary of your experience in the Prayer Diary of your journal.

23

THE WORD MADE FLESH
time: twenty-five minutes
materials: Bible (Mark 2:1-12)

In the passage we are reading in this section, John describes Jesus as "the Word become flesh." In this extended exploration (23-23d), we will explore what that description implies about Jesus and his teaching. Why does the Word become flesh? Is it not enough for God to speak the Word? And what does the taking on of flesh imply for us?

• We begin our exploration with a story of healing that brings out the relation between the body and the spirit. In our preparation today we will use a new exercise that relaxes the body through the mind. We have already experienced how the body can have a calming influence on the mind in the corpse pose. Now we reverse this action.

This exercise works through the power of suggestion. Begin by lying down comfortably; lie on a hard surface, such as a floor, to counteract the natural tendency to fall asleep. Now use the mind to progressively relax your body. First scan the body for any areas of tension, beginning with the feet and working upward. Don't try to use force; just suggest gently that each part relax. As you proceed, imagine the tension easing.

After you have scanned the body, spend a few minutes imagining your body becoming heavier and heavier. Feel the whole body sinking into the floor. It is very heavy. Scan the body once more: Feel your feet heavy and leaden, move up to the legs and on up the body, experiencing the heaviness.

• Now we're ready to begin our meditation. Read the Scripture passage; we will use our relaxation to enter into the story. We are the paralytic; the deadness and heaviness in our body will help us enter into the feeling of being paralyzed. Feel the helplessness. You have been paralyzed all your life. Your body is totally dead to you. What has your life been like?

But there is hope, for your friends tell you that Jesus is coming to your town. They tell you he can perform miracles, making the blind see and the lame walk. They want to bring you to Jesus. Will you go?

You lie on a stretcher. They pick you up and carry you through the town. You can't look around, only up at the sky. But you can hear the excitement of those around you. What are you experiencing as your friends take you to meet Jesus?

The stretcher stops. You must have arrived at the house where Jesus is. You hear the crowd and feel the excitement. Your friends lean over the stretcher and tell you that because of the large crowd they can't take you inside to see Jesus. How do you respond to this news?

But someone suggests that perhaps they could take you up to the roof and lower you through the ceiling. Are you willing to have them do this? Yes, you want to do anything to be cured. So they lift you onto the roof. It's a little frightening, but you are eager to meet Jesus. The thought that he might heal you keeps any fear at bay.

They are ready to lower you through the roof. They tie ropes onto your stretcher. You feel yourself lifted up and then lowered into the house below. You can sense the commotion around you as you descend. But you are only thinking of one thing: You want to see Jesus and talk with him.

Someone comes forward and bends over your litter. It must be Jesus. What does he look like? You wait. Finally he says, "Your sins are forgiven you." How do you react to what he says? You have been brought here to be healed of your paralysis; now Jesus says your sins are forgiven. Is there any connection between these two things for you?

The crowd's murmur now sounds harsh and threatening. You hear the word *blaspheme* a number of times. You know you are the center of the controversy. A Jew knows that only God can forgive sins. Yet Jesus has told you that your own sins are forgiven; he has done what only God can do.

Jesus turns away from you now. He speaks to the crowd. "Which is easier to say: Your sins are forgiven you, or get up and walk?" Ask yourself that question now as you lie paralyzed. Theologically, it is impossible for a human being to forgive sins. But what if he said, "Get up and walk"? There is nothing theologically wrong with this. Healings are possible. And they seem to your eyes more miraculous and marvellous than forgiving sins. You could witness a physical healing if it occurred; you could not see your sins forgiven. Besides, you want to walk; that is why you came here! Think now about what Jesus has asked.

Jesus here confronts both faith and doubt. Which is easier for you to believe—that your sins are forgiven, that your crippling thoughts and desires and emotions are made whole; or that if you take a step forward on those paralyzed limbs they will hold you up? What difficulties would you have if Jesus only forgave your sins today and left you lying helpless on your bed? Would you be satisfied if he only said "Get up and walk"?

"So that you may believe, I say to you arise and walk." Jesus knows our dilemma and responds to it by working on the physical plane, the plane where we live and in which we believe. Does his action here imply that he also has power over the spiritual plane? What, if any, connection do you see between the two?

• Now feel the strength coming into your body. Along with the bodily change, do you sense a change in your outlook on life? Do you think your past has been forgiven? Things are going to be different now. Just how will they be different? How do you think this will affect your future?

Has your past been forgiven? What has happened because of this forgiveness? Can you sense that you might be able to walk *because* your sins have been forgiven?

• As you feel the life coming into your body, slowly raise yourself from the floor and conclude this meditation by giving expression to your feelings of gratitude. Use your newfound body to express you‑ feelings. Praise the Lord through its movements. If you feel a little self-conscious about dancing, that's all right; do what you are comfortable with. Your movements need not be grand or graceful. Experience your body giving thanks; you'll discover it's easier to do than you thought.

As you perform these movements of praise and thanksgiving, be fully conscious of what you are experiencing through your body. Does your body enable you to be more thankful? Does it make thanksgiving easier? Can your body and its movements increase your feelings of joy and gratitude? Is there a barrier between what you feel inside and what you are able to express with your body? Do you experience a separation and dichotomy, or is there an interrelatedness?

23a

THE ANGELUS
time: three one-minute periods
a day for one week

This and the next exploration should be done concurrently. We will be exploring the interrelation between body and spirit in our own lives. In this exploration we will use a popular Christian prayer called the Angelus. The original Angelus is a series of prayers recited three times during the day to recall the angel's visit to Mary to announce the coming of the Savior. Many Catholic churches still ring their bells in the morning, at noon, and at dusk for the Angelus. This prayer allows us to reflect on the good news the angel brought to Mary and to all of us.

• We have modified this prayer for this exploration. For the next week we will take a minute for reflection three times a day: when we arise, in the middle of the day, and when we retire. During that minute of reflection, consider these words from John's gospel: "The Word becomes flesh and dwells among us." What would it mean for the Word to take on flesh at this moment of the day? How present to you is the Word (or meaning) on this day and at this moment? How might your life be different today should the Word become flesh in your life?

159

Our concern in this exploration is not so much with the Word as it appears in Jesus or anywhere in the past. Our real focus is here and now, this moment and this day. What would be different if the Word were not merely heard, understood, or believed in but instead took on flesh-and-blood existence? You might consider the question in the light of a teacher or leader who enfleshes the meaning of life. But also consider the question of whether you yourself might enflesh and breathe that Word, that meaning, in your own life.

Is the Word present in this moment of your life? What would it mean for the Word to be enfleshed here and now? We ask these questions not so much because we demand an answer; that is not crucial. These questions may, however, direct our search. They can reveal the importance, in our own life, of a meaning that goes beyond the mind and descends into our body to take control there and transform our life.

23b

ICON MEDITATION
time: twenty-five minutes a day for one week
materials: an icon of Jesus the Lord

This exploration should be performed along with the Angelus, which it complements. Icons are a form of prayer from the Eastern Orthodox Church. An icon is a representation of a holy person or a scene from the gospels. But it is not like the pious art of the West. To us the icon seems quite highly stylized. But the idea behind the icon is that it is a picture of the soul of the saint. When we look at an icon, we are not simply looking at a picture of a holy person; we are looking at the sanctity that enfleshes itself in the body of that saint. The icon is a representation of the saint transfigured—the saint as he or she is in the kingdom rather than in the world. The icon is a window into heaven, and often the eyes of the icon are windows into the soul.

In using an icon for meditation, you might feel that a two-way process is occurring. You are gazing at the icon, but at the same time you feel that the icon in some way is gazing at you. The saint in the icon sees you at the same depth as you see the saint. The icon sees you in your own holiness. It sees beneath your flesh into the part of you that is of the kingdom of God. Meditating with an icon is often an experience similar to that of Zacchaeus: You are known through and through, known for who you really are.

• Place the icon at eye level about two to four feet away. Prepare for the meditation as usual, paying particular attention to the relaxation of your body. Do you notice how the body is able to calm the mind and spirit? Be aware of the interrelatedness of body, mind, and spirit.

• For the meditation itself, spend ten to fifteen minutes each day gazing into the face of the icon. Allow feelings to surface. Acknowledge them, but do not become involved with them. Keep your attention on the face.

What is revealed to you in the face? Do you feel a particular power, a presence, a holiness coming to you from the eyes? Do you sense you are being seen by the icon? Is the icon seeing the you that is shown to the world, or is it seeing deeper?

Try to surrender judgment in these meditations; judgment often prevents us from experiencing. You do not have to tell yourself that you are simply projecting the image, or that your psyche is playing games with you. Nor do you have to believe that the icon is revealing the face of Jesus to you. Judgment can come later. Right now, give yourself over to the experience of meditation.

John says that in Jesus the Word takes on flesh. Can you experience in this icon the holiness, the meaning, the peace, the healing, the care and concern we have discovered as the kingdom of God? Allow the icon to become a window into the kingdom as well as a healing mirror for your own soul.

In this meditation we seek no answers. Our meditation is beyond all thought. It exists in the peace and quiet of Jesus' presence. There is no need to discover during this time whether Jesus or the icon is the Word become flesh. For this week only be aware, open, and receptive to whatever happens as you sit before the icon.

EXPLORATION **23c** DIALOGUE WITH OUR BODY
time: thirty minutes
materials: Journal (Life Experience)

● We continue our exploration of enfleshment by turning to our own experience of life in a body. First take a few minutes to center yourself. Sit comfortably and focus your attention on your breathing. Now review your day.

For our relaxation we'll express our day so far through bodily movement. What feelings and moods have you experienced? Can you translate them into motions and gestures? Express your day through your stance, your posture, your movement. You might settle on one feeling or emotion, or you might dance to trace a number of feelings experienced throughout the day.

If you have experienced anger, reenter that experience and allow your anger full expression. Yell, scream, pound on a pillow; just don't harm yourself or anyone or anything else.

Use your body to express your feelings and experiences. You might center on a feeling that was not really important today, but that you would like to explore further. Let the feeling expand until it fills your whole being. What is it like to feel this way? Can you experience the feeling more deeply now than you did today?

• Now sit down and open your journal to the Life Experience section. Entitle this experiment "Dialogue with My Body." Take the first five or ten minutes to call to mind your body's history. Write the story of your body in ten to fifteen short phrases. Begin with "I was born." List any serious illnesses, difficulties with the body; sports triumphs; bodily discoveries; significant experiences of touch and sensing; experiences of being held; being overweight, dieting; experiences of exhaustion, exhilaration, sex; achievements such as dancing, acting, singing. List no more than fifteen significant events.

• We have prepared the ground for our dialogue. In the dialogue we can explore our own particular enfleshment. What has it been like to be incarnated in this body? How do you feel about your body? Begin the dialogue by telling your body how you feel about it. Are you proud of it? Do you wish it were different in some way?

• When you have spoken, wait in silence. Soon your body will respond to you. Write down what your body says. It may have feelings about the way you have inhabited it. It may speak to you about the way you have treated and cared for it. Allow the body its voice. Avoid judgment or censorship.

Here is your opportunity to express what you really feel and think about this flesh you inhabit. How attached do you feel to this body? How important is it to you? What are your hopes for your body? What part do you want it to have in your fulfillment? In turn, allow your body to respond to your thoughts and feelings; it has a mind of its own which it will reveal to you in dialogue. If you feel uneasy at the thought of such a dialogue, you can begin the dialogue with those feelings of uneasiness. Why don't you want to dialogue with your body? Your body might have something to say about those feelings.

The dialogue we have begun in this experiment can be continued through our pilgrimage. Many of us have come to consider one element in our makeup as most significant: the mind, the spirit, feelings, thoughts, or the body. In Jesus' teaching and especially in his healings we see the body assuming a fundamental importance. The body is highlighted when Jesus is called the Word enfleshed. To follow Jesus, then, will mean coming to an appreciation of our own enfleshment. Is it important? Are we just a mind trapped in a prison of flesh, as some who have called themselves Christian have maintained? Or are we an embodied spirit that exists and grows through being enfleshed? From what we have seen, Jesus would side with the second view. If we take him as our teacher, our body will not be considered insignificant. Indeed, as we shall see and as we have begun to experience, our body can be one of our primary aids on our spiritual journey.

23d

THE WORD BECOMES FLESH
time: thirty minutes
materials: Journal (Prayer Experience)

• Prepare for this exploration as usual. In the Prayer Experience section describe your feelings, hopes, experiences over the course of these explorations that have focused on the body. How would you feel about the Word becoming flesh in a guide or teacher? How would it appeal to you to become an enfleshment of meaning? How might your life be different if this could happen? Do you think it is necessary that the Word become flesh for any real growth and change to occur? Must the Word become flesh in your family and community and the world itself? We are not yet asking whether Jesus is the Word made flesh. We need more experience before we are able to make that decision. We want to explore the difference between the Word becoming flesh and a philosophy or wisdom concerning how to live a human life. What is the difference between adhering to and believing in a way of life or wisdom and having that wisdom become incarnate in one's life?

24

THE PARABLE OF THE TALENTS
time: twenty-five minutes
materials: Bible (Matthew 25:14-30)

The parable of the talents continues our investigation of embodiment. It shows that when Jesus refers to the kingdom and its work he does not mean some special work. He does not ask us to retire from the world. Indeed, Jesus' illustrations of the kingdom have been quite worldly: farmers sowing wheat, people being mugged and helped, merchants seeking capital, and in this story, investing money. There should be no doubt by now that Jesus considers the kingdom something very much a part of everyday life. It is not "religious" if that means churchy as opposed to earthy. And it is not something other-worldly—something we enter after we die and leave this world. The kingdom is vastly different from the world. But the nurse, the minister, and the Samaritan all inhabit the same earth, the same town, yet two live in the world and one in the kingdom. So the kingdom must not be a different place but a different way of envisioning where and how we are to live. Let's explore this idea further in our meditation today.

• Prepare as usual. When you are ready, read the story in Matthew.

• We will enter into the story first by means of the third character. He is living in the world, so we can easily relate to him. He is given one bag of gold to keep. Instead of gold or money, however, let's use that old English word *talents* and take the advantage of the unintended pun to focus on the gifts and talents that have been bestowed upon us. Think about the gifts you have been given. The first gift is the gift of life itself; move on to examine your particular strengths and talents. These might be musical ability; a friendly nature; intellectual excellence; the gift of teaching; artistic ability; the gift of healing. Look over the talents you have developed, and then find a talent you have not developed. Perhaps you are not confident you even have this talent; you suspect you have it, but you have not cultivated it.

• Now become the third person in our story. You are afraid of the great gift that the master has entrusted to you. Imagine the master giving you this talent. How do you feel as you are given the talent? How do you feel about the responsibility?

Look at the other two people. Their talents are greater than yours. You know that someday yours will be demanded back. What if you should lose it? Enter now into that feeling of fear. Has fear kept you from developing the talent you suspect you have? How might you lose that talent should you risk developing it?

In your fear, you take the talent you have been given and bury it in the ground. Sit on it. Keep it hidden. Don't allow it into the rest of your life. What is your life like when you live this way? What do you gain by keeping the talent safe and hidden? What do you lose?

Now the master is coming back to collect his talent. You dig up the talent, and you take it to him. Are you proud of yourself for not losing anything? Are you happy that you have passed this test? Enter into this character's feelings.

The master is very angry at what you have done. Experience his wrath now. Tell him you knew he was a hard master and you were afraid so you hid the talent for fear of losing it. He doesn't accept your explanation. He takes your money away and gives it to the other two people. Then he throws you out.

This seems harsh to you. After all, investment and development of talents is a very risky business. Yet your master doesn't seem to believe that at all. At least you could have put the talent in a bank where it could earn interest. Why didn't you think of that? Was it because fear prevented you from thinking about it?

Let's see if we might discover the reason for the master's harsh behavior. He might be justified in responding this way if the third servant had acted quite stupidly. The servant was paralyzed by fear. But is that fear really stupid? If the parable is truly an image of the kingdom of God, then we can see that kingdom in the lives of the other two servants, and this servant would then be a member of the world. The third character did not risk the talent because, being a member of the world, he knew he might lose it. He kept it safely hidden through fear. But was that fear justified?

The other two servants both allow their talents to develop, and they double their initial sum. The master believes that if the third servant had done likewise, he too would have doubled his original investment. This is not what the world would say. The world works on the law of chance: You win a few, lose a few. The master believes you win all the time. So he is harsh with this servant because he feels the servant's fear is unreal. In the master's eyes fear is stupid and senseless.

• This teaching is hard for us. It goes directly counter to the school of the world. Let's explore it by entering into one of the other characters. Go back now and dig up that buried talent. Take it out of the ground and make it a real part of your life.

Allow it to develop and, in keeping with the story, imagine it increasing twofold. Imagine what kind of life you might lead if you allowed that talent as well as all your other talents to flourish and develop. If there is any fear, throw it away. Tell yourself it is unreal. What would happen in your life if those talents were wholly successful and enriched you twice over?

• What is the difference between these two ways of living? What is present in one way of living that is absent from the other? Which would lead to a happier existence? What prevents you from living the second way? What part do shame, fear, risk, fulfillment, envy, frustration play in these two ways of living? You may not be able to express in words what you feel. That's all right. Remain with the feeling and allow it to expand so that you can feel it more deeply as you continue to explore it.

166

What keeps you from living in the kingdom in spite of the fact that you have experienced it as a happier and better way of life? What holds you back and forces you to act like the third servant? When you have found the barrier, take a close look at it. Is it real? Just for fun, throw it away. What happens?

Do you see any way that you might dare throw away some of your fear about yourself in real life? Do you want to move closer to the kingdom? What draws you toward it? What keeps you outside? Is there any way you can move closer to the kingdom?

• To conclude, enter into prayer with your Father. Is there anything you would like to ask for? Ask for help in removing the obstacles that keep you outside the kingdom. Do you also want to thank him for revealing the kingdom to you through Jesus in this parable?

25 THE HIRED LABORERS
time: twenty-five minutes
materials: Bible (Matthew 20:1-16)

The parable of the talents raises a problem we have felt with Jesus' teaching. It makes us uneasy because it is violent, and if we investigate other parables, Jesus even seems to recommend immoral courses of action. Of course, the stories can be explained, but in every case we are left with the fear that we are really explaining *away*, that we are merely making the best of a bad situation. So let us now confront this uneasiness and disturbance by experimenting with a parable that brings it out in the open. What does Jesus mean to do by creating such conflict in us?

If you do the exploration on your own, use the hand movements and enter into the story by passing over into a laborer hired at eight in the morning.

• This story is very effective in a group setting. As we have seen, the kingdom is not something just for the mind, so let's experience this story through our body as well. Divide the participants into three or five different groups, depending on the number of people. For three groups you need a person or group to represent the landlord and foreman, a group hired at daybreak, and a group hired at the eleventh hour. For five groups add groups hired at the third and sixth hours.

The foreman begins by hiring the first group to pick the crop. They raise their arms over their heads and begin to pick the fruit. For the remainder of the meditation, they keep picking this way. Allow three minutes to pass before hiring the second group.

Now hire the second group. They too begin to pick fruit, their arms stretched over their heads. After six minutes, hire the third group. After eleven minutes hire the last group. At twelve minutes the foreman blows the whistle to signal the end of the work day. All the workers line up to receive their wage.

The wages are paid to the eleventh-hour group first. Use candy for the wages. Give each person who comes forward one piece of candy. Those who have picked for twelve hours receive the same wage as those who have picked for one.

Allow one of the laborers from the all-day group to voice his or her opinion about what is happening. Those laborers may feel cheated or ripped off; allow them to state their complaints. Finally the landlord should respond as he does in the story.

In acting out the story, encourage participants to allow their feelings to surface. Have them imagine this as a real situation. We would all feel cheated if we were in that first group. We might hesitate to voice such sentiments because we felt ashamed or guilty about them. But to understand the parable, we should explore these feelings and allow them to expand.

● Now sit down for a few minutes and explore your feelings about this situation. What was it like to be hired at the last minute? How did you feel most of the day as more and more people were hired and you were left behind? What were your concerns? How to feed your family? How to get the money you needed to live? Then how did you feel when you were given a decent day's wage?

If you worked all day or most of the day, how did you feel during the day? Were you happy that you had found work and were promised a good wage? How did you respond when everyone received the same wage? Were you angry? Resentful? Why? Did you ever consider that this wage, which is enough to live on, might be necessary for these other people regardless of how long they labored? How do you feel about this idea now?

If you were the landlord, see if you can understand how he or she could act this way. It is hard to enter into this character because he or she is of the kingdom rather than the world. But can you begin to see things from this person's perspective? Which does this person value more: strict justice, or people and their needs? What would it be like to live as this person?

● Now form small groups. Each group should have one member from each of the divisions of the meditation groups: a landlord/foreman, all-day laborers, an eleventh-hour laborer. The group members can share with one another what it was like to be those characters in the story. While a member is sharing, the other members should pass over from their own character into the character being described. The other members can ask questions that might clarify the narrator's experience. But the group should not allow conflicts between different characters. The all-day laborers cannot challenge the fairness of paying the eleventh-hour people or the landlord. In the discussion the object is not to justify any one viewpoint but to experience all the different viewpoints.

This story challenges human concepts of justice. If the landlord represents the kingdom, then the kingdom is pretty unfair by human standards. Moreover, the story implies that we must give up our traditional ideas of justice. The all-day laborers must either accept their wage or refuse it; they have no right to demand more.

The story sets the kingdom and the world in violent conflict with each other; they are incompatible. We are presented a challenge: Is the kingdom appealing enough to sacrifice things we hold very dear, such as our ideas of justice and fairness?

What about the shock we experience as the kingdom and the world are juxtaposed? Is the idea of the kingdom as we have explored it worth the conflict involved in relearning what is right and true? Would you rather ignore the kingdom so that you can hold on to your idea of what is good and proper? Jesus does not hesitate to challenge everything we hold sacred if it stands against the kingdom. If we take him as our teacher, we will find ourselves time and again placed in positions of conflict. Are we willing to put up with this conflict?

Jesus uses these violent techniques and ideas to awaken us. The gospels often picture Jesus acting like an alarm clock to waken the disciples. If necessary, he uses fear to rouse us: Consider the ending of the parable of the talents. Our fear may be stupid and wrong from the vantage point of the kingdom, but it can still rouse us to action.

In the current story the antagonism is not so much to arouse us as to challenge us to rethink our attitudes. The kingdom is beyond our justice, which gives to each according to what is earned; the kingdom distributes according to need rather than according to what is deserved. We like to feel we have earned what we have received, and we do not like the idea that others who have not earned something receive as much as we do.

If we would enter the kingdom, we must lay aside these demands. After all, what is the difference between the third group, which has been brought into the kingdom, and the first group, which is still caught up in the world? There is no difference in wealth. The only difference is between an attitude of thankfulness and an attitude of resentment based upon what is thought to be fair. The members in the first group could enter the kingdom simply by dropping their sense of being wronged. Actually they have not been wronged; they have received a decent day's wage. But it is a hard transition to make.

• Turn to your Father now in prayer. What have you learned about his kingdom through this story? What would you like him to help you with? Do you dare ask him to show you that the kingdom is indeed better than your sense of right and justice? Can you dare ask to rise above the world's understanding of fairness and justice?

EXPLORATION **26** **BEFORE THE CROSS**
time: twenty-five minutes
materials: Journal (Life Experience)

An old Sufi story addresses our dilemma concerning the challenges we meet on the path of growth.

Nasrudin, a holy man who appears to his neighbors as a fool, knocks on his neighbor's door. "My daughter is getting married and we need a great pot for the banquet. May I borrow yours?" asks Nasrudin. The neighbor hesitates but finally lends Nasrudin the pot.

A few days later Nasrudin comes to the neighbor's door with two pots. The neighbor is surprised, but Nasrudin explains, "While your pot was staying with us it gave birth to this second pot." "That's wonderful," says the neighbor as he gladly accepts both pots.

A year later Nasrudin again approaches the neighbor's door. "My daughter who was married a year ago is now about to have a child. May we borrow your pot again for the celebration?" The neighbor is delighted to lend the pot.

A week passes, two weeks, a month and Nasrudin does not return the pot. One day the neighbor spots him in the marketplace. He demands his pot back from Nasrudin. "Oh, but haven't you heard the bad news?" asks Nasrudin. "While your pot was at my house it suddenly died and we had to bury it."

"That's ridiculous," says the neighbor. "Who ever heard of a pot dying? You are lying, and I want my pot back."

"But friend," replies Nasrudin, "you showed no surprise a year ago when your pot gave birth. How can you be amazed now when that same pot dies?"

When things are going the way we want and hope, we have no problems accepting the miraculous or making allowances for what we do not believe. But when we are made uncomfortable, when the kingdom goes against our grain, we have reservations and we balk.

We were willing to believe the good news we have seen and heard from Jesus: a kingdom of overwhelming generosity, a kingdom of care and healing. But what about a kingdom that has no room for our type of justice, no place for our fear? The kingdom promises a better life than we currently have from the world. But the price demanded is the surrender of some dearly-held ideas. Nor is this conflict a minor part of Jesus' teaching. He often arouses violent opposition, and this ability to create conflict brings him to a violent, untimely end.

The kingdom in these parables stands as a sign of contradiction to the world and all the world holds to be true and valuable. That sign of contradiction does not stop with Jesus' teaching; he himself becomes the sign of contradiction. For the signs of contradiction we have experienced in the parables of the talents, the laborers, and the Good Samaritan come to a focus and climax in the death of Jesus. And that sign of contradiction takes symbolic form as the cross upon which he is killed.

• In this exploration we will use the symbol of the cross to clarify our position at this point in our pilgrimage. In the Life Experience section of your journal, draw a cross down the center of a page. Label the upper left-hand corner "Things Jesus promises in the kingdom." Label the lower right-hand corner "Things the kingdom demands I surrender." In the upper right-hand corner write "Things the world promises and delivers." In the lower left-hand corner write "Things the world cannot give me."

• Prepare for the exploration as usual. Then begin to fill in the squares created by the cross in your journal. What that you really desire have you experienced as part of the kingdom? What do you cling to that has no place in the kingdom? Now do the same for the world. What that you desire does the world offer? What things can the world never give you?

In this exploration we are not yet making a decision for or against the kingdom; we are only clarifying certain issues. As we continue our pilgrimage, feel free to return to this exploration to add any further experiences or insights.

EXPLORATION

27

THE FIRST PUBLIC APPEARANCE OF JESUS
time: twenty-five minutes
materials: Bible (Luke 4:16-30)

We will conclude our initial exploration of the kingdom of God by returning to our meditation in Exploration 16a. There we heard Jesus' proclamation in the synagogue. He read from Isaiah and announced that in their hearing the prophecy had come true. Today we can continue with that story.

Certain episodes in life later come to be seen as summing up our whole life. The cliché "That's the story of my life" gives voice to this experience. Our story today is just such a microcosm of Jesus' life. Like the ministry of Jesus which it inaugurates, the story begins with a proclamation of the kingdom of God. But Jesus' preaching then arouses the conflict and opposition we ourselves have experienced on our pilgrimage. Now the story shifts emphasis to the person of Jesus himself. Let's follow that movement in our meditation.

• Prepare as usual. When you are ready, read the story in Luke.

• We enter the story as we did before, by passing over into the person of one of the villagers. You are gathering with your neighbors to worship in the synagogue. Enter the building and take a seat. During the next few minutes enter into prayer with your Father.

Now the service begins. The old man in charge goes to the Ark and removes the holy scrolls containing the Scriptures. A young man comes forward and takes the scrolls. You do not know him personally, but you know that he is Jesus and that he comes from around here. He is a rabbi, a teacher, and you eagerly await the wisdom he will share with you.

Listen to him as he reads from the prophet Isaiah. Now he puts down the scroll and says that today this text is being fulfilled. You know from your upbringing that this text speaks of the Messiah, the savior Israel expects to deliver her from bondage to the Romans. Yet here is this local boy claiming to fulfill the text. He is really saying that he is the long-awaited Messiah.

You are surprised by his words. You hear whispers around you. "Isn't that Joseph's son? Wasn't he a carpenter?" Could it be that this great day all Israel has longed for has finally arrived? You feel a certain joy. You hope what he says might be true. Explore this initial good feeling now.

But now Jesus speaks again:

> No doubt you will quote the proverb to me, "Physician, heal yourself!" and say, "We have heard of all your doings at Capernaum; do the same here in your own home town." I tell you this . . . no prophet is recognized in his own country. There were many widows in Israel, you may be sure, in Elijah's time, when for three years and six months the skies never opened, and famine lay hard over the whole country; yet it was to none of these that Elijah was sent, but to a widow at Serepta in the territory of Sidon. Again, in the time of the prophet Elisha, there were many lepers in Israel, and not one of them was healed, but only Naaman, the Syrian.

What is he saying? He is insulting you. You aren't good enough. The Messiah you have been awaiting all these centuries will come for others but not for you. Who does he think he is? You feel your anger rising. He says you have no part in this kingdom for which you have prayed and waited so long. And who is he? No one special. Just one of the local boys with a swelled head. You feel the anger rising throughout the congregation.

As a group you rise up to chase this Jesus away. The anger of the crowd is contagious. You are ready to kill this upstart for all the trouble he has caused. The crowd streams from the synagogue and grabs Jesus. Move with the crowd as it heads for the top of the cliff. They are going to throw him off the cliff. In your anger you believe he deserves it.

The excitement is high as you near the cliff. But something strange happens. You are far from Jesus, so you can't see just what it is. But now people are saying he's got away. That seems impossible; the only way out is through the mob. How did he escape? Once again you are confused. Just when he was in your power, the man vanished. Conclude your meditation now.

In this story we can see Jesus as a sign of contradiction, both in his preaching and in his actions. The story is prophetic of what happens to Jesus eventually: He is arrested and executed. But according to his disciples, he escapes even death and conquers. If we choose to follow Jesus we will move ever deeper into the mystery and the meaning of this contradiction. Our willingness to explore and live with that conflict is necessary if we are to continue with him.

174

We have concluded our initial encounter with Jesus and with the kingdom of God he announces. We have experienced that kingdom not so much as a place but as a way of living. We also know now that the kingdom is in certain key ways contrary to the world's way of thinking. Jesus' vision offers something new.

Earlier on our journey we explored different ways of seeing the world, and in the story of Adam and Eve the visions of innocence and experience. Now Jesus proclaims a way of seeing beyond experience. In many ways his vision resembles that of innocence, but it is hardly naive or regressive. We will refer to it as the *vision of the kingdom*.

We have experienced the attractiveness of this kingdom as a way of living. It appeals to us because of our dissatisfaction with the world's vision and because it promises fulfillment and happiness. But we have also seen that to enter the kingdom means surrendering many cherished beliefs and axioms of the world. We find ourselves in a dilemma.

In a way, the kingdom might discourage us. After all, here is a place where forgiveness flows naturally, where harsh judgment is left behind, where people care for one another heroically, where wealth is distributed freely rather than hoarded for private enjoyment, where miracles occur: The lame walk, the blind see, and the poor hear the good news that God loves them. This kingdom is very attractive. But what have we to do with it? We find it next to impossible to forgive; our anger eats up our peace; often the only miracle is that we can indeed go on. The kingdom is not only not of this world; it is also, unfortunately, not of our lifetime; it seems so far from what we are capable of. How could we ever expect to enter into such a kingdom?

The difficulty of even understanding the idea of kingdom might make for further discouragement. So it might be helpful at this point to explore the idea a bit more deeply.

For one thing, we should realize that the people who heard Jesus speak knew from firsthand experience what a kingdom was; in their culture, kings and kingdoms were a fact of everyday life. For us, by contrast, the idea seems remote, so we have to use our imaginations to make it come alive.

Furthermore, recall that Jesus is a storyteller and a poet—as we have already seen in our pilgrimage. Like other poets, he uses words that are rich in meaning—rich because they can mean several things all at once. The word *kingdom* is one of those poetic words. For Jesus it has at least three meanings. Sometimes it is clear that *the kingdom is already here.* Many of the people that Jesus heals, and many of the people he mentions in his parables, are already in the kingdom. Jesus speaks of them as being leaven in the world, as being the light of the world. So they are clearly still in the world but are also in the kingdom.

But *the kingdom lies in the future too.* Jesus tells us to pray, "(May) thy kingdom come"; we are to look forward to a fuller coming when God's will will be done on earth "as it is in heaven." True, the leaven is at work in the mass of dough, the light is shining in the world, but the whole mass is not yet leavened, and much of the world is still in darkness. The followers of Jesus, then, are to help prepare the world for the full coming of the kingdom on earth, when all human beings will accept the will of God and live in peace and love in union with Jesus. And finally, at the end of time Jesus will come in glory, the earthly kingdom will come to an end, and there will be only the *eternal kingdom.*

The kingdom of God on earth is already with us, then; those who accept and follow Jesus, even though imperfectly, are in it. But it also lies in the future; the kingdom is to come more fully on earth. And finally the earthly kingdom of God gives way to the heavenly, eternal kingdom.

In the next part of our pilgrimage we will examine just how a person becomes a member of the kingdom. And we will discover how difficult and long a process it can be. It may take most of us the rest of our lives to journey toward that kingdom. But it need not be so. In reality, entering the kingdom is easy. Unfortunately, we find it hard to believe what we hear about the kingdom, and so we don't risk entering that kingdom. We make the entrance difficult and long. But before we consider the hard and difficult road, let's take a look at how easy it might be as we consider one of the greatest miracles of the kingdom: Christmas.

Our Father knows about our difficulties. That's why he gave us Christmas. It wasn't originally part of the package; the earliest Christians had no such feast. In fact the Church told them to stay home during the Roman Saturnalia: It simply wasn't the place for a good Christian to be. But finally the Church gave in, baptized the Saturnalia, and made it Christmas. But that didn't stop the good Christian opposition to Christmas. After all, it is a Catholic holiday; Catholics even invented it. And the word means *the Mass of Christ*. The Puritans didn't like that. They tried to repress Christmas, to outlaw the feast. But they didn't succeed. Today many Christians still don't like it: Give it back to the pagans, they say; it's commercialized and just an excuse for merchants to make lots of money. Of course, some Christians aren't ready to give up yet. They fight to put Christ back in Xmas.

But no one can hold it back, make it go away, or change it. For Christmas is a miracle. For a short time each year the kingdom of God comes among us on this earth. It becomes more present and visible than usual. Look around you next Christmas. This is the kingdom we have been examining and exploring: Here it is in all its glory.

But it looks just like the world, you say. Of course it does. It's still the same old world. Yet there are subtle changes as well, and they make the difference. People exhaust themselves and their bank accounts in giving to one another, and most do it with deep-down cheer rather than reluctance. That is Christmas; it is also the kingdom. No one diets at Christmas. Instead we indulge in fruitcake and eggnog. In Old Testament times, Israel hungered for the kingdom as a land flowing with milk and honey: eggnog and fruitcake will do as well. The air is filled with blessings as with cards and spoken greetings we wish one another a Merry Christmas and a Happy New Year. We pray for a year of peace and fulfillment for everyone in the world. That is Christmas; it is also the kingdom. Separations and divisions cease for a time; a Buddhist lama living in Berkeley sends Christmas cards with a Tibetan tale of wisdom and peace. And Arab and Jew, English and Irish, North and South, East and West put down their weapons for a few hours so that peace might reign. That is Christmas; it is also the kingdom. And miracle of miracles, the child in every one of us comes out—the innocent child, the expectant child, the wide-eyed child, the believing child. That is Christmas; it is also the kingdom. For unless you become as a little child you cannot enter the kingdom of heaven.

But there is more to Christmas. It is not just a preview of the kingdom; it is the kingdom. Yearly it visits our tired world for a few days to speak to us of another way of living, a happier way. And miraculously for a few days each year we are as close to the kingdom of God as many of us will ever be in our lifetime. That would be enough. But it is not all. For Christmas itself is the miracle.

And it did not begin with Jesus. Long before him the ancients celebrated Christmas as they witnessed the rebirth of the sun and the conquest of light over dark four days after the winter solstice. Christmas continues today undiminished, even though many who celebrate it do not know Jesus, let alone believe in him. Christmas is its own miracle, and Christmas works its own miracles.

Consider a story that in certain parts of the world is almost as popular today as the story of Jesus' birth—a story of Christmas that never mentions Christ, yet a story that for many has come to be *the* story of the spirit of Christmas. It's about a wicked old man whose name has come to stand for all that is mean and miserly: Ebenezer Scrooge. Here is one man who is of this world and has nothing to do with the kingdom of God.

Yet consider what happens to old Ebenezer. One Christmas Eve, after he has grumbled himself through the day, Ebenezer has a dream. That's all. Just a dream. Ebenezer himself says it was probably caused by some undigested bit of dinner, that's all. But in the dream Ebenezer sees what he has come to. He weeps for his childhood, for the loneliness and the cruelty he has endured. He sees in "Christmas present" that in spite of the suffering, hope lives on, sharing warmth and light. And finally, Scrooge squints with fear into the future he is creating out of his own misery and the suffering of others.

Well, Ebenezer awakens from that dream, and he begins to live. He has left the world behind and moved into the kingdom. He gives extravagantly, like the prodigal farmer. He becomes a friend to the poor and needy, like the landowner in the parable of the hired laborers. He no longer judges himself, or anyone else for that matter. Instead he laughs even—no, especially—at himself. And as all kingdom dwellers do, Ebenezer works miracles. He heals Tiny Tim just as Jesus heals the lame and just as Peter and John and all the saints heal and work signs. Ebenezer has passed over from this world into the kingdom because of a dream—all because of Christmas.

Is it so hard to enter the kingdom? During the rest of the year the parables of Jesus, our own fears, the world's wars and failures say "Yes, it is very difficult." But Christmas says "No." For it is no further away than a dream of Christmas, a wish of "God bless us one and all," and becoming like a little child. Something this big that happens every year cannot be stopped. Ebenezer cannot "Bah humbug" it out of existence; the Grinch cannot steal it; the gates of hell will not prevail against it.

Christmas can come true for us as well. There is no need to go through the difficult process of repentance we will explore soon. There is no need to spend years trying to enter the kingdom through all sorts of disciplines and meditational techniques. It can be as simple as a smile.

There was once an old priest who was thought to be insane by most of his fellow priests; they called him "Crazy Bill." And he probably was mad, but he was gentle and harmless, so there was no need to put him away. Instead, he was sent to the seminary, where there was a lot of room, and where he could be useful by hearing the seminarians' confessions. He couldn't get into much trouble doing that.

Now, seminarians tend to be very serious people. After all, they have left the world behind to become priests. They are the hope of the Church and they fully expect to save it, if not the entire world as well. A seminarian has great responsibility as he struggles with his vocation, his temptations, and even his sins. At Christmas one year all the seminarians had to go to confession to Crazy Bill. All the seminarians lined up in the chapel, and Crazy Bill went into the tiny confessional. Then, one by one, each serious seminarian went to confession to Crazy

Bill. Since it was Christmastime, Crazy Bill gave each seminarian the same penance: "Go into the chapel," he said, "and kneel in front of the manger. Then smile at the baby Jesus."

Imagine the scene as one by one each solemn, mature, manly seminarian leaves the confessional, shuffles reluctantly down the chapel aisle, drops to his knees in front of the crèche, and sneaks a smile at the plastic doll. As he rises and turns around he sees all the other seminarians who have already confessed sitting at the back of the church laughing at his predicament. The only way to salvage his wounded pride is to join his confreres in the back of the church and wait for the next victim to leave the box and begin his humiliating pilgrimage of penance.

But Crazy Bill might not have been crazy at all. He could be a great Zen master. For the Zen master knows that for every path to enlightenment studied and practiced in the monasteries there are millions of other paths outside the teaching. Maybe Bill knew that if these serious young men could have dropped that seriousness and enjoyed a simple smile at the baby Jesus they too, like Scrooge, might then and there have entered the kingdom. For it takes no more than a dream, no less than a smile, and suddenly you're there in that place where all dreams end and the living begins.

PART FOUR

Jesus' Program for Transformation

Now that we have some ideas about the kingdom of God, we can turn to the first part of Jesus' proclamation. He announces his ministry with the phrase "Repent, for the kingdom of God is at hand." What does *repent* mean? How do we go about repenting in order to enter into the kingdom?

In ordinary usage today, *repentance* means about the same as "feeling sorry for our sins." But *repentance* as Jesus uses the word is not just a feeling sorry or an admission that we have done wrong.

To repent also means to turn back. It implies something more radical than being sorry. To repent could mean to turn back to our source, to return to that time before this present situation. Zen masters ask their pupils to meditate upon their face before they were conceived. Perhaps repentance is something like this—a radical turning around in order to return to something like that state of innocence we left behind so long ago.

The original Greek word also gives us a hint about this action of repenting. *Metanoia* means "a change of mind." We have seen that the kingdom of God is not a different place but a different way of seeing. Then to enter into the kingdom, we need to change our way of viewing things—much more than changing our mind in the ordinary sense of that phrase. The change of mind that entry into the kingdom calls for is a radical rethinking of all our most accepted, commonsense thought processes.

28

READING JOHN
time: twenty minutes
materials: Bible (John 1:19-28)

As we have done in the other parts of this pilgrimage, we will begin
our present investigation by continuing our reading of John's gospel. In
today's passage we move out of the prologue and into a different kind
of narrative. In the prologue John spoke abstractly about such things as
the Word, light, enfleshment, law, and grace. Now he moves out of
that rarified philosophical atmosphere and into a world of people and
human events. We meet the strange figure of John the Baptist, who
announces the coming of the kingdom. In this scene he is being
questioned by the Jews. They want to know whether he is the Christ; is
he the Word made flesh?

Similarly, our own pilgrimage will now take on a more earthly
coloring. We have been exploring the presence and importance of
meaning in our life, and we have experienced through Jesus a vision of
God's kingdom. Now our attention moves to the dynamics of human
living. How can we go about passing over from this worldly way of
seeing into the kingdom's way of seeing? What is involved in the
change? Before, our interest was philosophical, although more practical
and existential than what passes for philosophy; now our concern is
psychological, although again more concrete and practical than
academic psychology. We will be reading and understanding our gospel
text and the other Scripture passages in this section from this
psychological viewpoint.

On the surface our present passage from John seems to be a
historical narrative. But Scripture is never solely restricted to one level
of understanding and interpretation. There is often a historical,
sociological, theological, and psychological level to the same text.

Early Christians were aware of these different levels and
employed them far more than modern readers do. For example, the
earliest Christians had no such thing as a New Testament to read. But
they did not feel at a loss, for they saw Jesus and his kingdom
prefigured in the writings of the Old Testament. Many New Testament
stories reveal a reliance and building upon the experience of Israel in
the Old Testament. As Jesus says, he does not come to do away with
the past but to bring it to fulfillment. Thus the New Testament makes
apparent what was present but hidden in the Old Testament. The entire

gospel can be read in the Old Testament provided we know how to read it there. The recovery of that lost art of reading is one of the goals of our pilgrimage. For a restricted reading and understanding of Scripture came with the general decline of imagination.

• Prepare for your reading now, using the first two phases of meditational preparation. Then read the passage from John, using all that you have learned about our reading of Scripture.

We begin our reading on a down-to-earth level with the narrative of a meeting. The Jews come to John the Baptist because they want to know whether he is the Messiah they have been awaiting. John tells them that he is not the Christ, the anointed one.

On the narrative level this passage concerns the forerunner of Jesus. John, appearing just before Jesus begins his own ministry, is a stark, ascetic figure. His preaching is of the fire-and-brimstone school, and his like has not been seen in Israel since the last of the prophets hundreds of years ago. In many ways the preaching of the Baptist and of Jesus are identical. For the Baptist also centered upon the kingdom of God and called all to repentance. In an age eagerly awaiting a Messiah, many assumed that John was the one they had been longing for. During the first years of the Christian Church there were still followers of the Baptist who claimed that he and not Jesus was the Messiah. John the Evangelist and his church are aware of this movement and troubled by it. Therefore John writes his gospel in such a way that there can be no mistaking the Baptist for the Messiah. For example, in all the other gospels, the Baptist baptizes Jesus. In John's gospel, Jesus is not baptized by the Baptist at all, because to be baptized by someone could mean that the baptized is lesser than the baptizer.

But how are we to read this passage psychologically? Instead of seeing the Baptist and Jesus as two separate people, what would we learn if we viewed them as elements within the composition of the human psyche? To read in this way, we never deny the other levels: Jesus and the Baptist are certainly still historical people. But we find that this narrative reveals something about the internal psychological makeup of the human psyche after repentance.

Of all the gospels, that of John often presents the most perfect and fulfilled picture of Jesus. In this gospel Jesus is often not the historical figure of the synoptic accounts but rather the risen Lord of the Christian community. So in this scene we are given a representation not of the average human psyche but of the perfect or "risen" human psyche—the mind of the kingdom.

When the Baptist is asked whether he is the Christ, he replies that he is not; rather, he is the forerunner and the servant of the Christ. Here is ego at the service of the self. It does not draw attention to itself and it does not grasp after what it is not. Instead, it knows its place and its role and fulfills both.

Seen in psychological terms, the Baptist is an image of the human ego, that part of the psyche that dominates in the worldly personality. Jesus (although he does not directly appear in this passage) then signifies the Christ or the self. In the worldly personality, the self is hidden or repressed, but as the person moves from the world into the kingdom, the self reveals itself and assumes control of the psyche. In this passage we see the relation between ego and self as it appears in the kingdom. This relationship is not our present psychological makeup but rather a vision of the new alignment that comes about through repentance.

But if this is the ideal psyche, what is an ordinary human psyche like? An old story in Walt Disney's *Fantasia* provides us with an image of our present psychological ordering. It is the story of the Sorcerer's Apprentice, who in the film is played by Mickey Mouse. Once upon a time, there was a great sorcerer who knew all the powerful magical spells by which wind, earth, water, and fire could be controlled. The sorcerer had an apprentice whose task was to draw the water that the sorcerer used in his spells. One day the sorcerer had to leave on business. He left the apprentice in charge, with instructions to fill the great basin in the house with water from the well.

After the sorcerer left, the apprentice began this great task. But drawing water from the well and carrying it across the courtyard and into the house is tiring and boring work. "Why should I have to do this?" the apprentice asked himself. "After all, I too want to be a great sorcerer some day, and I will never become one if all I do is carry this water back and forth. There must be some spell in my master's book that would finish this chore with no further effort on my part."

So the apprentice looked through his master's books on magic, and sure enough, he found just such a spell. He cast the spell on the old broom standing in the corner, and the broom proceeded to grow itself arms and legs. "Fetch the water!" commanded the apprentice, and the broom obediently went about its task. Proud of his accomplishment, the apprentice assumed his seat in the sorcerer's chair and fell asleep as the broom continued to fetch water.

Soon the apprentice began to have strange nightmares. He dreamt he was floating and then drowning. He awakened in fright to discover himself up to his neck in water. The broom had done its job only too well. The basin was overflowing, and the house was awash. How to stop the broom! But by what spell? The apprentice panicked. He had not considered this situation and didn't know the proper spell. He tried everything he knew, but to no avail. Finally in desperation, he chopped the broom in half. There, that should hold it. But not so, for the two halves each developed arms and legs, picked up their buckets and proceeded to fetch more water.

The entire house would be flooded! How could the apprentice save himself? Ah, that's just the point. There was nothing he could do to save himself. He was over his head not only in the magic spells but in the water too.

Just as all seemed lost, the sorcerer appeared in the doorway. With one wave of his hand he dispelled the flood, and the house returned to order. All was once more silent and calm except for a threat in the air. For the apprentice knew what he had done and what he deserved. He had learned his lesson. A quick kick from the sorcerer booted him from the chair. Chastened, he picked up his bucket and began to do what he was supposed to do: gather water for the basin.

This is a story about our human condition. The apprentice is our present ego. It wants to be in charge of our life; indeed, in the absence of the self, the ego has taken charge. When the ego takes charge, it creates the world in its own image, and so we live in the world rather than in the kingdom. That is why our life is so unsatisfactory. For the ego is truly unable to control our life. Whether we know it or not, whether we have awakened from our sleep or not, the truth is that we are drowning. The ego is not evil and certainly should not be destroyed: It serves a very necessary purpose in our lives. But that purpose is similar to the apprentice's task in the story. The ego may want to be in charge, may want to be sorcerer, and may even succeed in putting on the sorcerer's hat and performing some magic. But it is incapable of performing the sorcerer's role completely and soon it gets into real trouble.

When we pass from the world into the kingdom, the ego is removed from its present ruling position in our psyche and is put at its proper job, which is to guide us through the mundane business of living and being a part of the human race. For only the self is able to provide us with fulfillment in the business of living; only the self is capable of directing our lives. Until the ego is removed from its position of power and the self assumes its rightful place, our lives are of the world rather than of the kingdom. As we continue our journey in this section, we will continue to explore the relation of ego and self as well as the way that relation can be righted.

● To conclude our reading today, rewrite the story of John the Baptist to portray the ego/self relationship as it exists in the world rather than in the kingdom. How would the Baptist respond to the question about the Christ if he were a worldly ego?

EXPLORATION **29** **ARE YOU THE CHRIST?**
time: twenty-five minutes a day for one week
materials: Bible and Journal (Prayer Experiences)

We have met John the Baptist and the way he sees himself in relation to the Christ; now let's turn our attention to the Christ. During the next week take the question "Are you the Christ?" as your tool for exploration. Let's see where we can find the Christ in ourselves, in the world, in the Scriptures, and in others.

The Christ means "the anointed" and is the Greek term for the Messiah. The term refers not so much to an individual, however, as to a spirit or a way of living—the mind of the kingdom. Many words are used to name this same reality. For example, Jesus is primarily the Christ because as God's anointed he announces and inaugurates the kingdom of God. But we might also call this Christ the Spirit of Jesus, or the Spirit of God, or the Holy Spirit. From our own exploration so far, we might call what we are looking for the person who is living in the kingdom as opposed to the world.

• Each day this week, after your usual preparation for meditation, take our question—"Are you the Christ?"—and go searching for the Christ. Where will you look? Wherever your search carries you. In this meditation we seek a deeper appreciation of what it would be like to live in the kingdom, and we approach the question by asking what kind of a mind or psyche the person in the kingdom manifests. We do not seek knowledge or facts so much as experience and insight. And since we are only beginning our exploration of the mind of the kingdom, this week is a review, from a new vantage point, of what we have experienced so far in our journey.

• First we can look again at the stories of and by Jesus. How does this Christ-mind make itself known in them? Enter into the stories and ask your question of each of the characters: Are you the Christ? Of course, in the stories about Jesus himself you may know immediately from experience or upbringing that he is the Christ. But see whether you can find out about the Christ from what you experience in the story. Don't rely upon past information; draw up your own image. In the story of the laborers ask each of the characters whether he or she is the Christ? Which of the people in the story live in the kingdom? Which live in the world? Which move from the world into the kingdom? And what does each of these kingdom characters tell you about the Spirit of the kingdom?

• Like the early Christians you also can look for the Spirit of God, or the kingdom mind, in the Old Testament. Here, especially among the prophets, you will find many descriptions of the kingdom mind. For example, Isaiah 52:13–53:12 is a song of the suffering servant that is considered a description of the ideal citizen of the kingdom of God. What does this suffering servant show you concerning the Christ? What is the place of suffering in the Christ life? Can the Christ life be destroyed and annihilated by suffering? What is the final outcome of the Christ life?

• Or search for the glimmers of Christ among the people you have known—your parents, teachers, friends. Have you seen traces of the Spirit of Jesus in them? We aren't necessarily looking for people who follow Jesus professedly, but for people who act like Jesus, who live his spirit of generosity, forgiveness, healing, and care. Move through your history in search of those individuals who in rare moments revealed this other kind of mind that is not of this world but opens onto the kingdom.

- From individuals you can turn to special moments or events in your life where the Spirit of God made itself known to you. These could be moments of ecstasy, of healing, of forgiveness. What are the moments you yourself have experienced that parallel moments in the stories of Jesus and so reveal the presence of the kingdom of God?

- Of course we can take the question inside of ourselves. Where is the Christ within us? Naturally, egos not as purified as that of the Baptist will want to claim to be the Christ. But we are wise enough now to know that the ego cannot be the Christ.

Within each of us there is a self, or as Jesus would say, the Holy Spirit. Without this Holy Spirit who is God himself we would not even exist. This Spirit is the same as the Spirit of Jesus. When this Spirit is revealed and takes its rightful place in our heart, we move from the world into the kingdom. Thus far in our life, perhaps this Spirit has only made itself known at certain moments—those rare moments when we acted as a member of the kingdom, when we surrendered judgment and condemnation, when we responded to others out of pure love and care. Can you remember such fleeting moments? What were they like? How are they different from your usual feelings and thoughts? Where can the Christ be found in your own life?

- You may also make the question a part of your prayer to your Father. Ask him to show you the Christ in your life. Thank him after each meditation for the Holy Spirit that made itself known to you. As we have begun to see and will continue to experience, this pilgrimage is not something you do alone. Jesus your teacher leads you step by step; your Father guides you and sustains your strength as he brings you closer and closer to himself; the Holy Spirit within you draws you home.

- On the last day of your meditation summarize your findings of the week in the Prayer Experience section of your journal. Entitle your entry the "Spirit of the Kingdom" and describe this Spirit and where you have experienced it throughout the last week.

30 EGO WORK: THE WISE AND FOOLISH VIRGINS
time: ·twenty-five minutes
materials: Bible (Matthew 25:1-13)

Since in most people the ego is so dominant, the distinction between ego and self is very difficult to comprehend. Some even deny it exists. Furthermore, since the ego is in power, it will not surrender easily and will use every trick it knows to maintain its control. After all, human transformation (as opposed to superficial change) is not an easy undertaking; otherwise it would not be experienced so seldom.

But Jesus is not only a teacher who points out the kingdom. He knows how to transport us to the kingdom as well. The revelation of the ego is the first step in this twofold process. We must first come to see our ego for what it is, see what it has usurped for itself; then we will be ready to shift it to its proper place and allow the Holy Spirit to take command.

A number of Jesus' stories are designed to reveal ego to us. The next few explorations will give us a glimpse of this ego that has us in its power. Actually, we have already experienced one of these stories: that of the hired laborers. As we entered into that story, the discomfort we experienced was a discomfort of ego. If we found something appealing, it appealed not to the ego but to the Holy Spirit, or the self. Naturally these ego-revealing stories are disturbing. They signal the end of the ego's tyranny; being far from stupid, the ego knows it is being threatened, and it will resist with all its might.

But let us put some pressure on the ego to reveal itself and its true colors. Our meditations now will not be soothing or quieting. They may disturb us greatly, arousing fears, anger, outrage. But such feelings are not in themselves bad. They initiate the battle with ego, and provided we observe our feelings and thoughts carefully, we can learn much about the ego from these meditations and can come to a decision whether to allow the ego its present power or whether to shift the balance of power to the Spirit.

• Now prepare for meditation, following the usual procedure. Then read the parable of the wise and foolish virgins.

• This is not a difficult parable to understand. We begin our exploration by passing over into the experience of the foolish virgins who are waiting for the bridegroom. These maidens will eventually take part in the wedding procession and celebration. But as sometimes happens, the ceremony cannot start because the bridegroom hasn't arrived. The maidens will carry lamps to guide the bridegroom to his bride. But these foolish maidens have not secured the oil to burn in their lamps. Now they pass the time by waiting idly rather than acquiring the oil they will need.

• Can you remember similar experiences in your own life when you have delayed doing something necessary? Maybe in school you had this experience when writing term papers or studying for tests. How did you justify the delay? Enter into this experience of sloth by finding examples in your own past and exploring them now.

Now look at your life today in terms of your pilgrimage. We often complain that there is no time to do the difficult work of spiritual growth. How faithful have you been to the meditations and journal work of this pilgrimage? How carefully have you worked to learn to read for transformation? Have you really done the work? Have you skipped much of it? Have you merely dabbled on the surface? How have you justified this behavior to yourself? How justified is your

justification?

Take a hard look at your present life. How much time do you waste standing around doing nothing? How much time do you spend standing in line at the bank, the supermarket, the theater, the water fountain? How do you spend this time? Have you considered how many hours a week you could gain in mantra meditation if you used the mantra when you were just waiting around? How many hours a week do you drive a car alone? Have you ever considered chanting your mantra at that time? It could relax and refresh you. How does what you do with that time help you? Why don't you want to do the mantra at that time? Enter into this discussion seriously and observe your reactions and arguments. The arguments themselves are not important; the important thing is what is going on behind the arguments.

• Where is the "standing around" in your own life? You must receive something from it or you wouldn't do it, would you? What does it do for you? How does standing around help you live your life? Enter into your resistance toward preparing yourself rather than just standing around or waiting. Why do you avoid it? Are you afraid?

Would it disturb your present life style to prepare rather than to wait? In this part of the exploration, explore what is so wonderful about waiting and so awful about preparing.

• Now the bridegroom is coming. Feel the excitement in the air. You realize that you're not ready. This part of the story has the quality of a nightmare. Allow that nightmare feeling to expand. Can you taste the frustration of being caught off guard? Feel the anxiety as you try to prepare yourself now. Ask the other maidens if they will lend you some of their oil. They tell you they can't do this because they won't have enough for themselves. How are you going to prepare yourself?

Run off now to get some oil. What are you feeling and thinking as you do so? What are your recriminations against yourself? What are your fears? Your shames? Your anger? What or who is the anger directed towards?

Now that you have finally found some oil, run back to the house and knock on the door. The bridegroom comes to the door. You ask to be let in, but he tells you that you are too late. He closes the door in your face. This is a terrifying scene; if we can capture some of its fearsomeness in our meditation, we might extricate ourselves from our waiting attitude.

191

• Can you learn anything from this scene? What in our own life can we use to rouse ourselves from our sloth and to seriously implement this growth in the Spirit that brings us into the kingdom (or in the parable into the wedding celebration)? How can we make the transition from ego dominance to Spirit control? What in your life can serve as an alarm clock to wake you up to the importance of this task?

• We can see the foolish maidens as ego and the waiting as one of the games ego plays with us. "There's plenty of time to do that work," ego says. "Relax and enjoy yourself. Waiting is fun." But does waiting accomplish anything? And is it really fun? Look at your resistance in this meditation and at your resistance *to* this meditation; both are caused by ego. Can you catch a glimpse of what ego looks like now? Can you begin to see through its games? It will be necessary to return to this meditation and the other ego-work meditations again and again throughout your pilgrimage and to use them to cast light upon your life and your actions if you are to come to know ego and all its ploys. It will not be conquered easily.

• Now let's pass over into the experience of the wise virgins. They have taken the trouble to prepare themselves for the bridegroom's arrival. What would their kind of life be like? How might it be different from the life of the foolish maidens? The wise maidens still have time to stand around. Their life doesn't seem that much busier than that of the foolish maidens. But compare the sense of purpose in life in these two ways of living. Since we do not for the most part experience this wise virgin role, it is difficult to enter into. But can you envision this way of living, and can you begin to see that it is a better way for you, that it is more fulfilling, and that the ploys your ego uses to keep you from living this way are just ploys?

EXPLORATION **30a** FURTHER INVESTIGATION OF EGO AND SPIRIT
time: twenty-five minutes
materials: Bible (Luke 10:30–35 and Matthew 20:1–16)

Today's meditation returns to two stories we have already used in our journey. But originally we entered these stories for a different purpose. Stories are unique teaching tools precisely because they are not limited to one specific function. A story, as opposed to a teaching or a doctrine, presents a whole world. We can enter the story and explore its world from many different angles.

• After preparing for your meditation, reread the stories of the good Samaritan and hired laborers. Today we will explore these stories for what they reveal about the two kinds of mind: the world mind dominated by the ego and the kingdom mind under the direction of the Spirit. In the good Samaritan story, the minister and the nurse are two examples of the ego. The Samaritan represents the Spirit. In the story of the hired laborers the ego is found in those who complain about their pay; the Spirit manifests itself in the landowner, and the workers hired at the last hour make the transition from the world to the kingdom.

• In your meditation today, enter each of these different visions. Explore what it is like to live with the ego in dominance and what it might be like to live under the guidance of the Spirit. We are searching for tastes and experiences rather than for theories or ways to behave. As you approach these stories again, you come from a different place in your spiritual journey. What do these stories have to say to you today? How do they help you recognize and understand these different ways of thinking and being?

In the story of the good Samaritan, help comes from the person thought least able or willing to supply it. Likewise, you might think the Spirit quite incapable of direction and leadership in your life. On the other hand, the ego may have convinced you of its own capability. But is this situation really true? Can the story lead you to explore a different arrangement?

• Look at the story of the good Samaritan psychologically. You are the victim lying in the street. What parts of your psyche are able to help you and heal you now? Let us say that the nurse is your body. Is it able to help you? To supply healing and rehabilitation? Let the minister represent your mind or ego. How does it respond to your situation? The Samaritan represents the Spirit, which for modern humanity is not at all essential—it is even regarded as a figment of a more primitive imagination. Yet in the story, help and rehabilitation and care come from the Spirit. Can the story seen in this way throw light on your own life experiences and provide a way of seeing the same dynamic at work there?

The leadership provided by the ego or the body is quite different in kind from the leadership provided by the Spirit. For one thing the ego dominates and rules tyrannically; the Spirit's rule is gentle and does not attempt to usurp power the way the ego does. Yet the Spirit's leadership, from our present vantage point, might look like weakness, incompetence, or stupidity. What does the good Samaritan story say about such attitudes in us? In what ways does the shape of this story help you to understand your own experiences of healing and rehabilitation?

• Approach the story of the hired laborers in the same way. See all the people in the story as different elements in your personality. It is not necessary to be able to identify them or label them precisely. The ego is the group of self-righteous laborers; the Spirit is the landowner.

Seen as a whole, the story becomes one of conflict between the ego, which wants to rule and call the shots, and the landowner, who is the only one entitled to govern and decide wage policy. Seen objectively, which person would you rather work for? Which would be more of a tyrant? Which would better look out for the interests of your whole person rather than the interest of one segment of it? Can you sense times of conflict between the ego and the self in your own life experience? In your own life, which force tends to win? Is that victory for your own best good and the good of others?

EXPLORATION

30b

EGO WORK: THE UNFORGIVING SERVANT
time: twenty-five minutes
materials: Bible (Matthew 18:23-34)

• Prepare for this meditation, following your usual procedure. Then read the parable in Matthew. We will enter into this difficult story by passing over into the unforgiving servant.

• You owe your master a huge sum of money—more than you could ever imagine being able to repay. You know that he could call you to account at any time. How do you live with this debt hanging over your head? What is the quality of your life in this situation? Look through your own experience for situations where you have been greatly in debt to someone. This debt need not be monetary; psychological debts are actually much more potent. Someone has perhaps saved your life or helped you out when you were in great need. Imagine that you owe this person whatever he or she gave you. What is your existence like, under the shadow of such a debt?

Now the dreaded day arrives and your master calls you to account. You cannot possibly repay the debt. The master is strict and demanding. How do you feel as you approach this encounter? Do you have any hope about what might happen? Plan how you are going to deal with the master's demands.

Enter into the confrontation. The master is uncompromising. Use everything you have to plead your case. Allow the argument to proceed between the two of you until you find yourself on your knees, all of your pride gone. The master threatens to sell you and your family into slavery. You can't save yourself, but you try desperately. If you have ever been in a similar, hopeless situation allow that memory to aid your meditation now.

Finally your master cancels your entire debt. Enter into that experience. Do you experience doubt? Tears? Relief? Joy? Be with that experience as you thank your master and leave the court for your home. Perhaps you want to sing or dance to express your joy and relief.

• Suddenly your mood shifts. As you are walking along you see a fellow servant who owes you twenty dollars. All of a sudden you realize he or she has never paid you back. You are poor. It is hard to make ends meet. Maybe you feel that this person is trying to take advantage of you. Experience the transformation from gratitude to righteousness. Is that transformation difficult to imagine? Have there been times in your own life when you have suddenly forgotten gratitude because you realized someone owed you something? Can you imagine yourself simply forgetting your gratitude as you realize that you have a chance to collect from someone else? In fact, couldn't it be that this debtor gives you an opportunity to regain some self respect? Although it was wonderful to be forgiven, it was also humiliating. You were totally at the mercy of another; you are alive today simply because of that other person's generosity. That is often hard to live with. But here is an opportunity to get back some sense of self worth. You can show your power, can gain back a sense of your control over things.

So walk up to that other person now and demand repayment. The other person says he or she cannot repay you. So enter into debate. You feel the person is trying to get away with something. Besides, you can't afford to be generous: You have a family to support. Demand your rights. After all, a loan is a loan. You have justice on your side; you have nothing to fear.

Your fellow servant claims he or she can't pay. Call the police and have the person taken to prison. If people don't respect their obligations, what will society come to? If you happen to remember your own debt, you will surely be able to see the difference between that situation and the present one. After all, your master is quite wealthy; he can afford to be generous. He doesn't have to depend on this money to support his family. What other arguments can you suggest to justify your position?

Perhaps you resist being put into this situation. You say to yourself, I'm very forgiving. I'd never act this way. But look closely at your life. Do you ever hold grudges? Do you always and immediately forgive those who have offended you? Or do you attach strings to your forgiveness: "Well, as long as it doesn't happen again." Are there times when you haven't forgiven completely? Have you ever been glad that someone was indebted to you because then you could feel your own power and righteousness?

• Now pass over into the person of the master. You hear that your servant has had another servant thrown into prison for debt. How do you feel about this servant you have forgiven? Do you want that servant to represent you? Do you feel he has repaid your kindness by this treatment of his fellow servant? Drag him into court and give him a piece of your mind.

• Now see the unforgiving servant as your own ego and the master as your Spirit. The servant should be an extension of yourself. Is he? Does he act as you act? Do you want him representing you to the world? Are you satisfied with the way he responds to overwhelming forgiveness? Do you think he is capable of learning anything? Well, then, throw him out of your service and pay him as he deserves. Throw him in prison until the last penny is paid back if that's the way he wants to live.

• The end of this story is not all consoling. If we have been able to enter into the story at all, we should feel discomfort at this solution. But stay with the discomfort. Is the discomfort really you, or is it just a part of you? Can you enter again into that unforgiving situation and observe yourself? Is it you who are unforgiving, or is it merely the part of you that is in control? Enter again into a situation where you did not forgive. Was there some part of you that wanted to forgive? Did some voice within you ask you to forgive? Did some voice tell you that your righteousness was really full of holes? It may have been a very weak voice, and you might not have wanted to hear it, and you probably didn't follow it, but wasn't it there? See if you can remember that voice. Isn't it a voice you would rather have representing you? Can you begin to be a little dissatisfied with the voice that does put you before the world? Can you begin to see that that ego voice is not totally you but only a part of you? If you can, maybe you can experience some of the master's dissatisfaction with his servant. Can you dare risk making your ego uncomfortable?

30c EGO WORK: THE LAST JUDGMENT
time: one hour   materials: Bible (Matthew 25:31-46), recording of "Dies Irae" from the Verdi or Berlioz *Requiem*, and picture of *The Last Judgment* by Michelangelo

Christianity is problematic for many moderns. True, the original message of Jesus has often suffered misperceptions and corruptions that make it unappealing. But there are authentic parts of Jesus' preaching that are quite disturbing and even distasteful; the concept of the last judgment is one of them. If we are investigating Jesus as a possible guide, however, it will do no good to ignore these less savory aspects of his teaching. As we have seen in the stories of Jacob and Job, His tradition allows for dissent and struggle. So let's enter into the contest.

Today and tomorrow we will look at a scene of the last judgment. You may either do the meditation simply or you may enter into this scene through the work of a great artist. Whether or not this scene is appealing to us today, it has provided many artists with magnificent inspiration.

• When you have prepared for meditation in the usual way, read the last judgment story in Matthew. Then enter into the story, using some of the techniques of passing over that we have employed in other meditations. What is your reaction to this scene? Are there elements you find difficult to accept or that you must reject? How does this story fit in with what you have learned from Jesus so far on your journey? Does the story give you pause about following Jesus? Where is the good news in this story? Or does it sound mostly like bad news? What emotions does the story create in you?

● Through the medium of music and art we can enter much more intensely into this scene. You might make your meditation on Michelangelo's great painting of this scene. Study the individual figures. Enter into their experience. Taste the terror, the triumph, the awe. In the music of Verdi and Berlioz, set to the medieval hymn describing the day of wrath (the "Dies Irae"), we can also experience the majesty and the pleading that this scene has evoked for generations of Christians. Whether you want to believe the scene or not, can you enter it through these artists' imaginations? Can you experience what it is like to live with such an idea? Does the threat of this judgment enable you to move into a new vision of life?

Look at your own resistance to this scene. What is that resistance like? Why do you find it difficult to believe in such a scene? Is it because you do not like this kind of God? Could there also be some fear that you might find yourself on the bad end of the judgment? Pretend, with the help of the painting and the music, that the scene is real; allow these great artists to share their experience with you and transport you through this perilous journey.

EXPLORATION **30d** EGO WORK: THE LAST JUDGMENT (continued)   time: thirty minutes
materials: Journal (Prayer Diary)

We will enter this story of judgment again after the usual preparation. But today we will explore it on a psychological level. Instead of regarding the persons in this story as individuals, we will consider them as parts of the human psyche. We will then see the story as the passage of a psyche from this world into the kingdom.

● Since the title of this story is "The Last Judgment," let's begin by exploring the use of judgment in our own lives. What part does it play? How prominent is it? Do you find yourself constantly telling yourself that you have failed, that you are not adequate? Do you think it often about others? Take the time and effort now to search out the different ways you use judgment. They may be hidden, but undoubtedly it is a major component of your thinking.

When you have a full picture of your use of judgment examine judgment impartially. Judge judgment. What good does it really do you? Does it do you any good to compare yourself either favorably or unfavorably with others? Does it really change anything? What if someone wanted to take your judgment away from you? How would you react? Why do you feel this function is so necessary to your life?

• Think back to the story of the hired laborers. Where was judgment present in that story? Did it do anyone any good? What would have happened if all those who worked were grateful for the decent wage they had received and didn't judge, compare wages and hours, and then complain to the landlord? Would all have been happier? Did their complaining do them any good?

Recreate that story again, but leave out all judgment. What does the world of that story look like now? Could it be that a difference between the world and the kingdom is that there is no room for judgment in the kingdom? Do you think that is what the last judgment—the final judgment before entering the kindgom fully—is all about?

199

Here is a hypothesis we might test: Entering the kingdom means passing beyond judgment, letting go of judgment. If you haven't yet explored sufficiently what is involved here, do it now. See if you can feel the resistance to letting go of judgment; that resistance is created by the ego. Try to clarify the resistance. What is its texture, its feel, its taste?

Can you picture the kingdom as a way of living without judgment? Imagine your own present existence without judgment, as it would be in the kingdom. How would your life change if you could let go of judgment? Follow Jesus' advice: Judge not, and you will not be judged.

• The last judgment itself is still a frightening prospect. Let's enter Jesus' story. The judgment begins with a separation. In Jesus' day the sheep and goats were allowed to graze together during the day. Then at night they were separated, for the sheep were kept in the barn and the goats remained outside. We will be separated and judged just as the sheep and goats are, but since we are now exploring the story psychologically, we are not dealing with total rejection and acceptance of people but rather with a separation and judgment of our psyche.

The separation is made on the basis of nourishing, clothing, and visiting the Christ. At first glance this appears to be a judgment based on good works, and many have understood it as such. But if this is indeed the basis of judgment, then is not this last judgment meant to scare us into being good? Is such an idea then really good news?

We have seen that Jesus brings a message so great that it is too good to be true. Yet the news we have heard here does not seem too good to be true. Yes, it is just: We should care for the poor, the hungry, the imprisoned. We have seen that such care is the very nature of the kingdom of God. If we were to become citizens of that kingdom, wonderful charity and care would flow from us out to all our fellows, as we have seen happen with Zacchaeus, the prodigal farmer, the good Samaritan, the landlord, and in the many healings of Jesus. But simply to demand such care from us does not sound much like good news.

Although citizens of the kingdom are socially conscious, Jesus in this passage is not demanding such behavior. The words Jesus speaks to his disciples before sending them out on their mission are similar:

> Whoever receives one of these children in my name, receives me; and whoever receives me, receives not me but the One who sent me.
>
> Mark 9:37
> *The New English Bible*

> I tell you this: if anyone gives you a cup of water to drink because you are followers of the Messiah, that man assuredly will not go unrewarded.
>
> Mark 9:41
> *The New English Bible*

> I tell you this: everyone who acknowledges me before men,
> the Son of Man will acknowledge before the angels of God;
> but he who disowns me before men will be disowned before
> the angels of God.

Luke 12:8-9
The New English Bible

These are not commands to feed the poor or clothe the naked so much as commands to receive the Christ into your life: to visit the Christ, to nourish the Christ, to clothe the Christ, to allow the Christ a place in your heart. And the Christ refers to the Christ mind or the Holy Spirit—the mind of the kingdom rather than the mind of the world. That part of us that honors and prepares for the Christ mind is the part that passes into the kingdom; the part that does not nourish and make room for the Christ—the ego—will be left on the garbage heap and burned as worthless.

This explanation of the parable seems to take the terror away. But does it really? How *much* of our lives is spent in the service of the Christ, concerned with healing, sharing, forgiving, feeding the poor, clothing the naked, visiting the imprisoned? And how much of our lives is spent in service of ourselves and our own ends? The ego has no place in the kingdom, and if it dominates our lives to the extent that we become simply egos with no place for the Holy Spirit, what will there be left to save from the garbage heap? Luke continues in the passage last quoted:

201

> Anyone who speaks a word against the Son of Man will
> receive forgiveness; but for him who slanders the Holy
> Spirit there will be no forgiveness.

Luke 12:10
The New English Bible

Generations of Christians have tried to understand this hard saying. Yet it seems to mean that failing to take a stand for or against Jesus can be forgiven. But if we turn on the Holy Spirit within us, if we destroy the self—the breath of God—at the core of our being, there can be no forgiveness, for there is nothing left to rescue for the kingdom.

• Complete this meditation by passing over into your own life. How have you nourished and visited and given drink to the Christ? How have you related to the Holy Spirit? How have you ignored, forgotten, even slandered the Holy Spirit within you? When you have acted this way—when you have refused forgiveness, denied healing, begrudged care—can you see that it was not really you but rather your ego acting in your place? Is that the way you really want to be represented?

Instead, what would it be like to nourish that Holy Spirit within us? Can you imagine how the Holy Spirit would represent the real you better? Does such a representation promise you a better quality of living than you presently enjoy? How would you feel if you could let the part of you that has ignored and suppressed the Holy Spirit be cast on the garbage heap and burned?

• Carefully examine your attraction and resistance in terms of this parable. The attraction is the Holy Spirit; the resistance is your ego. Describe the contest within your own psyche now. Use the Prayer Diary section of your journal.

EXPLORATION **30e** **EGO WORK: THE LAST JUDGMENT** (optional)
time: one and one-half hours
materials: recording of the Second Symphony of Gustav Mahler

Today, if you wish, we will enter into the music of Gustav Mahler to see how one artist found the greatest good news in this rather frightening story of the last judgment. Mahler's symphony is a gigantic pilgrimage through death, judgment, and resurrection. He also described in words his experience of the last judgment, and it is certainly a different kind of judgment than the more traditional representation seen in Michelangelo, Verdi, and Berlioz. But is Mahler's mystic insight into Jesus' story really that far off base? Here is how Mahler describes the fifth movement of his symphony, where the judgment scene occurs:

We are again confronted by the terrifying questions, and the atmosphere is the same as at the end of the third movement. The voice of the Caller is heard. The end of all living things has come; the Last Judgment is at hand, and the horror of the Day of days breaks forth. The earth trembles, the graves burst open, the dead arise and march forth in endless procession. The great and the small of this earth—kings and beggars, the just and the godless—all press forward. The cry for mercy and forgiveness sounds fearfully in our ears. Gradually the wailing becomes more terrible—our senses desert us, our consciousness dies as the Eternal Judge approaches. The last trumpet sounds; the trumpets of the Apocalypse ring out. In the eerie silence that follows we can just barely catch the sound of a distant nightingale, a last tremulous echo of earthly life. The gentle sound of a chorus of saints and heavenly hosts is then heard: 'Arise, yes, you will arise.' Then appears the splendid glory of God. A marvelous light penetrates us to the heart—all is quiet and blissful. And behold: there is no judgment—there are no sinners, no just, no great and no small; there is no punishment and no reward. A feeling of overwhelming love envelops us with understanding and illuminates our souls.

203

● But Mahler is no writer and his words do not do his vision justice. Prepare for meditation and then lie down and allow this great, alienated mystic to lead you into the mysteries of life, death, and transfiguration on the wings of his inspiration.

30f EGO WORK: THE CURSING OF THE FIG TREE
time: twenty-five minutes
materials: Bible (Matthew 21:18-22)

We have chosen one of the most perplexing incidents in Jesus' teaching to end our series of ego meditations.

• Prepare for the meditation as usual; then read the cursing of the fig tree.

• What does this incident mean? It has been explained in many ways throughout the ages, and for many it has proven a source of embarrassment. In Luke much of its sting is taken away: It is made into a parable, and the ending is softened. Spend some time on your own with this story. Wrestle with it in the same way Jacob wrestled with God. Engage yourself in the struggle. What have you learned and experienced on this pilgrimage that gives you entrance into this story?

• After you have spent some time on your own, focus on the fig tree as symbolizing a citizen of the kingdom. In the story there is nothing wrong with the fig tree as a fig tree. Jesus comes by it in the early Spring; it is not the season for figs. The poor tree had no reason to bear figs at this time; if it had fruit on it now it would have to be a kind of fig tree such as is not known on this earth.

If Jesus uses the fig tree to show what he expects from the citizen of the kingdom, this citizen no longer corresponds to what we call a human being—the citizen, in Jesus' eyes, would have to be more than human. To be a member of the kingdom would go against the grain of our humanity.

From our exploration, consider some of the ways in which the kingdom calls us to transcend our humanity. What does the kingdom demand regarding justice? (The hired laborers.) What is the place of nurturing and caring in the kingdom, in terms of giving and receiving? (The good Samaritan.) What amount of risk and trust does the kingdom demand? (The prodigal farmer; the talents.) What does the kingdom demand in terms of your capacities? (Fig trees bearing fruit in the springtime.)

Here are some other things we will find that are characteristic of the kingdom and seem more than humanly possible: The member of the kingdom lives without judgment. If someone wants your cloak, give away your shirt as well. If someone strikes you, turn the other cheek. Be vigilant constantly. "Man does not live by bread alone." And would you be willing to fast forty days in the desert?

• Allow a full and powerful image of this kingdom, in a sharp contrast to life in the world, to develop in your meditation. Then allow your resistance to confront the image. How does this vision of the kingdom scare you? What arguments do you throw up against the possibility of the kingdom? Activate your defenses fully; only in this way can you gain a clear idea of what they are like. In this meditation the argument itself is not as important as how the argument reveals your resistance. When you see the resistance you will be able to decide whether it truly represents you or whether you can see something of yourself beyond that argumentative, scared, clinging piece of ego. Is this defensiveness really you, or is it only the defense of ego? Is there still a part of you that believes in and longs for an existence like that seen in the kingdom in spite of the seeming difficulty of passing over from this worldly existence into the kingdom?

The cursing of the fig tree certainly puts the situation in the most dramatic terms. Jesus is heading towards his own arrest and death. He has been with his disciples for the last three years, teaching and healing. But he is afraid that even now they do not see what is involved. The cursing of the fig tree is an almost desperate act of teaching, as Jesus hopes to make them see just how different life in the kingdom is and how worthless and even cursed our present life in this world is.

• Such a hard teaching might lead us to despair of ever being able to follow it. But we are not left on our own. Jesus has promised us that we can bring our desires to our Father. He will hear us and respond to our requests. Have you come to him throughout these ego meditations? Have you asked for his help in this great work? Why not? Come to him now in prayer. Bring him your fears, your confusion, your hopes for transformation. Open your heart to him. Ask for his help and support.

EXPLORATION 31 **THE TWO SONS**
time: twenty-five minutes
materials: Bible (Luke 15:11-24)

In our last series of meditations we explored what we have called the ego. Jesus of course does not use this psychological term; we employ it only because it gives us a handle to work with. But Jesus' stories provide many insights into the human psyche, differing according to his purpose in telling the story. In the present story we will see a different kind of psychic map. Try to remember that our terms should not be regarded as concrete psychic entities but as metaphors for describing human thinking and behavior.

Now that we have explored the Christ mind, or Holy Spirit, and the world mind, or ego, we can begin to examine the process by which a person passes over from the domination of one to the influence of the other. How is it possible to partake of the kingdom in this lifetime?

• After the customary preparation, read this famous parable of the two sons (often called the parable of the prodigal son).

• We will enter the story by first passing over into the experience of the younger brother. For a few minutes consider the little child that lives inside you, for there is a small child in there who has never grown up. Mature adults keep that child almost totally in check; he or she is not allowed much presence in our lives. But the child is alive within us whether given power or not and can make demands and throw tantrums just like other little children.

Locate that little child now—the one who's always asking for its own way, the one who knows nothing of responsibility or other "adult" concepts, but whose world is one of needs, wants, and demands. As adults we often say no to this child, or if we do give in, we later regret our actions.

• Now allow your little child to play the role of the younger son. Go up to your father and let him know how you feel. You don't want to hang around the farm working all the time. You want to have fun and enjoy your inheritance while you are still young. Ask for your share of the money. Make this son's thoughts and desires your own. Give your own child his or her voice.

Father gives you your inheritance. What do you want to do with it? Let your child's imagination run wild. What has it always wanted to do? Take a trip around the world? Wield power over others? Give rein to your deepest fantasies, for you now have both the money and the ability to make them real.

But now you begin to feel the pinch. The money runs out. You have no support. What you are going to do? Perhaps you are ashamed.

You have missed your chance. How does your child react in this kind of situation? Does it blame itself? Does it shrug off its failure and refuse to take responsibility even now?

Things are pretty bad, and you have found a job feeding the pigs. As if that is not a bad enough job, it is directly against your religion, which considers pigs as unclean animals. Nobody wants to slop the pigs, but you are reduced to eating what they leave over. What pride you had is now more easily swallowed than the food.

Remember difficult moments in your life when you have had to face the realization that you have acted foolishly and done wrong. Now even you realize that you are incapable of taking care of yourself. You have to go to someone and admit the horrible truth that you have failed, that you need help, forgiveness, and healing. What has it taken to bring your child to such insight? How does it feel to acknowledge how foolish you have been? What are your fears in such a moment? Your hopes? Do you put more faith in the fears, or in the hopes?

Begin the long walk home to your father. What are you thinking as you make this journey? The younger son rehearses his confession. He wants to convince his father to allow him to work on the farm. Use the son's words to help you enter into his feelings. Repeat the words over and over in your mind as you journey homeward: "Father, I have sinned, against God and against you; I am no longer fit to be called your son; treat me as one of your paid servants" (The New English Bible). Do you deserve such a concession? Is such a concession the best one you can hope for in this kind of world? Is the hope too optimistic? What will you do if your father refuses to listen to you?

You can see the house, but it is still a long way off. Is that someone running down the road toward you? It looks like your father. But why would he be doing something like this? The figure draws nearer. It is your father! Here comes the big moment. How do you feel now? You are entirely at his mercy. Will he be forgiving, or stern? Quick, before he has a chance to say anything, blurt out the line you have been preparing all the way home. Now.

In response he grasps you and hugs you and kisses you. He calls out to his servants to kill the fatted calf and prepare for a celebration. Can you believe this good news? Are you sure it is really happening?

• Enter into your own past to find a similar experience. What have you found it most difficult to be forgiven for? It might not be anything you have done. It might be an attitude, the way you are, a feeling. But what do you feel is beyond forgiving in yourself—that you can't even forgive yourself for it? Bring it before you now and place it in this story.

Feel it totally and overwhelmingly forgiven. Feel yourself joyously welcomed home. Explore this experience. What is it like? Is there any sense of guilt left? Is there any feeling that you will have to pay back what has been lost? Do you think your father is going to demand that you prove yourself before he trusts you again?

Is there any sense other than total and perfect acceptance? What does that perfect acceptance feel like? What does it do for you? How does it change you: the way you feel, the way you see yourself, the vision you have of the world and others? Do you think it even has the power to transform your actions in the future?

EXPLORATION **31a**

THE TWO SONS (continued)
time: twenty-five minutes
materials: Bible (Luke 15:25-32)

● Unless you are continuing the meditation immediately after the last exploration, prepare as usual for this session. Now we will pass over into the experience of the elder brother. A part of us identifies with this character as well. If the younger brother corresponds to the child within us, then this elder brother corresponds with our adult or what Freud called the superego. This brother above all knows and tells what is right and wrong. Here is the voice that chastizes when we fail, criticizes when we miss the ideal, reprimands, scolds, and even punishes the child in us. It is not hard to hear this voice; in many of us it is the strongest voice and perhaps the only voice we hear.

Enter into this part of yourself now. Feel the judge, the parent, the censor, the one who urges you on. This part of you is very mature and adult, it is entirely rational and believes that it has only our best interests at heart. It prides itself on its sense of responsibility, of duty, on its discipline, on its well-thought-out actions, and above all, on its decency and goodness.

- Now pass over with this voice into the role of the elder brother. You are out working in the field. Your younger brother has left many years ago. "Good riddance to bad rubbish," you said then, and you feel the same way today if you think of him at all. What that kid needed was a good beating to knock some sense into him.

You feel pretty good about yourself. After all, if you hadn't stayed and sacrificed much, the farm might have gone under. You've done what needed to be done, and you can rightly take a real pride and satisfaction in it.

The sun is setting. Stop your plowing and prepare to head for home. As you approach the farmhouse you notice great activity. What is happening? People are preparing for a huge party. Stop one of the farmhands now and ask him what is happening. He tells you, "Your brother has come home. Your father has ordered the calf killed for the celebration tonight."

What is your reaction? Do you feel joyful about the return? Do you feel justice has been done? What about all those years of sacrifice? Were there any parties for you? Were there any real expressions of gratitude from your father? Explore and expand these feelings as you approach the farmhouse. Allow your anger to surface and build. That kid is going to get off scot-free. How can you see that he receives what he deserves?

Here comes your father. Walk up to him and tell him just how you feel. Don't hide anything. Convince him that he's acting foolishly. Make him see what he is really doing.

Your father listens to you. But then he says he can't help feeling wonderful. After all, this son who was thought dead all these years has come back to life. He now wants you to come into the house, embrace your long-lost brother, and join in the festivities.

Do his words move you? What would it cost you to join in that celebration? Is it worth the price? What do you save if you keep your integrity and walk away? Will you go into the party, or leave?

If it is difficult to appreciate the elder brother's experience, it is because you are not really entering into it for fear you will go against the "Christian" interpretation of the story. The elder brother has much at stake, and so do we if we would enter the kingdom. It will cost him the same thing to enter the party as it will us to enter the kingdom. Can you appreciate the price?

It is the elder brothers who are successful, outstanding citizens of this world—is it worth *letting* go? How can you let go even if you wanted to? How can you ignore your sense of what is right? How can you swallow your hurt pride and forgive? If that brat worms himself back into your father's good graces, will he eventually cheat you out of your share of the inheritance? Father might divide the property again, you know. Will he talk Father out of more money so he can blow it as he did the first inheritance? How can you be sure he is really sorry? How can you be sure he is ready to appreciate forgiveness? Is he really able to mend his ways and act responsibly, the way you do?

EXPLORATION **31b**
THE TWO SONS (continued)
time: twenty-five minutes
materials: Journal (Prayer Experience)

Jesus makes no mistake when he leaves the story with no ending. It points up the seriousness of our dilemma. It is our sense of justice and righteousness just as much as our childishness that keeps us out of the kingdom. Nor is that justice merely a matter of politics, as we might have thought when we considered the hired laborers. It is a question of psychology as well: Why can't the child and the adult in me be reconciled and forgive each other?

• After the customary preparation, enter the meditation again by passing over into the father's experience. The father loves his sons simply because they are his sons. There is no reason for a parent's love; it simply flows. Consider your sons as they were before the younger left home. You loved them both. There was no competition between them for your affections. You loved the elder son's devotion and steadfastness. The younger son's enthusiasm and *joie de vivre* endeared him to you. Your sons complemented each other. Together you made a happy family.

Consider the two parts of your own personality: the child and the adult. What is lovable about each of them? Explore the strong points of each and allow yourself to love them as the father loves his sons. They are each a part of you and should naturally be loved by you.

Enter into the sorrow you feel when your younger son wants to go away. You let him go because you know that love cannot force or bind. Let that child within you leave now. You know that it will make mistakes. You know that it will get into trouble and be hurt. But you love it enough not to bind it to you. Let it go now, and wait in hope.

What is the waiting like? Does the pain ever go away? Can you taste the father's hope that someday his son will return? Is there any bitterness in the waiting? The father waits in pure, simple hope. Imagine such waiting.

One day you are standing on your front porch. You look down the road, as you have every day since he left. Ten years have gone by, but you have not given up hope. You see a tiny figure coming down the road. You know deep inside who it is. Run down that road. What are your feelings as you run toward him?

Here is your son. You love him. There is no recrimination, nothing but pure joy that the waiting is over and he has come home. Enter into your joy as you embrace your son, welcome him home, and call for the calf to be slaughtered.

Now you see your older son coming toward you. His face is troubled. You wish he could share in your joy. Tell him about that joy. Tell him you hope he will share in your happiness and make it his own. Tell him how you long for him to come inside and embrace his brother.

• Jesus did not tell the ending of this story. So write the ending now. Try to imagine the scene if the brothers could embrace. What would it be like? Explore the completeness of this scene with all the family reunited. What would it be like if within yourself all these different voices could embrace in love and harmony? What if all could accept the child as a child, and a good, lovable child at that? What if all could accept the older brother with his sense of seriousness and responsibility and love him for that? Describe the scene that would take place at the party if all this could happen.

32

THE DEATH AND RESURRECTION OF JESUS
time: thirty minutes
materials: Bible (Mark 11-16)

This process of reconciliation between our different voices is not easy. It does not happen through mere imagination. It becomes the focus of Jesus' ministry and life. We have looked at the stories about Jesus as well as the parables he told and the signs he performed. But all these are secondary to the story of Jesus himself: his death and resurrection. For it is this story that has brought many to believe Jesus and his message.

This story has become for Christians the central story in terms of which all the other stories are read and understood. Our search began with a consideration of the place and importance of meaning in our life and world. For a follower of Jesus, that search finds its most adequate and fullest response in this story. In this story we come in contact with the power that can effect our transition from this world to the kingdom. Obviously, a story this central and important cannot be unfolded and examined quickly, or even in the course of this book. From now on our pilgrimage will seek to draw closer to this story, whose full appreciation enables our transformation. During this week of meditations, we will only begin to explore its possible meaning for our growth.

Today we will read the story itself as told by Mark. His is the shortest and possibly the earliest written account. Obviously the story was carefully passed from one disciple to another for many years before being committed to writing.

● We have made progress in our new kind of reading; let's use our new skills to help us enter into this story. Prepare as usual for meditation; then turn to the gospel. Read slowly, perhaps aloud. If you are doing this with a group, take turns with the reading. As you read, pause often to reflect on the meaning of what you are reading. Is your mind wandering, or is it applying itself to the task at hand? With the group, reflect on the significance of the narrative. Beware of reading into the story things you have been told or know from the past. Rely only on what you read and on your personal experience.

32a

MEDITATION ON A FAVORITE SCENE
time: twenty-five minutes
materials: Bible (Mark 11-16)

Today choose one particular scene or story from this passion narrative
for meditation. Choose something you particularly liked yesterday. You
might pick the Last Supper, Peter's denial; the crucifixion itself, or the
resurrection. Take a scene that has already spoken to you, a scene you
will be able to relate to easily. There are no directions for this
meditation. Over the course of our pilgrimage you have learned a
number of ways of entering stories. Now it is time to begin work on
these stories on your own. If you meet with a group, you might share
with one another your meditations and the insights arrived at.

32b

MEDITATION ON A DIFFICULT STORY
time: twenty-five minutes
materials: Bible (Mark 11-16)

Today you will choose another story for meditation. Instead of
choosing one that appeals to you, choose one that you find difficult.
You may feel you do not understand it. Perhaps it makes you
uncomfortable. You might feel resistance to the story. Whatever the
case may be, choose that story and explore it today in your meditation.
When your group meets, you can share the story with others. Perhaps
you will find light through your meditation. Perhaps someone else can
help you explore it.

EXPLORATION **32c**

THE SHAPE OF THE JESUS STORY
time: twenty-five minutes
materials: Bible (Luke 4:16-30)

- Today we will explore this narrative as that central story of Jesus in whose light all the other stories can be understood. Let's go back to Exploration 27 where we meditated on Luke's story of the beginning of Jesus' ministry. Review that meditation now; re-read the exploration if necessary.

- Then perform the usual meditations in preparation for our experiment and read the story again in Luke.

- This time let's discover how Luke's story shares the same plot structure as the story of the passion and resurrection. What is the structure of Luke's story? Describe its movement. How is that structure and movement the same as that of the passion and resurrection? In the first story, isolate each moment in the story's progress and then find the corresponding moment in the larger story of Jesus' death and resurrection. When you have discovered all the parallels, spend the rest of the meditation moving back and forth from story to story in order to taste both their oneness and their unique variations upon the common theme.

EXPLORATION **32d**

THE ONE STORY
time: twenty-five minutes

Today we will choose our own story of Jesus and discover how it echoes this central story. We have done many story meditations. You must have a favorite story, or you might want to choose one whose real depth of meaning still eludes you.

- Whatever you decide, pick a story and explore its similarity to our central story of Jesus' death and resurrection. If you choose a parable of the kingdom, how does it reveal that this central story is also a parable and description of the kingdom? How do the healing and miracle stories reveal this story as the central miracle or sign of the kingdom? Of course, not all of the stories of Jesus have the same plot structure as our central story; some stories highlight only a certain movement of the central story's plot. Where does the story you have picked fit into the passion and resurrection narrative? How does your story take on a deeper facet of meaning when it is seen in relation to the death and resurrection of Jesus? Does the passion and resurrection story take on more meaning when you view it in the light of your original story? If you share this meditation with a group, have the members tell one another about their experience.

32e

THE WICKED TENANTS
time: twenty-five minutes
materials: Bible (Matthew 21:33-46)

● Our parable for meditation today is particularly difficult. Read the parable. At first it appears extremely judgmental. At the story's end, when Jesus asks what should happen to the evil tenants, we might agree with the disciples: They should be punished and thrown out. This ending is often taken to be the point of the parable.

● But in our meditation let's probe a little deeper. This parable reveals its full meaning only when it is seen in the light of the death and resurrection of Jesus. Look to Jesus' quotation in verse 42 for the key to understanding the story. The meaning of that passage carries the real meaning of the story. Does Jesus assent to his disciples' answer, or is he leading them to a different perspective?

This story penetrates deeply into the mystery of evil and human existence. The world has conditioned us to think always in its terms: Good must be rewarded and evil punished. But does the story really say this? Could the story be saying that by penetrating through evil we will not be destroyed, but rather find salvation? Notice the word *marvelous* in Jesus' quotation. What is marvelous in the story? Why? How does this story help you penetrate deeper into the passion and resurrection story?

This is a very difficult meditation. But enter the story in the way we have already done in our other meditations, and try to find a way to read this parable so that it too could be called good news.

EXPLORATION **32f** SUMMARY
time: twenty-five minutes
materials: Journal (Prayer Experience)

• Today after your customary preparation, summarize in your journal what you have experienced and discovered throughout this week. You might want to re-read Mark 11-16. What does this story say to you? How does it respond to your quest for meaning?

• Consider the question of reversals that we have met in practically every encounter with Jesus. Each of his parables stood the world, as we know it, on its head. Each of the miracles was a miracle simply because it seemed to refute the laws of this world. Does the story of the death and resurrection of Jesus follow this same pattern of reversal? Does it depict the world as we know it, or is it similar to the kingdom as we have come to know it? What does the story of Jesus' triumph over death say to you at this point in your exploration and pilgrimage?

33

THE WOMAN CAUGHT IN ADULTERY
time: twenty-five minutes
materials: Bible (John 8:1-11)

We have now encountered the central story of Christianity. But we still need to explore its meaning as it has been understood within the Christian tradition. At its simplest, it is another story of the kingdom. But it is also a story of the perilous passage from this world into that kingdom. The story itself contains the details, but being guided through the story will help us understand it better.

At this point in our pilgrimage we may not yet be ready to commit ourselves to the kingdom, although we have seen that the journey from the world to the kingdom can be made at any time and in the matter of a second. For the voyage is of the heart, and we have been exploring Jesus through the intellect and the imagination. We haven't yet made the decision to make the journey under Jesus' leadership. Before we do, we will need to know more about what such a passage would involve.

As we examine what this story has meant to Christians, our guide is no longer Jesus. He makes the voyage, but he does not explain it. Instead a great Christian teacher will guide us.

But before we meet this teacher, let's consider what we want to discover. We have spoken of the journey as a passage from the world mind to the kingdom mind. We can also speak of it as the displacement of the ego and the environment of the Holy Spirit. We can also call it repentance or *metanoia*. But all these metaphors merely describe the process from without. We know that something is happening, and we see the difference in people before and after they have made the transition. But what is this process itself?

Traditionally this story of Jesus is placed in the gospel of John, but many recent Bibles place it either in the footnotes in John or by itself elsewhere. Whether or not it has a place in the four gospels, the story itself is one of the most beautiful and popular in the Christian tradition. We will explore it today to focus our inquiry.

• Prepare as usual for meditation and then read this short piece of good news.

• First enter into the story with your imagination. When you have become familiar with it, turn your attention to the final line. Jesus says to the woman, "Does no one condemn you?" "No one," she says.

"Neither do I," says Jesus. "Go and sin no more." It is one thing to forgive the woman's sins, but how is she able to leave that scene and sin no more? Think of it—adultery was supposedly a part of her life. She probably did not commit the sin because she was wilfully evil. Rather, she was forced into it by her life situation. How can she walk away from that scene and be expected to change her life?

True, she is alive only because Jesus has saved her. But if the message of Jesus is really good news, what about that final command to go and sin no more? That sounds like a very hard demand. If it is not to sound like bad news, it has to be understood as only a direction for living rather than a command to reform her life. The reform has to happen in those few seconds, in the midst of the people, and in the face of certain death.

If the news of Jesus is really good, that woman must walk out of that square freed of her past and able to choose her future. How does that transformation take place? How is she renewed in this confrontation? Explore that transformation in your meditation. Use whatever techniques you can to experience that split second of transformation. What is it like? What happens inside that woman?

218

There are many possibilities for transformation in this story. By walking away, every person there admitted to being a sinner. Yet only one person joins the kingdom. The rest are convicted of their sin and acknowledge it by leaving—but there is no transformation in their lives.

• In your meditation pass back and forth between the woman and the townspeople. What is the difference between being convicted of sin and being forgiven?

EXPLORATION **34** **THE GOSPEL OF PAUL**
time: one hour
materials: Journal (Prayer Experience)

As we have discovered in the story of the woman taken in adultery, in the story of the two sons, and elsewhere, transformation is blocked by the self-righteous part of the psyche. Fortunately, our new teacher,

Paul, has great experience in self-righteousness. He himself often played the elder brother. Like those townspeople in the previous exploration he even lifted stones to kill followers of Jesus. But confronted by Jesus and his words of forgiveness, he became the greatest Christian teacher.

Hopefully on this pilgrimage we will eventually undergo transformation ourselves. But at the moment, we are still examining the path. We need more knowledge of what is involved as well as more insight into ourselves before we are ready for this perilous crossing. As we said, this crossing is made with the heart, but our work is still of the head. So let us explore this process of change and then to the best of our ability decide whether this process can transform us and whether we wish to be so transformed.

Our new teacher, Paul, is not exactly a gentle teacher. He becomes enthusiastic about his subject and often rubs people the wrong way. He may make us furious with him. But that is all right. For Paul will allow us to wrestle with him just as his ancestor Jacob wrestled with the stranger.

Paul is a perpetual fighter. In his youth he fights against Jesus. Then he fights for Jesus. But he is always fighting. He challenges us to take him on, not for his own glory but for the glory of his Lord.

• That is just the nature of this exploration. Listen to what Paul says. If you do not agree with him, argue with him in your journal. But argue from your own experience. Paul does not appeal to books or ideas, although he may use them to put forth his point; he appeals to his own experience of transformation. If you argue with him, you can use no weapons: no books, no ideas about how it should be. You must argue with your bare fists: your own experience of what it is like to be human.

You may already be acquainted with Paul. If so, what you hear today is not exactly what he says in Scripture. For he is above all a communicator. If he were to preach today, he would use our own ideas and concepts. If you hear something today you do not think he would have said two thousand years ago, argue with him. Use his letters to back you up. But be careful. Are you really saying what he said? Are you understanding him in the context of his time? Or are two thousand years getting in your way? Don't be shy. He won't be easily hurt or vanquished. He enjoys a good fight. But he likes to win. Nothing would make him happier than to bring you to the ultimate victor, Jesus Christ his Lord.

We know Paul primarily as a letter writer. All of his writings preserved in the New Testament are epistles to the Christian congregations. He would respond to their problems with his letters. He was of course writing to people who were already Christian, but they had still not understood the full implications of Jesus' good news. Therefore, Paul needed to teach and correct.

• We are now firmly grounded in basic Christianity, so let's see where Paul can lead us as well.

Greetings! May the happiness of the risen Christ, who has raised us all from sleep and death into real life, be with you all! You have already heard the good news of Jesus—that though he was innocent, he was put to death, but his Father vindicated him and raised him from the dead. Now that dawn of new life that comes with his resurrection applies to everyone. The resurrection puts a seal on his preaching; his kingdom is a real kingdom. It has already made its appearance in this world, and even death itself cannot stand against it. That kingdom is available to you and I right now give thanks to the obedience of Jesus—obedience to the point of death on a cross. You have heard the words of Jesus: Change your way of thinking and enter the kingdom.

But, you think, that is just the problem. How do I go about this awesome and fearful work? I cannot lift myself up by my own bootstraps; yet that is just what Jesus seems to be asking for. This Jesus is too much for me. If I take him seriously, I am led to despair. I cannot possibly do what he asks. I know in my heart that he is right, but I am not strong enough for the task.

Do you know what I, Paul, have to say to you? I say you have not yet heard the good news. Your despair is not real. It is just an excuse thrown up by your ego to protect itself. You can do what Jesus asks. Why? Because there is nothing to do. It has been done for you. So give up your whining and listen to me.

There are really only two questions. First, what work has to be accomplished in order to come alive and enter the kingdom? And secondly, where will I come by the resources, the energy to enable me to do this work? What can I use to fuel my journey into the kingdom?

I originally put this dilemma in a different way: This is my situation. I know what is good, and I know what is evil. But such knowledge does me no good. For in spite of what I know, I still find myself doing what is evil, and I am unable to accomplish what I know to be good. Who will save me from this predicament? You want to know who will save you? Who, in fact, has already saved you? Who has abrogated the journey? Jesus Christ! Thanks be to God!

Let us take a closer look at how we are put together. There are really three different centers involved in creating our life. First of all there is the body center or what I call the flesh or *sarx*. This center's task is to control and run our physical organism. It is located just below your navel. You experience this center whenever you are involved in a complex physical activity such as a sport, playing a musical instrument, riding a bicycle, typing, or even walking.

221

The second center is located in the brain; I call it the *psyche* or the soul. This center is in charge of your psychological functions as well as your thinking functions. In many of us this center has assumed total control; the ego work you have been doing has been aimed at this center.

The third center is located in your heart; I call it the *pneuma* or the Spirit because it is in charge of your spiritual being. Ideally, the three centers should work in harmony. Each should do its own job and cooperate with the others to help them do theirs. But we soon discover that we are not in harmony. The third center, being the most spiritual, should govern the other two. But it is also the least-developed center, so one of the other two has taken control of us. Of course we have all known people who are totally dominated by one of these centers; if it is the *sarx*, we see a person who lives only for physical gratification; if it is the *psyche*, we see an egghead; if it is the *pneuma*, we see a neurotic romantic whose emotions have totally taken control.

As we see the human condition, these three centers are not functioning in harmony with one another. Ideally, the *pneuma* should be the leader over the *psyche*, and both should rule over the *sarx*. But instead we often see one dominating at the expense of the other two, and this imbalance creates all sorts of problems because the centers are then trying to regulate things over which they have no competence. For example, the heart may try to think, the mind may try to feel or control a physical skill, the body may try to think or feel. You can easily experience this sensation of imbalance in the body center. Normally your walking is dominated by your body center, but try walking with your brain in control. Be conscious of each movement as you walk. Before long, you will be stumbling because you have put in charge a center that is not able to do this job. Multiply that situation and you have an idea of our fallen nature.

Here is the explanation of why I can know something to be good and yet cannot do it. My knowledge is head knowledge, and the head alone is not able to govern my whole being. How do I shift my being so that my spirit comes to assume its rightful place over my mind and body? For only then will all my centers be able to assume their proper function and bring me peace and happiness.

How are we going to accomplish this task? Where will we get the energy needed for such a great work? Such transformation will require an enormous amount of power and energy. Well, that energy is available through the work of Jesus. If we could plug into Jesus' energy, the current crisis in the Christian churches—a crisis of stagnation and lack of zeal—would be over. Christians today walk around depleted and spent. "How will we be able to reform our lives and live the gospel message?" they moan. "How can we transform the world when we do not have enough energy to work on ourselves?"

Of course there are other Christians who have all sorts of power. They are filled with the power of Jesus and they use it. They tell the world it is going to hell in a basket. They jibber-jabber in tongues and call that the good news, but they cannot seem to find compassion enough to love or even tolerate those different from themselves. These people scare me more than the lifeless ones. For they do not have the power of weakness, which is the power of Christ. They have laid hold on the power of self-righteousness, the power of the establishment, the power of the Pharisee, the power of the world.

We have an energy problem. Put in simple terms, we wish to drive a car from New York to Los Angeles. What fuel can we burn to make the trip? What fuel will release enough energy to bring us from the world into the kingdom?

Jesus has shown us the world as it truly is, and he has also provided glimpses of the kingdom. The world is dark; the kingdom light. The world is false; the kingdom true. But how can this truth assume ascendancy in our hearts?

What resources will enable us to live a life in the kingdom? Consider some of the behavior of the kingdom: loving selflessly, forgiving freely and fully, surrendering anger and blame. This is the program in black and white. For two thousand years Christians have tried to explain it away. We have intimated, if not boldly asserted, that Jesus did not really mean what he obviously meant. How straightforward could he be? There is no hidden agenda here. "If there is anger toward another, do not bring your gift to the altar. Go and bury the anger. Only then are you ready to bring your gift to the Father."

There is a way through. It begins with a call. You remember how Jesus called Zacchaeus. Zacchaeus wants to see Jesus and find out more about him, but he is afraid to come too close, so he climbs a tree. As Jesus passes by he sees Zacchaeus and calls him by name. Zacchaeus is surprised and confused. What can he do now? He has been exposed. He wanted a nice unobtrusive perch, but now he is the center of attention. His life is disturbed, and it will never be the same again. He has been called.

Every one of us has been called. We might not have heard the call yet, but it has gone out. And it is not just a call to the human race in general. The call is much more

223

personal. You are called by your own name. The call comes from the heart of Jesus. He knows you. He loves you. He wishes to stay in your heart.

Here is my story of that call. This is the old me, Saul. I am setting out for another day of killing Christians for the greater glory of God when all of a sudden I am knocked off my horse—literally and figuratively. There in the dust of humilation and confusion I hear my name being spoken. "Saul! Saul!" came the cry. It happened to me. It is happening to you. Do you also need to be knocked off your horse to hear it?

As long as we believe that this call goes out to people in general, or worse, to people more gifted than ourselves, we protect ourselves from the good news. As long as the call is only something we read of in books or imagine in our meditations, it is dead. I'm talking about your life here, not the life of Everyman and Everywoman, whoever they might be. For the power of Jesus to have any effect, we have to pass beyond what he might mean for humanity as a whole to what he is for me as a unique individual. How do we do this? By realizing that, like Zacchaeus, you have been discovered and called. Now come down out of your tree and meet this man.

When I got knocked off my horse and heard my name called, the next thing I knew I was struck blind. This was amazing, for at just that moment I realized that I had been truly blind all my life. But I had to wait until my sight was physically taken away on that road to Damascus before I could know my real blindness and then begin to "see." Blindness showed me how blind I had been. Blindness in my eyes enabled me to begin seeing with my heart.

You must pass through that same painful process. Acknowledge that you are blind, lame, lost. How else will you ever realize you need a physician? You've become expert at living with your handicaps. You even label managing to survive as living! And you give thanks in your heart that you were not born deformed!

Here is our greatest difficulty. If we were visibly crippled, we might be closer to being healed. At least we would know our true condition and take steps to overcome it. But we consider ourselves whole and so need to overcome nothing. Our sickness wins out and convinces us that this is life. In the kingdom of the blind, the one-eyed is king. But do you know you have only one eye? Who will tell you?

What does it mean to acknowledge our blindness? In traditional language it means confessing one's sins. It means admitting we are not whole, but fragmented, human beings. We do not have the means to help ourselves. We are incapable of making ourselves happy.

This situation cannot be corrected by head knowledge. We have that already in overabundance. It is rather a matter of the heart. You may have no trouble at all saying you are a sinner: Christians do it easily at every liturgy. But it is one thing to say it, quite another to feel it. And deep down inside we do not want to feel it. We fear it. We are ashamed of it. We have so hidden our flaws from the world that we do not even see them ourselves anymore. And since everyone else is in the same situation we support one another in our lies, thinking that if our sins are hidden we can transcend them. But like the emperor's new clothes they are on exhibit to anyone who has the eyes to see and the ability to speak the truth (a quality happily limited to children and saints).

225

If we ignore our incompleteness and try to cover it over, our effort is doomed from the start. The flaw is still there whether we face it or not. And there is always the danger that it will be found out or that it will crack any foundation we attempt to lay on it. I am not speaking about the laundry list most people take to confession or to God; it is not becoming angry or masturbating or forgetting one's prayers. The real sin is that profound sense of dis-ease we feel deep within. The real sin is the entirely selfish way we live, not because we choose to, but because we feel so insecure and unlovable that we cannot help but try to survive this way. The real sin lies so deep and hidden that some would say it does not even exist. But if it doesn't exist, why can't we find true and lasting happiness?

When we finally come to acknowledge our blindness, we do the only thing we can in such a situation: We surrender to the nearest available help. "I can't see. Please take me home," we plead. On the road to Damascus I had to do just that; I gave up my entire life. Things could not proceed as usual, for I knew I was blind. My powers and my abilities were for nothing if I could not even find my way home.

Jesus does not demand agreement or argument. He wants more. He wants us to trust him and surrender our entire life to him. He wishes to guide our living. He is different from other teachers we know. When we ask a teacher a question, we often have a fair idea of the answer. So we ask our question to test the teacher more than to find the answer. If the teacher does not agree with us, we are ready to debate the relative merits of the different answers. But there is no room for such testing in Jesus' school. We either surrender and accept, or we walk away. Many times the overwhelming temptation is to walk away. But where will you go?

Give up your prejudice, your commitments, your claim to knowledge. Like me, put your life in the hands of a man you cannot see. On that road, blinded, I could not afford to challenge anyone who would take my hand. It was enough that a hand was offered. It belonged to Barnabas, a Christian, one of the group I was on my way to exterminate. But I had no choice. Barnabas took care of me.

Does your fear of what will happen if you should surrender keep you from this moment? We all have memories of times when we opened ourselves and met with rejection, ridicule, or even blackmail. We have learned our lessons well; we no longer reveal ourselves or give over our power. But that very blockage prevents us from obtaining the energy we seek. Sooner or later we are bound to discover that we cannot save ourselves. We can try all our life; we can delude ourselves that we are making it. But how are we going to save ourselves in the hour of death?

Look at the woman caught in adultery. She's lucky. There's no question of having to surrender here; she's been caught and condemned to death. She couldn't deceive anyone now if she tried. So she surrenders and awaits the execution. Every fear in our body tells us that the moment we surrender, the moment we reveal our vulnerability, we will be killed. This woman knows too, but what can she do? She is certain to die anyway.

When you surrender to God, when you reveal who you are in all your frailty, the question in return is not "Why are you like this?" No, the question is "Does anyone condemn you?" And to our response of "No" comes the reassurance "Neither do I."

If only we could believe this response of Jesus! If only we could look at ourselves without flinching and know we're accepted for who we are! It goes counter to everything we have learned and experienced. We have been taught time and again that we are not all right. We have been forced to construct a social face to show the world. But behind that false face lurks one that we dare show no one, not even ourselves.

227

When our sins are known to the whole village, when we tremble in the square as we await our execution, there is nothing we can do. The miracle is that not one thing is required. As the adulterous woman lies there in her sinfulness, she discovers that she is really loved. In that knowledge all the games and false images can be dropped. She is who she is. That is enough. Jesus sees her and does not condemn; he does not lay a burden on her shoulders. He simply points the way to a fuller existence. As she leaves the public square, she does not even consider returning to that sinful existence. She has the power to create a new life. That power is not a matter of belief; it is a transforming experience.

There is an unresolved issue in this story, however. The losers are the elders and the townspeople. They came in dragging this poor woman, willing to sacrifice her to score a point with Jesus, but *he* is causing *them* trouble. They do not want to see themselves as sinners; they are good, upright people. Yet, Jesus in this confrontation once again forces them to look within: "Let those among you without sin cast the first stone."

They are condemned; they are no better than this poor woman. Think of the shame, the guilt, the fear in that crowd during the next few minutes, as one by one the stones drop from convicted hands. It will take days or even weeks for these good people to cover up what has been revealed there and to regain their self-esteem.

These people hear the call, but tragically, through fear and cowardice, they do not stay around to hear the good news: Does anyone condemn you? Blinded by one glimpse of their sinfulness, they scurry to bury it deeper, ignoring it in the bustle of daily life. All they manage to salvage from this encounter is shame and perhaps a deeper resentment against this Jesus, who compels them to see themselves as they really are.

Why didn't they have the courage to stay in the square so that they too could hear the word that sin is not condemned but forgiven? Here is the all-too-common tragedy of human life. We are so afraid of condemnation that we are absent when sentence is passed, and so miss the unconditional pardon. But there is hope. I was once a Pharisee. I once took part in the stoning of sinners. But I have heard the pardon pronounced, and I won't stop shouting until everyone else has heard the good news.

You know, the greatest problem Jesus encountered in his ministry was people like you and me. He was very successful when he dealt with sinners such as this woman. But in his dealings with us, he meets real resistance. We are the people who become angry with Jesus, and our anger seems justified. For we see him providing an easy pardon to all these undeserving sinners. He not only forgives them; he stays on to associate with them afterwards. He ate with Zacchaeus and stayed at his home. I would have said to him, "Wait a minute. Look at these people around you. It's one thing to forgive them. But do you have to associate with them, too? What's wrong with me and my friends that you have to stay with this cheap, cheating tax collector?"

"Jesus, you can easily save a great sinner," we mention. "But what happens to those of us who do not qualify for Degenerate of the Year? You can forgive a whore and she walks away transformed, but what about me? What great sins can you lift from my shoulders? I haven't done anything heinous, so when I am forgiven my little peccadilloes, nothing happens. I am not reborn. Where do I find sins to fuel my journey into your kingdom? You yourself acknowledged the problem when you said that those who have little to be forgiven have little to be grateful for."

Jesus is aware of this problem, and I believe that he has responded to it. Let's reexamine the parable of the two sons. Consider the elder brother, who embodies the sinfulness of the upright man. His sin is his very self-righteousness. He has worked hard; he has become a good person through great effort.

"I've done it on my own," he says. "Granted, it's been hard work, but I've succeeded. The farm is a success because I've stayed with my father. I've passed up many good things, but that's what life is about. It isn't supposed to be easy. So there's no excuse for this snivelling young kid. He had his chance. He didn't listen to his elders. He failed. That's the breaks."

This elder brother's sin is unforgivable because he doesn't even see himself as sinful. By contrast, the woman caught in adultery acknowledged her sin and opened herself for healing, and the younger son acknowledged his sin and returned home to suffer the consequences. But if you don't need forgiveness, how can you possibly accept it?

The truth is that this elder brother is no better off than his younger brother. In terms of the real work to be accomplished—becoming a full human being—the elder brother has not done a thing yet, and he has a lot of making up to do. For one thing, look at the enormous pile of resentment rotting away inside, polluting his life with its stench. He resents his younger brother's pluck in taking the

229

money and running away. He resents the farm that has consumed his youth. He resents his father for not appreciating his great sacrifice.

But the younger brother knows he has failed; the elder counts himself a success though his life is making him sick. The real task, the only task, is unfinished in either case. And it remains unfinished as long as we fondly hold to the greatest obstacle: believing that nothing is wrong or that we can do it on our own.

Unless we come to the disturbing realization that we have failed and that we cannot do it on our own, we will muddle through the rest of our lives never able to enter the kingdom. Like alcoholics, we cannot admit the truth until the bottom falls out: The marriage ends; the children leave in disgust; the job is taken away. Until then we can fool ourselves. As long as we cope with our lives, we can blind ourselves to our weaknesses and inadequacies. So we continue to live half a life—closer to death than to what Jesus would call living.

Now let me show you how Jesus ministers to us, the elder brothers. Go back into that story and resume your identification with that brother. How do you see your younger brother? You see him as a sinner, don't you? Well, who do you think that younger brother really is? I tell you: it's Jesus himself. As I once wrote, "For our sake God made Christ into sin so that in him we might be made into the holiness of God."

Jesus was willing to take the role of the younger brother. Immediately I can hear the objections. "But the younger brother was a sinner." And I say, "Look at the evidence." Jesus was put to death not only as a sinner but as a blasphemer and insurrectionist. He suffered a death reserved for criminals. In the eyes of Mosaic Law, he was cursed and cut off from God, for the Law says, "Cursed be he who hangs from a tree." Isaiah says, "We found no beauty in him so we put him to death."

Our inability to see Jesus as a scandal keeps us from experiencing his saving power. We see Jesus as a wonderful guy who would make a great addition to our next dinner party. We reassure ourselves that if we had been present at his trial we would have stayed with him even to the cross to offer encouragement and consolation.

But we are blind! What gives us the audacity, the self-righteousness, the lack of knowledge to see ourselves acting any differently from the disciples? What makes us think we are better than Peter who denies him or, for that matter, Judas who betrays him? Or myself, who stoned his followers? Pilate refused responsibility and washed his hands; Herod was unaware of what was happening. And we ignorantly think we would have behaved differently? This blindness stands in the way of our salvation.

As long as Jesus is not a scandal, he has no power over us. Only by confronting the blasphemy of Christ as sinner can we see our own self-righteousness for what it is: sin. Jesus like a scapegoat lifts the curse from every human being, younger and older brother alike. But he can't be driven off to the desert and forgotten. As the younger brother, there he is, wounds and all, coming home. He has taken my elder-brother resentment from me and what does he give me in return? My Father's constant love, the assurance that his own victory over death is shared with all his brothers and sisters. Through his love and obedience I am recreated and reborn. He has reconciled my Father with me.

I have discovered I cannot save myself. I have discovered that my judgment does me no good. I have discovered that to hold grudges against my brother only harms me in the end. I have come to enjoy the banquet because my long-lost brother has come home. Both sons have returned. They have come home as sons to their loving father, who will be for them not a tyrant, but a Father who will enable them to develop to their fullest and share in his joy. And what brings them all together here? Why, the fatted calf who gives its life so that a family might celebrate the joy of reunion. Thanks be to God our Father who brings us this great victory through our Lord Jesus Christ.

You can continue to make this long pilgrimage. You can continue to do the meditations. You can continue to learn how to work on yourself. You can look at your judgment, you can transcend your anger. You can do whatever you want to save yourself and move toward the kingdom. Or you can stop right now. You can admit you cannot possibly do the job, and it will be done for you by your brother, by your Lord. And then, from the overflow of that love, you will live naturally, without judgment or resentment and in generosity and self-sacrifice for all. That is the real good news.

EXPLORATION **35** THE BAPTISM OF JESUS
time: twenty-five minutes
materials: Bible (Mark 1:9-11)

Now we'll return to our initial story of John the Baptist and Jesus. Here are elder and younger brother reconciled. There is no conflict here between Jesus and the Baptist nor between the ego and the Spirit. The ego points freely toward the self as the place where the Spirit is made manifest. John says that although he came before Jesus, Jesus is far greater; he, John, has only paved the way. Similarly the ego paves the way for the Spirit; the one who comes after takes rank before.

In the Christian tradition the process we have been investigating in this part of our pilgrimage reaches its climax in the ceremony of Christian initiation with the sacraments of Baptism, Confirmation, and Eucharist. To conclude our exploration here, let's look at the moment of Baptism, first as it played a role in Jesus' own journey and then as it plays a role in the life of a disciple of Jesus.

• After the usual preparation, read the account of Jesus' baptism in Mark's gospel. The baptism of Jesus is the first public action in his ministry. He has grown up in an obscure town in Galilee. His family is ordinary. Since his father is a carpenter, Jesus has more than likely been apprenticed in this craft. Perhaps he has also studied as a rabbi or

Jewish teacher. At a certain point in his youth, he feels called by God for a special task. He may not know what this task is. He may also question whether it is a real call.

• Begin your meditation now by entering into this experience of Jesus to make it your own. Now you have left home to pursue your call. You stand one day with many others on the banks of the Jordan river, listening to the preaching of John the Baptist. "You brood of vipers! Who warned you to escape from the approaching retribution? Prove your repentance by the fruit it produces! Don't presume to claim Abraham for your father. God could make children for Abraham out of these stones. The blade is laid to the root of the tree; any tree that fails to produce will be chopped down and thrown into the fire. I baptize you with water for a change of heart; but one mightier than I comes after me. I am not fit to loose his sandals. He will baptize with the Holy Spirit and fire. His shovel is in his hand and he will winnow the threshing floor; He will gather wheat into the granary and cast the chaff into the fire."

You have come to the Baptist hoping for a confirmation of your call, so you join the throng of people who press forward for baptism. Now it is your turn. You wade out into the water. The Baptist takes you in his powerful arms and immerses you in the water. As he raises you up out of the river you see a great light and hear the voice, "You are my Son. I am pleased with you." You look around. No one else has seen the light or heard the voice. But you did; here is the sign you have been awaiting.

Explore your feelings of joy and acceptance. How do you experience the peace of this scene? What is it like to have this feeling of total acceptance and belonging? What does it feel like to know who you truly are—that you are the Father's son and totally loved? Does this experience strengthen you? Does it provide a ground for you to stand upon? What meaning does the experience open for your life?

• This experience is not limited to Jesus. Some have turned Jesus into a freak—someone different from ordinary mortals. Thus what happens to Jesus is not what happens to us. But such is not the case; Jesus is the model and exemplar. But he is also the firstfruits, as Paul says. He is the first of many who will follow him in exactly the same experience.

For he opens the gates of the kingdom to everyone. Each of us can come to this baptism experience of Jesus in our own Baptism into Jesus.

36

THE LOVE OF GOD
time: twenty-five minutes

• To conclude your exploration, let's consider the Christian experience of God's love and concern for each of us. The idea for this meditation comes from Julian of Norwich, a wonderful mystic of the Middle Ages, who suggests that we think about Jesus' suffering and death. Christians have often pointed out Jesus' tremendous love of humanity as the motive for his action. But Julian asks you to imagine that you are the only person in the universe who needs salvation. Only you require a teacher, a savior to forge a path through death into the kingdom. Enter into this lonely experience. How will you be able to join all the rest of creation in the glory of God's kingdom?

• The second movement of Julian's meditation is to realize that Jesus would do everything he did for you if you indeed were the only one in need of redemption. Think back to the parable of the lost sheep. When you are in love with a person, it doesn't matter that there are fifty or a hundred or a billion who are found. The one who is lost, the person you love, must also be found. And if necessary, you will risk and lose your life for that love. In your meditation, experience that total, unrestricted, unqualified love of Jesus for you. What effect does the knowledge and experience of such love have on you?

• Complete your meditation by giving thanks to your Father for such a guide, teacher, and, perhaps, Lord. If there is anything you wish to ask for, feel confident as you remember Jesus' words.

We have explored the message and program of Jesus. We are ready to take our first step into discipleship, to hear the call in our lives, to respond to the call, and to hear the assurance that we are accepted and loved.

PART FIVE

The Call to Discipleship

When we began this pilgrimage, we examined the place and importance of meaning in our life. Then, through the Scriptures, we came in contact with a new vision of living and of perceiving life. Jesus calls this vision the kingdom of God. In the last section, we examined how we might begin to pass over from this world into that promised kingdom should we take Jesus as our teacher, guide, and ultimately Lord. Now we are ready to enter into discipleship with Jesus to learn the vision and to make the transforming journey. *Now is our time of decision.*

XPLORATION **37**
WHAT DO YOU WANT?
time: twenty-five minutes
materials: Bible (John 1:29-39)

On our pilgrimage, John the Baptist has been our guide, witnessing to the presence of meaning in the world. In this passage, he points toward Jesus as the center of that meaning. John has already introduced us to Jesus. From our vantage point as witnesses, we have observed him both in word and in action. Now the Baptist points toward Jesus as though for the final time, so that we, like the Baptist's disciples, might approach Jesus ourselves.

How are we drawn toward this man? Has he satisfied us that he is a capable leader, a guide to fulfillment? Can we follow and accept him as our Lord?

• Prepare as usual for your meditation. Because the Baptist tells his two disciples that Jesus is the one they have been waiting for, they go to Jesus, hoping to become his disciples. Create this scene in your imagination. What do you bring with you into this encounter? What are your feelings as you approach Jesus? What doubts and questions still remain? Do you feel peaceful? Anxious? Excited?

• Once the scene is set, move on to the question Jesus asks, "What do you want?" Take this question as the center of your meditation. Allow it to resound within you for the remainder of the session. Just what do you want from this man? What do you want in a teacher? What can he give you that you need from him? What is your heart's desire? What do you hope to gain by following Jesus? What can you learn from him?

EXPLORATION **37a** WHAT DO YOU WANT? (continued)
time: twenty-five minutes
materials: Journal (Prayer Experience)

Today we shall continue yesterday's meditation through work in our journal.

• After the usual preparations jot down an outline of yesterday's meditation. Write a letter to Jesus in response to his question "What do you want?" Do not rush the process. This is a crucial question; allow yourself time to answer it thoughtfully. What were the reasons you undertook this journey? What additional motives and reasons have you discovered on the journey? What do you hope a continued journey under Jesus' leadership might bring you?

38

EXPECTATIONS
time: twenty-five minutes
materials: Bible (Luke 9:57-58)

A passage in Luke's gospel concerning discipleship will carry us deeper into our own decision-making process.

● Look up today's passage and read it before preparing for meditation. Then prepare as usual.

● As Jesus and his disciples travel along the road, they meet a man who exclaims "I will follow you wherever you go." Take his one line now and use it to enter into his experience. Is this a cautious statement? Is the man hesitant? What does his exclamation tell you about his present feelings? Are there instances in your own past that led you to a similar kind of exclamation? What were they?

This statement overflows with enthusiasm, energy, and emotion. The man is practically beside himself. His statement has not emerged calmly from the depths of his own mind. He is on fire; he is inspired. He may have heard Jesus speak or he may have witnessed one of the miracles; perhaps he has heard about Jesus from someone else. Whatever the situation, he hopes and feels that this is the teacher he has been waiting for.

● Review your own journey to this moment. You have witnessed Jesus in action and heard his words. Allow your enthusiasm to expand to equal this man's. Enter into his exclamation, "I will follow you wherever you go." There is no need to feel it is your own enthusiasm. To pretend is sufficient. But climb into his skin so that you may be able to recognize a corresponding hint in your own experience. Do you believe Jesus may be the answer to your yearning? How eager are you to follow him?

You, too, have said, "I will follow wherever you go." Perhaps you said it to someone you were in love with. How did you feel when you made such a statement? How did it feel to put yourself on the line, to declare your intentions openly without any hedging or qualification? Bring those memories into the meditation to deepen your experience.

This is no rational statement. The man does not speak from a well-considered opinion; he is caught up by feelings and desires. He does not mean what he says, although at this moment he does not know that. In the future will come second thoughts, rational suggestions, real concerns, and problems. He will then qualify or even retract his words, regretting this fervent burst of spirit.

Enter, nevertheless, into his enthusiasm, magnanimity, and joy. Make his statement your own; by doing so you open yourself further to Jesus.

• Now hear Jesus' reply. "Foxes have their holes, the birds their roosts, but the Son of Man has nowhere to lay His head." Remain a few moments with these words. What do they say to the man and to you?

At first, they don't seem to respond to the man's declaration. Jesus does not rebuke the enthusiasm, but he does not accept it at face value either. Jesus makes a veiled statement that the man does not know what he is opening himself up to. "Your expectations are not entirely realistic," Jesus is saying. "You say that you will follow me wherever I go, yet your picture of what I have to offer is not what indeed I can give you."

240

We have all sorts of romantic ideas about what it means to follow Jesus. But they may not be the reality at all. We do not know what Jesus may demand of us. All we know from his reply is that he will unsettle us. Other creatures have a place to rest their head, but those who follow Jesus give up even that security. To go after Jesus, we must surrender the possibility of home at least as we have come to know it. The birds and foxes by nature have nests and holes, but not the pilgrim *on the way to the kingdom.* Jesus has departed from the expected reply before in the story of the hired laborers, the wise and foolish virgins, and above all the fig tree. Following Jesus means to venture into the unknown.

• Allow yourself to respond to Jesus' words now. What feelings and thoughts do they arouse in you? What do you say to Jesus in reply?

• Conclude your meditation by bringing yourself into prayer with your Father. Is there anything you want to ask for? How does he respond to your feelings?

38a

SLEEP AND WAKEFULNESSS
time: twenty-five minutes
materials: Journal (Life Experience)

Let's explore that image of sleep Jesus hints at in his reply. We might be disturbed by his statement because we take it as a literal threat to our domestic security. But consider instead the image of sleep. This image arises again and again throughout the gospels and the rest of the New Testament. One of the earliest Christian hymns calls us to

> Wake from your sleep,
> and rise from the dead
> and Christ will shine upon you.

All humanity is asleep. We pass our lives in slumber until Jesus awakens us. If we follow him, we cannot afford the luxury of falling asleep again. He himself often puts off sleep to spend the night in vigil. The birds and foxes have places to sleep, but those on the road to wholeness cannot afford that luxury.

If we are not ready to put sleep behind us, we can't do what will be demanded of us. Maybe we feel let off the hook by this interpretation. We may not, after all, have to sell our houses and live in poverty to follow Jesus. We can live in the same place we do now; we can keep the same job; we can remain with the same family; we can enjoy the same friends. But we can no longer sleep in any of these situations. The person on the way to wholeness has no place to lay his or her head.

• Explore the areas of sleep and wakefulness in your life. In your journal, list the ways and the times you are asleep. How important are these sleeping times? What do they give you? How would you feel if you were deprived of them? Then explore the ways Jesus might wake you up or prevent you from sleeping.

How do you feel about Jesus' statement? Does it threaten you? Does it excite you? Explore your responses. Do not hold back negative feelings. Allow Jesus' words to disturb you. What happens out of this disturbance? Remain with the disturbance and observe it. What happens? Does it become worse? Does it go away? Does it turn into some other feeling? Use the disturbance to enter more deeply into yourself. Instead of being merely negative and fearful, disturbance can become an aid to growth.

39 LEAVING THE DEAD BEHIND
time: twenty-five minutes
materials: Bible (Luke 9:59-60)

Jesus takes the initiative in the second call to discipleship. He looks at the person and says simply, "Follow me."

• Read the gospel verses and prepare as usual. Picture yourself as an interested bystander with Jesus being in the center of the crowd. You might find yourself in this story to be quite unlike the man in Exploration 38. You can't summon the courage to approach and ask Jesus if you can be a disciple. So you join this group that is merely observing him.

• Explore this situation in your meditation now. Fill in the details of the scene. You yourself want to come to some decision about Jesus: Should you risk following him?

All of a sudden Jesus' call breaks through your private thought-world: "Follow me." Just where and how would that call break through to you? What are you thinking at the time? Has that call occurred to you outside of this meditation? How has it broken into your awareness at those times?

What is your immediate reaction? Are you upset that you have suddenly been thrust into the spotlight of attention? How do you feel about being called? Are you ready to respond? Once that call is issued, there is no more time to think and ponder. What do you say? Will you immediately obey? Will you refuse? Will you try to delay and make some excuse? Allow sufficient time to enter and explore each of these responses. If emotions arise, be with them; try to discover what they are saying to you. What images come to mind? What thoughts?

In the story the person replies, "Let me go and bury my father first." This seems a realistic request. After all if a father dies, it is the duty of the child to give him a proper funeral. Before we can forsake everything else to follow Jesus, there are a certain number of loose ends that need straightening out.

This is a common response to the call to follow. We want to follow, but we are not quite ready. Yet the call from Jesus is simply, "Follow me." There is no qualification allowed. The only adequate response is to follow.

• Complete your meditation now by entering into the tension of this situation. You want to follow, but first you must bury your father. Taste this experience. Explore all its components. Is there fear here? How much tension is created? Is there a possibility of anger?

39a

LEAVING THE DEAD BEHIND (continued)
time: twenty-five minutes
materials: Journal (Life Experience)

Today we carry the meditation into our journal. The young person has told Jesus he must look after his father's burial. What things do you find necessary to accomplish before you see yourself free and able to follow Jesus? What business do you have to conclude? What preparations do you need to make?

• In the Life Experience section of your journal, list all the things that need completion before you can follow Jesus. What stands in your way and prevents you from making a full commitment right now?

39b

LEAVING THE DEAD BEHIND (continued)
time: twenty-five minutes
materials: Journal (Life Experience)

Jesus responds to that young person and to us as well, "Leave the dead to bury their dead." Your duty is to spread the good news of the kingdom of God. Such a response may strike you as harsh, even cruel. But Jesus is not counselling carelessness or neglect of filial duties. He is instead responding to this person on a deep level.

He perceives that for this person, the burial is actually an evasion of the call to discipleship. We all evade such a call in this way. We all have unfinished business, important business, crucial business. "We would like to follow," we say, "but we can't just now." And our excuse is iron clad to all but the eyes of a master such as Jesus. He sees through our apology and recognizes the game even we do not know we are playing.

But it is a game, and Jesus unmasks it even at the risk of seeming cruel. What is dead is dead. It does no good to busy oneself about what is dead in one's life. All the shuffling and rearranging of deadness will do no good. Jesus calls us to life. There is no preparation for that. It is simply a matter of following.

Jesus' judgment is harsh. We *do* have to get things in order; what we have listed in our previous meditation is important; it may even be crucial. There may be no way to leave the work undone without shirking our responsibility. But Jesus does not leave room for dialogue or argument. The young person is allowed no response. Jesus has spoken; the follower's concerns are exposed for what they are: evasions and hiding places.

● Let's now risk having what is dead exposed by Jesus. Bring what you have written into the light of his gaze. Allow him to sift your concerns. Will staying behind to put these things in order really help you? Jesus says we are the dead living among the dead. We seek life and he holds it in front of us. But before accepting it, we say, "We have certain things we must do first."

There is no preparation you can make for living, says Jesus. There is no tidying up that will help in this work. You must leave everything dead behind in order to seek life. When you have found life, you may return to these concerns and then you can deal with them. But that is of the future. Follow me!

• Read again the things you need to do before following Jesus. Allow Jesus to see beneath the surface. Allow his words to reveal your motives. Is he right? Can the dead take care of the dead while you seek life? In what ways are the things you have listed dead? How do you remain dead by busying yourself with these things and postponing a decision to seek life from Jesus?

40 UNNEGOTIABLE CONDITIONS
time: twenty-five minutes
materials: Bible (Luke 9:61-62)
and Journal (Life Experience)

• The third encounter in Luke's gospel gives us an opportunity to explore yet another dimension of the call. At first glance it seems that this person's response to Jesus is the same as the son who wanted to bury his dead. "I will follow you, sir, but let me first say good-bye to my people at home." Once more the person tries to condition the call—I am not quite ready to follow completely. I want to modify your stark invitation.

In our last meditation we looked at the things that prevent us from following Jesus right now. In this meditation let's instead examine the conditions we want to put on our following the call. For some reason we feel unable to follow Jesus without first laying down certain conditions we feel must be acknowledged and made allowance for.

• In the Life Experience section of your journal, list the conditions you feel you must put on your following of Jesus. Are there certain things you cannot do? Are there certain things you cannot give up should Jesus demand it? Do you have limits you feel Jesus must honor should you become his disciple? List all the things that you are unwilling to surrender in order to follow Jesus simply and totally.

Unfortunately, Jesus does not take these conditions any more seriously than he did the obligation to bury the dead. "No one who sets his hand to the plough and then keeps looking back is fit for the kingdom of God." Harsh words, to say the least. Either Jesus has very little insight into how difficult his demands are, or he sees how difficult it is to extract us from the world. How can he be so unwilling to even consider these conditions that we see as so crucial and necessary?

There is a Sufi story that may provide us with a more objective viewpoint on our conditions and on Jesus' unwillingness to compromise.

Long ago a group of people had to move from their beautiful island home and migrate to a quite ordinary and poor island. Someday they would be able to return to their homeland, but that day was hundreds of years in the future. And since the thought of the life they had lived on their island made their existence on this present miserable island even more intolerable, the islanders soon began to "forget" how good life had been before. After a while, the previous life became only a wonderful dream to their children and grandchildren. But the descendants still cherished the wonderful news that someday it would be possible to return, and so they preserved the great art of shipbuilding so that when that day finally arrived, all would be able to make the journey home.

But as hundreds of years passed, the memory of home grew dimmer and dimmer. In fact, many now claimed that there had never been a homeland. It was just a dream to keep people from enjoying the present life. As the dream grew more and more unreal, the art of shipbuilding came to appear as so much useless knowledge and activity. People stopped building the ships; what would they do with them anyway? There was nowhere to go. And soon they even forgot how to build them.

But all was not lost. A few people preserved the dream and cherished it, passing it on from believer to believer. Since no one knew the art of shipbuilding any longer, the only hope for return to the island lay in swimming.

Finally these few dreamers who had preserved the old ideas announced that it was time to make the return to the homeland. Of course, most of the islanders by now did not even know about the homeland. They looked at the swimming instructors with amused curiosity, perhaps had a good laugh, and then went about their daily business again. The swimming instructors told the people about the beautiful island that was their real home. While most thought the instructors a little crazy, a few people here and there believed them. And these believers presented themselves for swimming lessons so that they might make the great journey.

Such a person would come up to a swimming instructor and say, "I want to learn how to swim."

"All right," the instructor would reply. "What bargain do you wish to make with me?"

"Oh, I don't really need to bargain. I just have this ton of cabbage that I must take with me."

"But why do you need these cabbages?"

"For food when I finally arrive in the homeland."

"But the foods of the homeland are infinitely more nourishing and delicious than cabbages, so there is no need to carry all of that cabbage with you."

"You don't understand; I need this cabbage for food. How can you expect me to voyage out into the unknown without my food supply? It seems I'm risking enough as it is. I may die. Besides how can I be sure that you are right when you say there is better food in the homeland? Have you been there? How do you know? And how do I know I can eat it? I'm afraid I must insist upon my cabbages."

"But it will be impossible for you to swim dragging those cabbages along with you. They will tire you long before you reach home; then they will drag you under, and you will drown. You cannot succeed this way."

"Well, in that case, I'm afraid I can't go. Because although you call my cabbages a hindrance, I consider them absolutely necessary to my well-being and survival."

Since most of the bargains with the swimming instructors ended like this, very few people ever learned how to swim and thus very few ever returned to the homeland.

247

• Put yourself into this situation. Jesus is the swimming instructor. He tells us he can teach us to swim to our true home. We reply we are eager to learn, but we must take along our cabbages. We have to do it on our terms. We are not being difficult. We know what we need to survive, and we need these cabbages. Look at the list of conditions in your journal. Can you now see more of your own cabbages? What things are you unwilling or unable to live without? What are the non-negotiable conditions—ideas? feelings? outlooks? people? It is easy for us to see the ridiculousness of taking a ton of cabbage on a swim. But it is very difficult for us to realize that all the things we consider so essential for our well-being are just as useless as this ton of cabbage.

EXPLORATION 41

THE RICH YOUNG MAN
time: twenty-five minutes
materials: Bible (Matthew 19:16-23)

• We can continue to discover the cabbages in our lives through another story. Prepare for your meditation and then read Matthew's account of the incident.

• First, pass over into the rich young man. Ask yourself: What has my life been like? Why, since I have all this wealth, should I want to follow Jesus? What is unsatisfying in my present life that urges me to search for a fuller existence?

Once you have entered into the young man's experience, then seek out Jesus. What is he doing when you meet him? As before, use your imagination to create the scene; setting the scene and establishing the atmosphere is an important component in entering the experience.

What do you hope for as you approach Jesus? Now that you are in his presence, go up to him and ask your question, "Master, what good must I do to gain eternal life?" Restate that question in your own words. Take a few minutes to formulate this question.

In response Jesus tells you to keep the commandments. Listen to that answer. Does it satisfy your longings? Why not? What is missing from such an answer? The young man feels the inadequacy of such a response. Through entering his experience can you also sense you want something more than to be just a good person? Why isn't it sufficient for you to be a good person who keeps the commandments? It may be quite difficult, if not impossible, to articulate just what you hunger after, but can you at least taste that longing now?

When you can experience the longing, tell Jesus about it. The rich young man says, "I have kept all these (commandments). Where do I still fall short?" Put his statement into your own words, based, if possible, on your own experience.

Now listen to Jesus. He tells the young man that if he would be perfect, he should sell all he has, give it to the poor, and come follow him. What is it like to hear those words? What might happen to the young man if he could obey Jesus' command? What urges you, if anything, to follow these directions? The young man says nothing in reply. Is there anything you can say to Jesus now?

• Take this story as a framework for your own situation. What might Jesus say to you had you asked the young man's question? The young man's riches were his cabbages; what would your cabbages be? Can you hear Jesus telling you what to let go of? Don't search for a response. Sit quietly without searching or censoring, and the voice will speak to you. Don't try to anticipate it, or guess what it might say; it may come and it may not.

If you fail to hear Jesus' voice, then consider your own cabbages. Which of them prevent you most from entering the kingdom? Remember, your cabbages are very real and necessary as long as you cling to them. They are not easy to leave behind. It may not seem a sacrifice in the eyes of the world, but for you they might be frightening and difficult to surrender. Which of the cabbages does Jesus demand you leave behind?

41a

THE RICH YOUNG MAN (continued)
time: twenty-five minutes

● Prepare for meditation as usual and then listen to this Sufi story that helps us gain perspective on our demands.

A group of people are sitting around enjoying one another's company. They decide to pass the time by telling each other the most essential thing in their lives, the one thing each feels unable to do without.

The first person says she could not give up her mother. After all, her mother had given birth to her and raised her. To her mother she owes her life.

The second person says that for him his wife is the one thing he could not part with. True, his mother gave him birth and raised him, but he did not ask her to do this. She did it on her own, and he bears her much gratitude. "But my wife is different," he says. "I asked her to become my wife and therefore I have a responsibility to her. I cannot forsake her ever."

Now the third person speaks, "I could part with absolutely anything in the world, except my navel." Gales of laughter greet his statement, for his friends believe he is joking. But his serious expression soon tells them he means what he says. He is not in jest at all.

"Well, you will have to explain yourself," they tell him. "We can see why this woman cannot give up her mother and why this man cannot forsake his wife, but why can't you part with your navel? That we need to understand."

"It is fairly simple really. Whenever I have a holiday so that I can stay home, I like to lie in bed, on my back, and eat celery."

"That is very well and good, but what can that possibly have to do with your navel? You can certainly eat celery without your navel."

"Oh, yes, I can eat the celery without my navel. But without my navel, where would I put the salt into which I dip the celery?"

The person who cannot part with his navel is the same as the swimmer unable to forsake the cabbages, the same as the child who must say good–bye to his family, the same as the young man unable to sell his possessions, and the same as we ourselves. To the rest of the world, clinging to one's navel is ridiculous and absurd. But to the one clinging, it makes sense. To one who clings to his navel, it is ridiculous to cling to one's mother or to one's wife. To others, these things that we cling to are quite expendable.

Now play with the story. Put yourself into that third person's place. Experience the tremendous importance of your own navel. Make it an unnegotiable condition for your peace of mind and happiness or even for your continued existence.

When you have entered fully into the importance of your navel, then take a look at the other people at this party. Imagine each of them mentioning one of the cabbages you listed in your journal in Exploration 40. Do you see these cabbages from a different viewpoint now? Can you see them as cabbages, and not really half as important as your navel? Can you even begin to find them ridiculous?

To our excuses—our cabbages and navels—Jesus responds, "No one who sets his hand to the plough and then keeps looking back is fit for the kingdom of God." There is no possibility of negotiation. It is impossible to swim to the island loaded down with cabbages. If one has put one's hand to the plough, it is necessary to look ahead to see where one is going. To look back will endanger the whole enterprise; we may hit a rock and break the plough. Jesus orders us to let go of our other commitments and conditions. Do we dare?

41b THE RICH YOUNG MAN (continued)
time: twenty-five minutes

- Let us return to the story of the rich young man. This time we will pass over into the role of Jesus. Imagine yourself as Jesus, a spiritual teacher who is able to recognize cabbages in the people who come to him. Imagine the scene from your new perspective. How do you feel at this moment?

Notice the young man in the crowd. Be aware of him as you continue your activity. What strikes you about him? How is he dressed? Can you sense that he is not only rich but that he spends money lavishly upon himself? What does that tell you concerning him? What other clues show this young man to be quite attached to his wealth?

He is approaching you. Feel attracted to him—he wishes to follow you and learn from you. You would like to have him for a disciple; you like his sincerity. Feel compassion for his longing and his search, but realize how difficult his growth will be. Hear his question; then tell him to follow the commandments, hoping this will satisfy him.

But he insists that he wants more than merely obeying the Law. So tell him to sell what he owns, give it to the poor, and come follow you, hoping all the while that he might be able to obey you.

From Jesus' vantage point, can you discover why the young man's wealth is the stumbling block to his perfection? Can you imagine how the selling of his possessions would free the young man, allowing him to become whole and to *pass over into the kingdom*? Experience Jesus' answer not as a harsh demand of obedience but rather as a difficult but necessary action this person must take before he can move along the spiritual path.

Watch the young man turn and walk away sadly. Allow your compassion to flow toward him. Experience how difficult it is for that young man to obey your words. Realize also that for him to be freed he must do what you have said.

- Use this story as a framework for your own confrontation with Jesus. As Jesus, see yourself approaching. How do you perceive this person? Feel Jesus' compassion, his nonjudgmental attitude, his perception of all this person's faults and cabbages. What can you say

252

to this seeker that will help him or her on the journey? What stands in the way of this person's perfection? What do you say when he or she asks you the question about perfection?

As Jesus, tell this person (yourself) what is necessary to complete the pilgrimage. You are not putting the person under an obligation so much as you are freeing him or her from cabbages. How can letting go of this obsession free the person?

This is a very difficult meditation, but remain with it. Try not to force the scene. Rather, relax and allow it to happen.

42

A NEW NAME
time: twenty-five minutes
materials: Bible (John 1:40-42)

We now return to John's gospel as we continue our exploration of the call to discipleship. On hearing John's testimony, Andrew, originally a disciple of the Baptist, follows Jesus. In his excitement he runs to his brother, Simon, to tell him he has found the Messiah. Andrew then takes Simon to meet Jesus. Jesus looks hard at Simon and says, "You are Simon son of John. You shall be called Cephas (that is, Peter, the Rock)."

When we decide to follow Jesus, we are transformed; we enter a new reality, a new way of living. As a sign of that fundamental change, we are given a new name. We will take this incident of the naming of Cephas (or "Peter," in Greek) as our next discipleship meditation.

• Prepare as usual and then read the text in John.

• Pass over into Simon's experience but take your own name with you. Your brother Andrew comes to you and says he has met the man who fulfills all the hopes and dreams of your people. Allow the joy and excitement of hearing this news to grow in your imagination.

Your brother leads you to Jesus. Jesus looks at you and calls you by your name. Explore that calling. What does your name sound like as Jesus speaks it? What does your name reveal about you? How does it describe you? Allow the sound of your name to resonate within you as you hear Jesus speak it.

• Become yourself again. Realize that Jesus is not satisfied with your present name. He is going to call you by a new name just as he calls Simon *Peter*. Listen for this new name Jesus gives you. Wait in silence and openness, and the name will reveal itself to you. When it does, you must test it: Is it indeed your new name? Speak it over to yourself. Call yourself by this name. How does it sound and feel? Does it name you? Does it call you forth into a new life? Does it open you to the kingdom? You may have to sift through two or three names before you hear your real new name. But stay with the process and eventually it will happen.

• When you have received your new name, repeat it over and over to yourself. It could be an ordinary name, such as Michael or Elizabeth. It might be the name of someone you know. It might be a name you have never heard before. Explore its texture. What associations does it have for you? What does it call you to? What does it call forth from you? When Jesus called Simon "Rock" he was calling him to become a rock. What does your name call you to become?

This new name is a symbol for the new life you undertake as you follow Jesus. Keep it with you and use it in your prayer. It is your private name, your inner name. If you are not yet baptized, you may even wish someday to adopt this name as your Christian name. But whether you choose to use it in public or not, it is the inner name by which Jesus invites you to enter his kingdom.

• Conclude your meditation with a prayer to your Father. You might thank him for this new name and ask that he reveal its true meaning to you.

43

PETER AS DISCIPLE: WALKING ON WATER
time: twenty-five minutes
materials: Bible (Matthew 14:22-33)

Having met Peter, let's use him in a week-long extended meditation on the life cycle of a disciple under Jesus' direction. We have met Peter's constant companion in Christianity already—it is Paul, his opposite in almost every way. These two men symbolize the poles of Christian existence. Paul is the radical, the firebrand, the preacher who knocks us off our horse and convicts us of our blindness so that we might be healed. Peter, on the other hand, is the pillar of the church. Jesus calls him "Rock" although as we shall see he is anything but a rock in the beginning years of this discipleship. We use Peter as our model not because he is exemplary, but because he illustrates that it is possible for an ordinary, fumbling, enthusiastic, unstable person to enter into the kingdom. Peter gives us hope. If he can make it, so can we.

• Prepare for your meditation and then read today's story in Matthew. Here we notice Peter's primary characteristic: he is impetuous, never timid or hesitant. Where others are cautious or hedging, Peter jumps in with both feet, even into the water as he does in this story. Enter into Peter's experience. Throughout this week's meditations we shall explore the theme of doubt and belief as it finds flesh in Peter's discipleship.

255

Today we will examine two areas of belief. Consider Peter's enthusiasm for belief. He is not afraid to tell Jesus that he too wants to walk on water. The other disciples are amazed that Jesus is able to do this, but there is no anticipation of duplicating the feat. This is not the case for Peter: "I want to walk on water too," he yells out to Jesus. And rather than rebuke Peter or tell him that such wonders are reserved for the Messiah, Jesus takes Peter seriously and invites him to come out onto the water.

• Put on Peter's feelings and enthusiasm now. Sense his boldness, his eagerness, his reckless daring. If you are by nature timid, it need be no real obstacle. Through your imagination, you can at least vicariously explore what such daring feels like.

• Use Peter's story as a framework for your own experience. What are your own dreams concerning discipleship with Jesus? Be as open, hopeful, daring and optimistic as Peter. After all, wanting to walk on water is no safe ordinary request. Nor it is a wish of the highest seriousness. In dignity it falls far short of wanting to feed the world or wishing yourself the most fulfilled person in the world. Peter has seen his master walking on water, and he thinks it might be wonderful to do it, too. Enter into your own realm of desires. What would you like from this man? Would you like to walk on water? Would you like to perform miracles?

As he did with Peter, Jesus takes your request seriously and encourages you. He grants your wish. Allow that desire to be fulfilled in your meditation. What is it like? How does it happen? Enjoy the experience.

• Once Peter goes out onto the water, he realizes what he is doing—it is impossible for a human to walk on water. So he panics and begins to sink. Enter into his experience. Imagine yourself walking toward Jesus over the water. What is it like? How does Jesus sustain you and allow you to accomplish this feat? Look in his eyes and feel there the confidence and the assurance you need. Feel your attraction to Jesus, your confidence that he will hold you up and allow you to perform this miraculous deed.

• Take your attention away from Jesus and look at where you are. Realize you do not know how to walk on water. Walk around the room and imagine you are walking on water. Don't think about anything except walking toward Jesus. Now put all your attention upon the action of walking. Let your brain dictate and totally control your walking. Give each muscle and joint directions for movement. Pretty soon you will find yourself floundering, losing balance, and perhaps falling. You have entered Peter's dilemma. Feel your confidence ebb away as you start to sink into the waves. Allow your feelings of failure, fear, and panic to rise until all you can do is call for Jesus to save you.

Peter sinks into the waves as soon as he gets in his own way: his self-consciousness does him in. What are the ways we might get in our own way on this spiritual journey? In what ways do we work to undermine our own progress? Our own accomplishment? Do we convince ourselves that we cannot do what is demanded? Do we destroy ourselves through self-criticism? Does our fear prevent any risk of growth and development?

Peter is responsible for his own failure. Let's consider some of the ways we, too, guarantee failure in our lives. Since this is a rather serious and heavy matter, we must try to keep our sense of lightness. After all, this is a humorous story; Peter is the clown of disciples. In your meditation, guard against self-vengeance. Instead take an amused look at the way your self-consciousness trips you. If you start to become hard on yourself, lighten your spirits by returning to the original story and having a laugh at Peter's expense.

43a

THE TRANSFIGURATION
time: twenty-five minutes
materials: Bible (Matthew 17:1-8)
and Journal (Prayer Experience)

The transfiguration of Jesus is one of the most beautiful stories in the gospel for it speaks of the heights of mystical experience.

• Prepare as usual for meditation, and read the account in Matthew's gospel.

• Using whatever techniques you can, enter into this event through Peter's experience. Imagine climbing to the top of the mountain. What are your thoughts and feelings as you make the difficult ascent? What is your first impression as you see the vision? Mystical experience is described by two kinds of emotion: fascination, which draws us into the experience, and terror and awe, which force us to shrink back.

If you have had such an experience, bring it to mind now; if not, use experiences of overwhelming wonder and dread to gain entrance into this scene. By imaginatively combining the two you might taste this transcendent feeling.

The transfiguration confirms for Peter, James, and John the greatness of Jesus—his holiness and splendor. For a moment he puts off the robe of flesh, and only the light that illumines the darkness is seen.

Review your own experiences with Jesus throughout your pilgrimage. Were there times when the light, the word, the meaning took on radiance in the person of Jesus? Have there been times of inner illumination because of something you experienced from Jesus in a meditation? We are not looking here for an overwhelming or mystical experience. Those are few and far between. We do not need to be knocked off our horse, as Paul was, to qualify for this exploration. But haven't there been times during your search when a little more happened than you expected, when you entered a meditation with certain expectations and were surprised by what actually occurred? Have there been instances when you have received far more than you put in? Have there been times when you could say with Peter, "How good it is that we are here!"

• Now, in your journal, describe one of those experiences. Tell of the preparations (though at the time they may not have seemed important). Explore the experience itself as deeply as you are able. Then detail the aftermath of the experience: how did it influence the way you perceived Jesus afterward?

EXPLORATION **43b** BELIEF AND DOUBT
time: twenty-five minutes
materials: Journal (Life Experience)

For our work in this exploration, we will examine another cry of faith. This cry is not by Peter. Instead it comes from the father of an epileptic child. The father asks Jesus for help, and when asked whether he believes, the father says, "Lord, I believe. Help my unbelief." Let us use this confession to clarify our own areas of belief and unbelief.

Let's begin with belief. This is easy to define and understand. Belief is not only what we believe to be true; belief includes that which we trust, that in which we have confidence, that upon which we know we can stand.

• Take about ten minutes to write your beliefs in your journal. Don't restrict yourself to religion; in some ways our religious ideas (unless they are deeper than lip commitment) are not really beliefs. For belief is not only of the mind but of the heart and body. We are willing to risk and entrust our lives to our beliefs. They may relate to other people, to God, to the world, to circumstances, to outlooks on life. Explore your beliefs now.

Unbelief is not quite the same thing as doubt or disbelief. If you doubt the existence of God, that is not necessarily an unbelief. Indeed, if you claim to be an atheist, your doubt of God's existence is not unbelief at all. Unbelief is something you feel lacking from your belief system. For example, you want to believe in the innate goodness of your friends, but you find yourself unable to trust them: that is unbelief. If, on the other hand, you normally suspect everyone, then your absence of trust is not unbelief but rather a consequence of your belief—you believe people are not trustworthy.

• In the first part of this exploration we described our beliefs. What are your unbeliefs? What are the things you desperately want to believe in but cannot do so? Explore your unbeliefs in your journal.

• Now examine your unbeliefs to see how they might be transformed into beliefs. Imagination is crucial in this work. We are not saying we can do this task; we are only imagining how it might be accomplished. Try to convert your unbeliefs into beliefs. If you want to believe in something only because you feel you should, it is not really going to be your belief.

The state of unbelief is very unsatisfactory; you do not want it to remain as it is. You can call out with Peter, "Help my unbelief." Make Peter's exclamation your own. Can you ask your Father to help you in your unbelief?

43c **PETER'S DENIAL**
time: twenty-five minutes
materials: Bible (Matthew 26:69-75)

If the transfiguration is the bright side of faith, Peter's denial of Jesus is the dark side.

• Prepare as usual for meditation and then read Matthew's account of the denial. You will remember that this story occurs during the passion of Jesus, just after he has been arrested.

This story helps us explore the place of failure on the spiritual journey. Denial is much more desperate than unbelief. When we deny, we stand against something we believe. We place ourselves in opposition to our faith, to our teacher, to our very selves.

• Let's enter into Peter's experience. Just a few hours before, we self-confidently declared we would stand by Jesus to the very end. What fear has now brought us to this point? Jesus has been arrested; the others have fled for their safety. We are confused, terrified, confronted by the servants in the courtyard.

• Have there been times in your life when you have been unable to stand up for what you truly believe? Taste these times. Did you feel like a hypocrite or a traitor to yourself? Did you deny a truth or a person without realizing what you were doing? What was your reaction when you realized what you had done? Was there forgiveness and healing? Where did it come from? From those you betrayed? From yourself?

How comfortable are you with the knowledge that you have done what Peter has done? Do you have to hide such knowledge from others? From yourself? Can you accept such denial as part of yourself? Do you think such actions disqualify you for spiritual growth?

If you must hide this denying part of yourself, what does this say about the wholeness you seek? Is there no place in that wholeness for betrayal and failure? Would a wholeness that acknowledged betrayal be more perfect than one that only acknowledged progress and success?

Peter at his worst illuminates what Paul said about becoming conscious of our limitations, our sin, our estrangement from wholeness. In the world's eyes, Peter's failure would disqualify him for discipleship. But as Paul has shown us, Peter's frailty, far from disqualifying him, may instead be a necessary step in his transformation. Failure thus becomes a glorious opportunity to learn. Because they are so painful, our failures are better teaching devices than our successes.

• Conclude your meditation by looking at the failures and betrayals in your own life. How did you react to them? Seen in the light of your present experience, were they really as negative as they originally appeared? Could you say that you grew as a result of these denials and failures? If not, can you imagine how they might have contributed toward your growth had you seen them in a different light?

43d

DO YOU LOVE ME?
time: twenty-five minutes
materials: Bible (John 21:15-19)

• This story takes place just three days after yesterday's story. It is Easter Sunday, and the news of the resurrection is spreading among Jesus' followers. Continue your role as Peter. How do you respond to this news? Are you ready to meet Jesus again? What will you say to him when he asks you about your denial? Does this news of resurrection make you feel better or worse concerning what you have done?

When Peter encounters his risen Lord, there is never a mention of his denial. Jesus knows what Peter has done: he predicted it at dinner on Thursday night. But he does not condemn Peter.

• Prepare for meditation, and then read the dialogue between Jesus and Peter.

• Enter into Peter's experience again. How do you feel at the beginning of this encounter with Jesus? Are you afraid that he might judge you unworthy? Or do you already feel the love Jesus is pouring upon you? Do you already in some way feel forgiven?

How do you answer Jesus' questions? Was there any time when you did not love Jesus? Did you love him even when you denied you knew him? What is this love like? Is it like trust? Is it calm and peaceful, or violent and marked by upheaval? Do you feel that this love is greater than you are? Could you call this love divine?

When Peter tells Jesus that he does indeed love him, Jesus asks Peter to feed his sheep. Would this love enable you to do what Jesus asks: to manifest the care, the love, the concern, the forgiveness that you experienced from Jesus and that you have to come to recognize as

261

constituting the kingdom of God? Do you think that by the power of this love you might make the kingdom manifest in your life so that others might see it and experience it through you?

Making the kingdom manifest does not mean speaking or preaching about it. It means living in the kingdom. It means responding to the needy as did the good Samaritan. It means looking out for what others need rather than what you think they deserve, as the landlord did for the hired laborers. It means living generously with your talents and life, as did the prodigal farmer and the two people who lent the talents. It means forgiving and reconciling with your brothers and sisters, as in the story of the two sons. Is this love you feel for Jesus powerful enough to enable you to feed his sheep? If it is not already that powerful, is it possible to hope that some day it may be strong enough?

EXPLORATION **43e**

PETER PROCLAIMS THE GOOD NEWS
time: thirty-five minutes
materials: Bible (Acts 2:14-36; 3:11-26) and Journal (Prayer Experience)

Today's story occurs after Pentecost when the Holy Spirit has been poured out upon the disciples. We will read how Peter first proclaims the good news of Jesus to the people of Jerusalem.

When we heard the good news from Jesus, it concerned the kingdom of God as an alternative way of living that promised the perfection and fulfillment our world was incapable of supplying. The good news consisted of parables Jesus told and signs he performed that provided us glimpses into that alternative reality.

As we read Peter's speech, we will notice that the content of this good news has shifted. Now Jesus himself is the good news. Instead of the parables Jesus once told, we hear stories about Jesus himself. But although the format has changed, the deeper reality has remained constant. Jesus is the good news because it is through his life and teachings and his conquest of death that the kingdom breaks into our lives.

• Prepare for your reading by spending five minutes with your mantra. Then enter into the scene. Peter is speaking to Jews, so he uses their tradition to communicate the good news. Some of his references might puzzle you, but the central message is quite clear: in Jesus a new day has dawned for us. For ten minutes, read carefully and meditate upon these speeches of Peter. Can you catch his excitement? Can you translate what he says into your own words?

Now turn to the Prayer Experience section of your journal. Take the next twenty minutes to compose your own proclamation of the good news. How would you tell your friends and neighbors what you have experienced through Jesus? You need not use any of Peter's words or ideas; use your own. You have had your own encounters with Jesus; try to communicate what you have discovered.

EXPLORATION # 43f

THE MIRACLE OF PETER
time: twenty-five minutes
materials: Bible (Acts 3:1-10)

In this meditation of our extended Exploration 43, we observe Peter's final stage of growth; he is now a full member of the kingdom of God. He is filled and motivated by the Holy Spirit rather than by his own ego. He is another Christ, able to carry on the work of Jesus. In the world, he is a sign of the presence and the promise of the kingdom.

• Prepare as usual for meditation, and then read in Acts about the healing of the lame man.

Again we pass over into Peter's experience: now it is you who heal the lame. But how do you do it? Is it under your own power (the power of the ego) or under the power of God? What is it like to be the healer? Do you feel in total control and determination of the situation? Or are you a channel through which the healing power flows? Would you be able to be a channel of healing if your attitude toward life were manipulative or grasping? If it were an open surrendering to the Spirit?

Switch over in your meditation from one attitude to the other. What blocks the healing when ego is in charge? What opens when the Spirit is in command?

Now let's return to the question of belief. Previously we considered belief in terms of what Jesus did. Could he really cure the sick, heal the lame? We came to perceive the miracles not so much as magical tricks of power but as signs of an alternative way of living. We bypassed our skepticism by moving to the meaning behind the signs. But what about the miracles themselves? Did they actually happen? Are they enacted parables? True, for us they are read and heard just like parables, so they have become a different variety of parable. But did Jesus work these miracles? Could his followers work them today?

• The real question is not whether Jesus performed miracles, but whether you believe that you might also be channels in this way for the kingdom's transforming presence. If you want to know why you have not already been a vehicle for miracles or why you have not witnessed miracles in others, consider how open you have been to receive miracles. How receptive are you to the possibility that you might be a vehicle for miracles? Spend the last few minutes of your meditation with this question.

• Return to today's story and experience the two ways of living—the one that is open to miracles and the one that blocks them. Remember, Jesus could not work miracles in his home town because the people were not able to receive them. If you embark upon the path of Jesus, miracles are promised as a part of your life. How could you be open to these miracles that transport you deeper into the kingdom?

EXPLORATION **44** DIALOGUE WITH PETER (preparation)
time: twenty-five minutes
materials: Journal (Life Experience)

We should be fairly well acquainted with Peter after last week's meditations. In Christian tradition Peter is somewhat more than another disciple; he is the leader of the community banded together in

Jesus' name. Perhaps this journey has appeared to you as an individual pilgrimage made under the tutelage of Jesus. But there is an essential communal dimension to the path of Jesus that we will explore. If we should decide to confess Jesus as our Lord, we would naturally move into membership in that community so that we might participate in the fullness of the Christian experience.

The calling of the disciples in John's gospel is not really an individual call from Jesus. The disciples are called out of a community of relationships in order to form a new community with Jesus. This experience of fellowship is important to Jesus' vision simply because of the great emphasis upon persons in the kingdom.

For Jesus, God is not just a certain concept or law or state of existence, but a person addressed as Father. Nor is the mind of the kingdom another philosophy or psychology, but, again, a person—the Holy Spirit. And the kingdom itself, inasmuch as it is a social entity, does not exist for the isolated individual but rather so that persons might live in relationship to one another. So it is in conformity with Jesus' vision that there be a community an individual could join in order to journey along the path of Jesus.

At the beginning this guide suggested strongly that the explorations be done, at least in part, with others. It is not impossible to do this work alone, but it is more difficult because one must be one's own inspiration. Group spirit and commitment do much to preserve the flow of energy and raise individual members when they stumble or become stuck. Besides, when we work alone, we lose the benefit of other insights and experiences; imagination is fed and developed through sharing.

• Explore the communal dimension of your pilgrimage, writing your thoughts in the Life Experience section of your journal. If you have done the work in a group, reflect upon that experience. Did the group aid you in the work? Did the group bring a wider horizon to your meditation than when you worked alone? Did fellowship and friendships arise out of the communal experience?

How did your central focus upon Jesus and his vision transform the group into a community of persons sharing a common goal and helping each other? In what ways might you see the group as a taste or anticipation of the kingdom? As you grew to know one another did a real community develop? What is this community like? How does it strengthen your ability to make the journey? If you did the work as an individual, reflect on how it might have been different had you worked as part of a group.

EXPLORATION **44a** DIALOGUE WITH PETER (observation)
time: twenty-five minutes
materials: Bible (Matthew 16:13-20)

This has been a search that again and again revealed the personal nature of existence—a loving Father, a flesh-and-blood guide, a personal Spirit, a communal vision. At the deepest levels, meaning, in Jesus' eyes, is the revelation of a person in relationship to another person. Now, through the technique of dialogue, let's continue our exploration and importance of community.

Even if you have been working alone, you have had contact with a community. First you have met Jesus and through meditation have dialogued and entered into relationship with him and his Father. But there has been another person as well. Ideally you might think of that person as the Holy Spirit who brings all of us toward the kingdom. But in this instance, think of that person as the one who writes these words and who has cared for you and wished to be able to bring you to the path of Jesus. I speak of myself, the author of this guide. For I have been with you in spirit all along this journey. My every thought in setting down these words has been to be for you a path to Jesus. Since I have now revealed myself, it is no longer necessary to pretend that I am impartial in witnessing to the kingdom.

Let me help you prepare for your own dialogue with Peter by showing you a sample dialogue. Since Peter is named by Jesus as the head of the Christian community, we shall enter into our dialogue by speaking to him.

Prepare for today's observation in the usual manner and then read the account in Matthew of Jesus naming Peter head of the church.

I myself was not raised in the church of which I am now a member. Nor have I always believed in Jesus. Perhaps the doubts and difficulties I have experienced in coming to terms with this community called *church* may aid you in your own journey. Commitment to follow Jesus is ultimately realized in joining the Christian community. Commitment and joining are not the same thing, but if we decide to follow Jesus, that decision will include a decision to affiliate with like-minded people who are at the very least publicly committed to the same path and vision.

Here is my situation in this dialogue: I have heard the good news of Jesus. I have been attracted by the kingdom Jesus proclaims. I have also heard the good news about Jesus—how death through him is destroyed and how the kingdom of God is not limited by this world or by death. I now want to discover my next step in pilgrimage. So I approach Peter, head of the disciples, and begin to speak with him:

> *Me:* How do I become a follower of Jesus?
>
> *Peter:* Through baptism. In baptism we are joined to Jesus in his death, and we are raised with Jesus into his resurrection. Thus we are incorporated into the body of Christ; we are his new people; we represent him in this world; we claim renewed life in his name.
>
> *Me:* But how do I acquire this baptism?
>
> *Peter:* We can do it for you.
>
> *Me:* But who are you?
>
> *Peter:* We are the Church Jesus set up to represent his vision and teaching in this world.
>
> *Me:* But wait a minute. Churches aren't my thing. They may be great for some people, but I'm no joiner. Besides, in all this journey I have never heard Jesus himself mention anything about a church. And as I look around me at those churches that claim they belong to Jesus, I don't see one that comes anywhere near Jesus' vision of the kingdom. The churches of Christianity are as much a part of the world as any other organization.
>
> *Peter:* You're right. The Church is definitely not the kingdom. And if the present Christian Church is any indication, the kingdom of God on earth is still a long way off. But Jesus in his lifetime inaugurated the kingdom through his teaching; through his death and resurrection he opened the possibility of the kingdom to everyone. The rest

267

of the mission—the carrying of this good news to those who can be freed by it—is not his responsibility. So he entrusts it to people like you and me. And it is not lost there because the Holy Spirit guides us and gives us speech and inspiration. You and I have heard the good news of the kingdom. We have seen that our sins cannot destroy us. We have confidence that Jesus has found for us a way to everlasting life. Won't you help us carry this news to those who have not heard it yet?

Me: You mean you want to recruit everyone to be preachers and teachers for Jesus?

Peter: No. That is not what we need. There are plenty of preachers and teachers. We need ordinary people, no heroes. Just ordinary, weak people. We will all fall far short of our task. Many of us will even betray the very things we cherish most. But that is all right, the kingdom we seek is a kingdom of persons rather than lofty ideals. And we are not alone in our work; we have one another. We carry with us that spirit of Jesus and the knowledge that he guides and sustains us.

We need you. You have something unique to share with us—your own individual experience. You already belong to us because you share our dreams. So I ask you to join us. Together we can help and support one another when the vision grows dim. We can encourage one another when the way is rough; we can correct one another when we become sidetracked from our true vision.

Me: But I'm still not convinced. From what I've seen of churches they involve too much ugliness, arrogance, institutionalism, and downright sinfulness. I've looked at your churches. I've seen them in operation. I wonder whether they are working for or even concerned about the kingdom you speak of. Sometimes I believe they have totally betrayed what Jesus stood for. I did not come to know Jesus through the Church. Why at this point should it be necessary to give my allegiance to it? I see as much hate and unconcern for people inside the Church as I do outside in the city streets.

Peter: Everything you say is true. But are you really that much different from those of us inside the Church? We don't join the Church because we are committed and saintly and holy; we join because we are sinful and hateful and we need all the help we can get. This may be the one institution with the easiest entrance dues in the world—all you have to do is say you want to belong. And the church may be the only institution that not only tolerates failure but is designed with failure in mind.

There was certainly something ludicrous about Jesus' appointing me to lead his Church. I am hardly the best of the disciples. I am hardly the most stable of his followers. John is more spiritual; Matthew has a better business sense. But he chose me. He even changed my name to "Rock." There's a laugh. "Rocky" might have been all right, but "Rock" hardly fits at all.

Nobody's in this community because he or she is good. If we were good, we would not need to cling together to keep from destroying ourselves and our vision. We need this community because we are weak, because we are filled with anger, self-hatred, and sin. But if we can cling to the teachings, the example, and the spirit of Jesus, there will be hope not only for ourselves but for the kingdom we give our lives to help build. And we need you to help us. And we will help you. If you take your dream of Jesus away with you, it may wither and die. If you share it with us, it will enrich both us and you.

Me: But there must have been some better way to go about keeping the dream of the kingdom alive. Why isn't it enough to study the Scriptures? Why do we have to drag in all the sheer stupidity that the church has promoted in the name of Jesus? I'm sorry, but the Church is a stumbling block.

Peter: You've hit the exact point about the kingdom and about Jesus. They are stumbling blocks. If you haven't stumbled over them, then you haven't really encountered them. This kingdom was awaited for over two thousand years, only to be rejected as stupid and blasphemous by the very people who nourished the dream. They dreamed of a

269

mighty savior who would lead his people out of slavery and into freedom. Instead the Messiah was himself led to defeat and death like a lamb to the slaughter. The Church calls herself the New Israel, but she surpasses the old Israel in blindness and faithlessness. Yet we must remember the old Israel was not rejected for failing to be good enough. Indeed, the old Israel was not rejected at all. The old Israel rejected Jesus; that is why the Church had to become the New Israel. But the reality of the community of faith being a collection of weak human beings has not changed. When the Church has the chance, she grabs for power like any other institution. She has wrapped herself in the trappings of worldly glory; she has pocketed money that should feed the poor; she has sided with the powerful against the people; she has paid lip service to the gospel and run whoring after the world. She has often wanted to sell her birthright for a mess of pottage.

But there is more to her than all this. She has given birth to hospitals and universities. She has shared her dream with artists and brought forth wondrous human creations that sing the praise of God. Through her, women and men have caught the dream of Jesus' kingdom and provided flesh for that dream through their lives. The Church has been killed many times, brought low in the dust of humiliation, fed on the refuse of pigs. Yet, like the prodigal son, she has come home again to be received and restored by her loving Father who never judges, because he can only love. You see, there's only one justification she has: Jesus loves her and has taken her as His bride. She is unworthy; she is incompetent. But she is also loved, and only that matters. Through all this history—the sordid and the sublime—the dream has been kept alive even until today. The Church—she's not that much different from the kingdom after all.

Jesus once compared the kingdom to a mustard seed. The Church too could be likened to that mustard seed, for in the midst of this gigantic and important world, she is insignificant. But this seed will grow and become a shrub. Then, says Jesus, all the birds of the air will come and make their home in that shrub. Imagine thousands of birds each trying to perch and make a nest in a pathetic and rather ugly piece of shrubbery. Such an image of the kingdom fits the reality of the Church.

This ordinary and not so important little bush that grows from a tiny seed is nevertheless the presence and promise of the kingdom in this world. It comes out of the weak, the ordinary, the ridiculous. It is entrusted to the likes of you and me.

I am not adequate to the task I have been given. And neither are you, for that matter. But if we can know our weakness, if we can acknowledge we are inadequate, and if we do not admit defeat but are faithful to the heritage Jesus has left us, then the kingdom will come not only in spite of our weakness, but because of our weakness.

You are attracted to Jesus because he said things that nourished you. He offered you a vision of the world that would enable you to grow into the kind of person you want to be. In a sense, the kingdom of God is the only humane kingdom possible, for it is built upon the reality—and that means the finiteness, the incompleteness, the smallness, the sinfulness—of human existence. We need you and your vision in that enterprise. Come and join us.

Me: Well, it isn't as easy as you describe. What you say makes sense. The Church is certainly as great a sign of contradiction as the kingdom or Jesus himself. But even if I were willing to join the Church there is still a real question: which one? I see a multitude of churches all claiming to be the Church of Jesus. Yet there is little unity or agreement between them. Which one should I join?

Peter: This is a different matter and it is slightly less important than what we have been discussing thus far. For most of these churches are in some way or other the Church of Jesus. Yes, they are split. Yes, they squabble and spit at one another. No, they cannot agree on much. Yes, they are a scandal to the world. But each in her own way tries to keep alive and make flesh the vision of Jesus.

If you were already a member of one of these churches and were being nourished by her I would say you

271

should stay within that church and join the efforts to remove the barriers and obstacles still rending the real unity of the Church.

On the other hand, if you have no particular affiliation with a church it is up to you to find one that can help you grow in the vision of Jesus. Perhaps you have made this pilgrimage with a group from one of the churches. That church would be the place for you to start.

How could this church nourish you? How does it challenge you to grow? Do you feel already a part of this church? Would you like to belong to this group of people—not that they are perfect or that they have the answers, but that you can identify with them and share their concerns and their vision? I think it would be most important for you to find a community where you can feel at home and feel that you are a real part of it.

Traditionally, there have been four tests to determine the true community of Jesus. They are contained in the creed—a summary of Christian beliefs: "We believe in one, holy, catholic and apostolic church." Those same standards could help you decide on a community to affiliate with.

We say that the Church is one, but obviously there is more than one church in our world today. The Church is no longer a visible and political unity. In the earliest days each apostle founded a community wherever he preached the good news and was heard. Gradually, as the Christian faith spread throughout the Greek and Roman world, there were many churches. In these churches there were various traditions, but they believed themselves one with each other because, as Paul the apostle once said, "There is one body and one Spirit, as there is also one hope held out in God's call to you; one Lord, one faith, one baptism; one God and Father of all, who is over all and through all, and in all" (Ephesians 4:4-6).

I myself was made head of the apostles by Jesus. And I eventually found my way to Rome, the center of the world at that time. There I died, and so the tradition arose that my successors in Rome were the sign of unity in Jesus' church—the unity that Jesus envisioned when he prayed "may they all be one."

I hope that someday all the Christian communities will again be united, and the body of Christ be one on earth. It need not be a monolithic structure where everyone must act and think alike. Nor need it be a reunified community gained at the price of surrender of what each tradition holds sacred. Rather, the Holy Spirit will lead us to preserve our individual traditions so that our unity becomes an enriching rather than a narrowing experience. As of today, only those in communion with the bishop of Rome share this preeminent symbol of unity, and they must not look at this symbol as a sign of superiority but as a challenge and a spur to achieve in deed what is now only possessed in dreams.

The Church is holy. Nor is this second standard obvious: You and I are examples of its sublety. However, when you consider Christianity's two thousand years of unbroken tradition, you find thousands of holy lives within its community. They come from every age, from every culture—from Europe to America, Africa to Asia; from contemplatives such as Thomas Merton to activists like Martin Luther King, Jr.; from householders and people of the world, such as Thomas More, to cloistered mystics, such as Teresa of Avila; they even include simple fools such as Joseph Cupertino, so dull he did not qualify intellectually for ordination. Before you join a church, ask to see its lineage: look at its models and exemplars. Are they people you can relate to, be instructed by, be inspired by?

And what about the third standard, the word *catholic*? This isn't a name but a condition. It means *universal*. It refers to the ability of the good news to adapt itself so that all kinds of people throughout the ages can experience its joy and be liberated from the bondage of the world. Jesus' vision is not a narrow idea to which the entire world must conform by putting aside its own thoughts, traditions, and ways of living. The good news of Jesus is the yeast that enables the bread of the world to rise.

To be a good catholic means to be open. When it is catholic, the good news of Jesus risks taking on new expressions so that it might become good news for all people. The path you take to arrive at this point is not the same path I traveled. It is created out of your own culture. It is alive with your own ideas about psychology, history, spiritual techniques. Many Christians throughout history would not even recognize your ideas or words, let alone understand them. But they are the path by which you have come to Jesus.

To be catholic means to be adaptable. To be catholic means to claim that nothing human is alien from the Good News. To be catholic means allowing a universality of expression to the Good News. To be catholic means to say with Augustine: "In essentials unity, in other things diversity, in all things charity." Look to the community you join to be catholic.

Finally, we say the Church is apostolic. Often in the course of history this characteristic has been defined in a purely external manner. Apologists would say that the office of ministry in the Church is passed on through a laying on of hands and that therefore the apostolic nature of a community depended upon its being able to trace the laying on of hands all the way back to the original disciples. Now, this lineage *is* important, but it is not the full meaning of apostolic. The real question is whether in all the adaptations of the faith and in the catholic reaching out to the world, the original message of Jesus has been preserved.

While being catholic means adapting the vision of Jesus so that different peoples can grasp it, being apostolic means being faithful to that original vision in all its purity. It is always tempting to be catholic without being apostolic. We are tempted to find in Jesus' message those things that a culture wants to hear, and to present only that part of the message. It is also easy to be apostolic without being catholic—to preserve the vision of Jesus in the very words and concepts of Jesus' time and to demand that other peoples leave behind their own culture and enter instead into the thought patterns of two thousand years ago. It is hard to be open to the new and yet faithful to what has been passed down.

Me: You've certainly given me much to consider. Thank you. But I'm afraid it's been a little overwhelming. I think I'll have to give the whole matter some more thought before I can decide upon my particular community.

Peter: Of course give it more thought. Look around you and consider. And remember, you must find a community where you can feel at home and where you can truly grow in your faith. Your church must be a community where you can be accepted, encouraged, taught, healed, and confronted by the vision of Jesus. It must be a church where you find a vision that disturbs and heals at the same time. You will find that *such* a church will be one, holy, catholic, and apostolic.

44b

DIALOGUE WITH PETER (execution)
time: twenty-five minutes
materials: Journal (Prayer Experience)

Now that you have some idea how a dialogue might proceed, try it yourself. Granted, the dialogue you read was staged and structured to present material needed for your decision. But in your own dialogue you are not searching for information so much as a way to sort out your feelings about affiliation with a Christian community in order to continue your pilgrimage.

• Prepare for the dialogue by entering into a state of relaxation. Then enter into Peter's shoes by recalling incidents you have already experienced in the meditations on Peter.

• When you are ready, turn to the Prayer Experience section of your journal. Begin simply. Greet Peter and tell him where you are at this point of your pilgrimage. Go ahead and ask him questions. As you go into the dialogue, do so without thinking, "I know how it will turn out." Such an attitude guarantees no surprises. Keep yourself open, giving entrance to the Holy Spirit who has guided and nourished this entire pilgrimage.

As you enter the dialogue, say what you have to say, then wait for an answer to arise from Peter. There is no need to search or create. Allow whatever emerges to be your answer. Try not to censor whatever occurs. You are engaged in a rather delicate and deep process of exploring the psyche and spirit. To do this, you must be gentle and encouraging. Roughness and manipulation will accomplish nothing.

Remember the dialogue is a work of the imagination. On the pilgrimage you have seen the power of imagination. Today you bring this power into a dialogue. You may not be able to deal with all the issues that arise, but the dialogue is open-ended. It can be continued and taken up again any time. Should you want to dialogue with others, such as the apostle Paul, Jesus, or people significant to you in the contemporary scene, you can initiate those dialogues as well. You will find the dialogue a tremendous tool of self-exploration in your spiritual journey.

276

• Of course, the ultimate and continuing dialogue is the one you have already initiated with your heavenly Father. Conclude today's dialogue by taking your experience to him in prayer. Ask for light in your decision. Thank him for all the blessings he has showered upon you so far. Confidently ask for what you need.

EXPLORATION **45**
NATHANAEL: THE TRUE SELF
time: twenty-five minutes
materials: Bible (John 1:45-50)

After our extended excursion into Peter's life and experience, let's go back to John's gospel to conclude our investigation of the call to discipleship.

The next day, says John, after Jesus decides to leave for Galilee, he meets Philip and says "Follow me." Philip came from the same town as Andrew and Peter. Philip goes to find Nathanael and says to him, "We have met the man spoken of by Moses in the Law, and by the prophets: it is Jesus, the son of Joseph, from Nazareth."

"Nazareth!" says Nathanael. "Can anything good come from Nazareth?"

• After your usual preparations, read Nathanael's encounter with Jesus in John's gospel and enter into Nathanael's experience. He embodies that part of us which is without deceit and which seeks the truth. Philip has come to him and enthusiastically acclaimed Jesus as the man who fulfills all the dreams and expectations of the Jewish people. Nathanael thinks that Jesus seems to be a rather ordinary person from a very ordinary town. Shouldn't the fulfillment of all our dreams be more dramatic than this peasant carpenter from down the road?

• Relate to Nathanael through your own experience of Jesus, especially if you have grown up in a Christian environment. Perhaps you have accepted Jesus as the Messiah in the same manner as you have accepted the law of gravity. Jesus is God himself. This is no news to you. But you know better than to look for your *dreams* in Jesus or his church.

At this stage of your journey, you are asked to believe that this man, Jesus, who founded the Christian Church with all its pettiness and hypocrisy, may indeed have the key to your happiness. You might say, "You don't expect me to believe Christianity has the solution to my quest?"

Even if we are practicing and believing Christians, we might ask a question such as this. For we have spent all our lives in this church listening to the words of Jesus. Yet we find ourselves in the same boat with everyone else: we are searching for happiness. Now what do we discover? That it has been under our eyes all along? That's ridiculous. If the key to happiness has been in Christianity all this time, why haven't we seen it? The Nathanael in us asks: Can anything good come from Christianity?

When Nathanael asks this question of Philip, the latter replies, "Come and see." He does not argue; he does not explain. He only brings Nathanael into the presence of Jesus. There Nathanael's question can find its proper response. So, with Nathanael, bring your doubt, your skepticism, into the presence of Jesus.

As Jesus sees you approaching, he remarks, "Here is an Israelite worthy of the name; there is nothing false in him." For you, like Nathanael, are honest; your search for a fuller life involves the pure and honest part of yourself. The portion that seeks to grow, to enter into the vision of Jesus, is without deceit. Here is your highest and best self. And that part now asks Jesus "How do you come to know me?"

Jesus replies that he was with you long before you came to him. Perhaps unknown to you he has walked along with you from the beginning of your search.

As we look back over our journey (and we, unlike Nathanael, have encountered Jesus before) we find that he has seen us even as we did not see ourselves. He has known this inner self, this Nathanael, even if we did not know him. Like Nathanael, can we understand that Jesus has indeed been with us not only from the beginning of this pilgrimage but the beginning of our life's pilgrimage?

Is Jesus just some historical figure or powerful teacher, whom we have encountered? Or is he more than that? He claims to be friends with that inner part of us incapable of deceit. Does he resonate with that deep self? Does he know that self better than we do? If he does,

he is indeed more than just a historical figure, more than an extraordinary teacher.

Remain for a while with these words of Jesus. Explore them and test them. If he speaks the truth, if you can glimpse his presence as companion and friend along your spirit's pilgrimage, then respond with Nathanael and name him the answer to your longing and search: your guide, your teacher, your Lord. When this seeking part of you approaches Jesus, it is promised even greater things than you have seen on your pilgrimage.

Now enter into that proffered vision. Ask yourself: What do I want from Jesus? What do I hope to gain? What is my heart's desire? Then listen to Jesus' words and let him assure you that the reality is even greater and the vision brighter than you can imagine. Allow this promise to speak to your heart—the place without deceit, the realm of Nathanael. Allow that part to respond to Jesus and follow him.

• Conclude your meditation by turning in prayer to your Father. If you are not yet ready to make a decision about Jesus, you may want to ask for help in arriving at a decision. If you have made a decision to follow Jesus, then thank your Father for the gift of Jesus in your life. And now the shape of your prayer will change. You have accepted

Jesus as your guide and Lord and teacher; you have placed yourself under his care; he is responsible for you. Jesus has taught you how to pray. Jesus has revealed his Father to you. So as you conclude your prayer to your Father, end it with the following words: "I make my prayer to you Father, in the name of Jesus Christ, my Lord."

EXPLORATION

46 EXPERIENCE OF PILGRIMAGE
time: indefinite   materials: Bible (John 1) and Journal (Prayer Experience)

You have completed your reading of the first chapter of John's gospel. It has been an overall guide for this pilgrimage. On the threshold of your decision to accept Jesus as guide and teacher, pause and consider where you have come on your journey. The present exploration will aid the review. Over the next few days reread the first chapter of John, review your entries in your journal, and reexamine some of the material in this book.

• Then in the Prayer Experience section of your Journal, communicate the essence of this chapter in your own words, with your own ideas, and through your own imagination. It is a challenging exercise, but it will enable you to make this material even more your own.

You have come to the end of this first stage of the pilgrimage, but as you can see, it is really more a beginning than an ending. Having taken Jesus as your Lord, you will continue to learn from him and be initiated further into his vision. Let's conclude this guide with a look at the path ahead. Just where does following Jesus lead?

If you are not a baptized Christian, you will be enrolled in the catechumenate where your Christian education will continue. As a catechumen, you are considered a member of the Christian church. During this period, which may extend anywhere from a few months to a couple of years, you will continue to explore the vision of Jesus and become acquainted with life in the Christian community. The teaching at this time will be a continuation of the material we have explored in

Parts Three and Four. You will also participate in the worship of the community, continue your growth in the life of prayer, and gain a taste of Christian service as you learn how to promote the kingdom through ministry in your own neighborhood and community. The catechumenate is also a time for making new friends and of growing to feel a part of the church of Jesus.

During Lent—a period of forty days prior to the celebration of the resurrection at Easter—the final preparations for initiation take place. When your sponsors in the faith decide that you are ready to be initiated into the fulness of the faith, you are enrolled on the first Sunday of Lent as one of the "enlightened." The period of learning and study is now over. During Lent you will undergo an intensive preparation for experiencing the sacraments of initiation at Easter. The preparation consists of the discipline of fasting, meditation on the Lenten gospels, prayer and discussion with the other candidates, and a series of rituals that bring one closer and closer to the climax of Easter.

The climax of the Christian pilgrimage occurs during the sacrament of initiation at the "Easter Vigil" service. In our description here we will imagine that service somewhat as it was performed in the early centuries of the faith. Today certain of these rites have been modified to accommodate modern circumstances, but these accommodations also obscure the original powerful symbols.

Before midnight on the Saturday before Easter, the candidates, together with the rest of the community, gather outside in front of the church building to celebrate the Easter Vigil. It is deepest night, but out of the darkness, the Easter fire is kindled. It is the sign that the light of Christ has conquered the blackness of death. From that fire, the huge Easter candle is lit. During the following procession each person will light her or his own candle from this symbol of Christ. The Easter candle is carried at the head of the procession as all enter the dark church. Three times during the procession the deacon sings "Christ our Light," each time at a higher pitch. And the people respond by singing "Thanks be to God." By the time the Easter candle has reached the front of the church, the entire building is aglow with hundreds of candles.

The celebration continues as the deacon sings an ancient thanksgiving hymn in honor of this moment when death is slain and Christ rises triumphant from the grave. We hear of the many prefigurations of this event throughout the course of human history.

We hear how Moses and the people of Israel were led across the Red Sea and into the promised land by a pillar of fire. The Easter Candle at this moment becomes the focus and center of meaning; it is the light darkness can't grasp; it is the presence of the Word in our midst.

In a series of readings, we hear again the history of our search and the many times the love of our Father has been revealed for all his people. We hear of the creation of the world when light first conquered darkness. We hear of the passing over of Israel from the slavery of Egypt to the liberation of the promised land. We long with Israel throughout ages of oppression and injustice for a savior who will inaugurate a new age. As the series of Old Testament readings concludes, everyone joins in singing the "Gloria" and for the first time in three days the bells of the Church are rung as the spirit of joy and celebration grows. We are ready to hear the good news of this night, first from the Apostle Paul and then in the proclamation of the Easter gospel with its joyous alleluias.

Now the time of the initiation mysteries is upon us. Enter into this moment now in your imagination. We shall go through the movement of these mysteries as they were celebrated in the earliest days of the church. Today their form is somewhat modified, but by entering imaginatively into their earlier fulness we will be able to taste this great moment.

You have been preparing for this moment for a number of years. You have studied the teachings of Jesus and have learned how the Christian community understands this man as both guide and savior. Throughout the last forty days, you have prayed and fasted in preparation for this night. Now the bishop calls all of you forward to the sacrament of baptism. As you come forward, the people pray to all the saints for you in the litany. The bishop blesses the water and asks that it be the vehicle for your transformation. He recalls how the Holy Spirit breathed on the waters at the dawn of creation and made them the wellspring of all life; how Noah and his family were saved from the flood waters that inaugurated a new era under the sign of the rainbow; how Moses and the Israelites were led through the Red Sea waters and into freedom. And now he asks that you be conformed to the image of Jesus through his sharing of his death and resurrection.

Before you lies the baptismal pool. It is shaped like a coffin, for it is the grave of your old self. But it is also pregnant with the waters of new life. You come forward; you confess Jesus as your Lord and Savior.

Having dropped your clothes, you descend into the waters. The bishop takes you in his arms and immerses you in the waters. Here is the moment of final surrender. Everything that you have done comes to fulfillment in this moment; equally, there is no preparation for this moment.

During the course of your pilgrimage you have come to see ever more clearly the boundaries of sin and slavery in your life. You have worked to recognize yourself and to know yourself. You have, through meditation, prayer, and fasting, taken part in the birth pangs of your spirit. But you have also come to see the tremendous scope of the journey. You have come to know that you could never make the journey on your own. For the path demands total transformation—passage through death into true life.

And so you come to this moment of surrender. Now you can let go. With Martin Luther, you can cease your struggles to perfect yourself; they lead only to misery and frustration. When you surrender into the bishop's arms at the moment of baptism, you are admitting you can't save yourself.

But miraculously as you let go, as you let all your attempts to find your own happiness fall away, something new happens. You are not destroyed even though you lie under the waters helpless to save yourself. When you are lifted up out of the waters into a new existence, you are no longer the person you were—that person lies dead at the bottom of the pool. It is no longer you who live; it is Christ who lives in you.

You are given a new identity; you are called by a new name: your Christian name. You are clothed with a white garment for you have put on Christ. You are handed a candle lit from the Easter flame for it is by the light of Christ that you now walk through life. You are sealed with the Holy Oil and experience the gift of the Holy Spirit come to power within you. For the first time, you are invited forward to join in the Eucharistic mysteries.

This moment is not magic. It brings this pilgrimage of transformation to its fulfillment, but not its completion. Now you are a citizen of two worlds. You have not yet passed over into the kingdom—but you are on your way, equipped with the knowledge and the grace needed to bring you safely home. In the meantime you live in this world but are not of it. You are still a sinner, but at the same time a saint. And you will spend your life from now on in pilgrimage with others who in their weakness make the same journey, nourished by the same daily bread.

PART SIX

The Path Ahead

At this point in our pilgrimage we have made our decision to follow Jesus as our teacher. If we were not already Christians perhaps we have now passed over in Baptism from death to life. We have emerged from the dark wood where Dante realized he was lost.

We have seen the light of the kingdom. And although our search is far from over, it is, from this point on, significantly different. The way ahead is not easy, but it is marked out by Jesus the trailblazer, and there are not only our friends who accompany us on our journey but other helpers as well. We have come far. We have passed the major point of decision. The way ahead may still be uphill toward loftier and loftier visions, but we have a commitment and a faith to ease the way.

For the next seven weeks we will look ahead: What is this new experience of Christian living that we have undertaken? The time of our pilgrimage is now Easter. We have been through the journey of Baptism. From Easter until the fiftieth day of Pentecost the Church completes the training of the new Christians. This section of the catechumenate is called the *mystagogia* or the explanation of the mysteries. We now learn how to continue our pilgrimage with the help of the Church's sacraments to guide and sustain us.

In the old mystagogia, through a series of homilies, the teacher would unfold the mysteries of Christian life. This is not a time of hard work and learning; that was during Lent in our work of deciding to follow Jesus. This is a more leisurely time when we can reflect upon our pilgrimage so far and look ahead to how it will continue.

47

A WEDDING AT CANA
time: thirty-five minutes
materials: Bible (John 2:1-11)

The wedding feast is one of Jesus' favorite images of the kingdom. We have already seen it in the parable of the wise and foolish virgins. We will use the first miracle of Jesus in John's gospel to explore the shape of the Christian path. In this incredibly rich story, the entire contents of the Christian life are suggested, and the story itself will provide guidance for us throughout this section.

• Prepare for your meditation as usual; then read the story in John's gospel.

• In our meditation today we will pass over into each of the main characters, experiencing the kingdom from each perspective. But to begin, let's enter the whole situation. This, like all the other stories of Jesus, describes the kingdom of God; the story as a whole is an image of the kingdom. Retell the story to yourself, making the scene as vivid as possible. What do the characters look like? How do they act? What is happening at the feast? How many people are there? Do you know any of these people?

• Once you have a taste of the story as a metaphor of the kingdom, begin to explore the possible perspectives. Pass over first into the bridegroom's experience. This is your wedding. How do you feel? Taste your happiness. What does your bride look like? How do you see your future with her?

Right now you and your bride are the focus of attention. All eyes are on you. There is great excitement all around. You are occupied greeting guests, celebrating, dancing with your bride. Enter into this wonderful, chaotic time.

But there is something you are not aware of: the wine has run out. This is a serious situation, yet you know nothing of it; you know nothing either of the great miracle that has happened at your own wedding celebration. Water has been changed into wine, wine that is much better and in greater supply than the old.

• Take the wedding as an image for your life. As the bridegroom, you are savoring life to its fullest. Yet right in the midst of your life, unknown to you, important things are going on that are affecting the quality of your existence.

Compare your own life before you were concerned with spiritual growth. What things that you now consider of paramount importance were you unaware of then? What things that at that time were very important have ceased to be important for you now?

The master of ceremonies approaches you. He compliments you on the great wine that is being served. How do you react? Are you surprised? You do not quite understand what he is saying. But you are becoming aware that something unusual has occurred at your wedding feast: the best wine is being served last.

In your own life, what were the hints that all was not quite as you thought it to be? What was your first inkling that something more was happening than you were aware of? Consider the hint the bridegroom receives. He does not receive the truth about what is happening—only that something *is* happening. The first hints of the spiritual dimension are often half-guessed and perhaps totally wrong, but they alert us to the possibility that something more is happening.

• Now we'll pass over from the bridegroom into the master of ceremonies. You are in charge of this wedding. It is up to you to see that everything goes well. Experience this busy role as you move about seeing that everything is going smoothly. You notice that the servants are carrying new jugs of wine into the banquet room. You want to ensure that the wine is good, so you cross the room to test it before allowing it to be served to the guests. As you taste the wine, you are immmediately aware that it is different. Enjoy this experience; sample the bouquet, the taste, the texture. This is marvelous wine. You are a connoisseur of wine, and this wine transports you to heaven. It is a far better vintage and grape than has been served till now. What is going on? This is crazy, but delightful; your friend the bridegroom has saved the best wine till last. Run to tell him and congratulate him on his fine taste.

• The master of ceremonies is aware that something has happened, but he is totally wrong in his understanding of what it is. To what stage on your own pilgrimage does this experience correspond? You have awakened to the possibility of a spiritual path, but you have no real idea what the spiritual journey is like. Perhaps, like the master of ceremonies, you made all kinds of incorrect assumptions. Use his experience now to remember the corresponding time in your own spiritual journey.

• Next pass over into the servants' experience. You are quite aware that there is new wine at this celebration, and you know where it came from. You have been a witness to the miracle Jesus has performed. You know that because of Jesus' action the wine is not only different, not only better, but actually miraculous.

The servants' experience may correspond to your own as you encountered Jesus first in this guide. You saw the signs of Jesus in his healing of Bartimaeus; you had to come to grips with their implications. What do the miracles proclaim? What do they reveal about the kingdom?

• Bring your own experience on encountering Jesus' signs into the servants' situation. How did you react to the signs? With surprise? Doubt? Did the signs invite you to follow Jesus and believe? What did the signs tell you about Jesus and his power to transform the ordinary into the extraordinary? How does the servant at this feast react to what she or he sees?

• As we pass over into the disciples' experience, we have arrived at our place on the spiritual path. The disciples have already met Jesus. They have sensed in him a power and a message that has prompted them to follow him. They also witness this miracle but to them it is more than a mere display of power. They witness the signs and hear the parables in the context of seeking the kingdom of God.

As disciples of Jesus, we look at this story as a reflection of the kingdom; we begin to see meaning in things that before might have appeared nonessential. The story takes place "on the third day," which is the way Christians spoke of the day of resurrection. Read in this way, the story is connected with Jesus' resurrection. So if we see the water as an image of life in the world (death), the wine is an image of the kingdom (new life).

The story concerns a wedding feast, and we have already found this image used by Jesus to describe the kingdom. In the miracle, Jesus transforms Jewish ceremonial water: In Jesus we see not only the fulfillment of Israel's dreams, but something more than could be anticipated. Throughout the Old Testament, the prophets use the image of the vineyard for Israel. Yet here the wine comes not from a vineyard, but from water. It is unexpected wine. It is not a change in degree, as the master of ceremonies thought, but a change in kind. Jesus is the unexpected, the more than expected fulfillment of Israel's dreams.

Look at the wine's abundance—180 gallons. We are reminded of other images of the kingdom and the abundant care of our Father—the prodigal farmer who casts his precious seeds to the wind and reaps a harvest one-hundredfold, the forgiving father who welcomes his son home with a lavish feast.

As you pass over into the disciples' experience, can you move into a deep appreciation of the meaning of this story? Pass from the story as a miraculous event to the story as a sign—an event that provides entrance into the kingdom. John concludes the story by saying that this is the first of the signs by which the disciples witnessed Jesus' glory. As a disciple, experience this glory. What is it like? Explore its infinite depths of meaning.

• From the disciples, we pass over into the role of Mary, who asks Jesus to intervene in the crisis. "They have no wine left," she tells him. At first glance this seems a rather mundane problem to bring to a spiritual teacher, even if he happens to be your son. It almost seems an abuse of Jesus' powers to produce wine for a wedding celebration. It is hardly of the same serious nature as healing the blind. Yet Mary dares take her ordinary, worldly care to Jesus and ask that he respond. Similarly, in our own work of transformation, we will ask for help in everyday situations, many of them of no more cosmic import than this lack of wine. As you enter into Mary's experience, bring to Jesus some problem from your present life situation. Ask him for help.

Jesus' response to Mary tells that more is involved than a simple act of kindness. He addresses her not as a mother but as "Woman." She becomes an image of the Christian and the church, which in John's thought is feminine, in relation to the masculine Father and Son. Mary is receptive in relation to the Father and his grace. Place yourself, like Mary, before your Father through his Son, and ask to experience the transforming power of the Spirit in the midst of your ordinary life.

Jesus' response to Mary does not seem encouraging: "Your concern is not mine." There are many stories, familiar to all, where people are granted their wishes only to discover by story's end that those wishes produced disaster. King Midas is only one example. In the spiritual life we must be careful what we ask for: we do not know

289

ourselves well enough to recognize what we need. Coming to know what we truly need is itself a major part of spiritual growth that comes about through hazardous testing.

Mary displays the proper attitude toward this work of transformation. She dares to ask for what she believes she needs even though the request is then sifted and weighed. Mary does not argue or abandon her request; she lives in obedience to whatever the response might be, and she counsels the servants to do the same. She surrenders all control once she has voiced her needs: the rest is in Jesus' hands. Her situation articulates that point on the spiritual path often described as the dark night in which the person no longer has control over his or her own growth but must surrender that power to God.

Entering now into Mary's experience, taste these different elements. You may have had such surrender demanded of you in the past. Those memories can aid you now. The feeling of surrender is dark. You do not know the outcome: there is no guarantee. But it is not a despairing surrender; it is simply obedient and hope-filled.

Taste this surrender; it will be a crucial part of your journey ahead. You have experienced it already on a simpler, less demanding level, and you have read of it in the preaching of Paul.

• We finally pass over into Jesus' experience as the miracle worker. As Christians we too shall become channels through which the good news flows into the world. We are the ultimate signs of the Father's love. We have already witnessed this transformation in Peter's life. For Peter, once transformed by the death and resurrection of Jesus, is able to act in Jesus' name for the healing of the sick.

From the way Jesus acts in this story, we can see how the disciples will act in later situations. The act of surrender initiated by Mary is continued by Jesus. He acts only according to his Father's will. Jesus is a vehicle for the miracle, just as Peter will be a vehicle for miracles. The realized Christian, too, surrenders his or her own will to live in conformity with the will of the Father. This surrender allows the grace of the Father to flow through the disciple: Miracles occur; the concept of the kingdom becomes more clear; and in the disciples one catches glimpses of that other life called the kingdom.

At this stage of our own journey, it may be quite difficult even to imagine such an experience. The thought of surrendering our will seems not only impossible, but terrifying. In our experience, such abandonment leads to imprisonment, loss of freedom, and great damage to our personality. There is no longer a question of surrender; it has already occurred. But instead of being destroyed, we experience a truly rich existence. Far from being annihilated, our will, now in conformity with our Father's will, is perfected.

An analogy from the physical world may help. Consider a skill at which you have become quite proficient: It may be sports, typing, or playing a musical instrument. You become so expert at the task that you need not think about what you are doing; it happens automatically. You are operating at some different level from conscious thought, and you experience this proficiency as a flowing with the event. In sports, this happens when you no longer need to worry about hitting the ball, but in the joy of the game become a part of a larger whole: The game plays itself.

If you have had such experiences, use them now to enter into the experience of Jesus. In Jesus that feeling of flow or of being part of the will of your Father extends to your entire life and everything you do or think. What does such a life taste like? How is it different from your present existence? What is lost in that life in the Father's will? What is gained?

291

• This story offers us an extremely rich meditation. During the course of the next week return to the meditation to explore each of these areas in more depth. Through imagination enter into this full picture of the spiritual path.

Without too much difficulty, we can discern the general shape of the catechumenate in this story. The bridegroom, the master of ceremonies, and the servants are at different points of awakening to the possibility of spiritual development. The disciples have committed themselves to Jesus and are learning from him. They would be catechumens. Mary is passing into the stage of illumination and initiation as she learns to surrender her will to Jesus and his Father. Jesus, in this story, represents the realization toward which we are striving. He is the embodiment of the kingdom. He is the fully developed person who manifests completely the image of God.

We can find similar journeys of spiritual growth throughout the Western tradition. The details may be different from map to map but the overall shape of the pilgrimage is remarkably similar. This similarity might lead us to ask whether these different maps basically describe the same journey.

Dante, in the *Divine Comedy*, also describes the spiritual path in terms of a voyage through the hell of self-discovery. As Dante is led through the "Inferno" he comes to see the consequences of the life he is creating for himself through his actions and beliefs. In the "Purgatorio" he begins to work on his life, gradually stripping away the concepts and ideas (the seven deadly sins) that lead to loss and destruction. In the "Paradisio" he is granted a vision of the kingdom of God and of his final destination.

The shape of this path is not even limited to the Christian tradition. We can find it in a thinker as alien from that tradition as Friedrich Nietzsche. Nietzsche stands against Christianity and proclaims himself the Anti-Christ; yet as he speaks of the development of our spirit, the similarities to the Christian path are striking.

Nietzsche uses three animals to describe the three stages of spiritual development. First there is the camel whose task is to assume and carry burdens. The camel says, "Load me down. Put everything on my back." For almost twenty years the adolescent attends school and learns everything the culture has to give. He or she is loaded with the knowledge and wisdom of the ages. The camel learns what is right and wrong, how things happen, what to think and what not to think. On the Christian path, as catechumens, we are instructed in the knowledge of Jesus and his church. We accept the burden of those teachings as our own; we believe in them.

When the camel is fully loaded with all that culture has to bestow, it runs off into the desert where it is immediately transformed into a ferocious lion. The lion's task is quite simple but extremely dangerous: It must kill the dragon. Of course this is the making of the hero—for people become heroic by slaying dragons. St. George and Siegfried are obvious examples of heroes. Jesus, after his baptism, goes into the wilderness for forty days to do battle with Satan, often represented as a dragon or serpent. Early Christian art pictured the harrowing of hell after Jesus' death as a battle in which Jesus wields his cross as a sword against the devil dragon.

And how will the hero recognize which dragon must be slain? On their scales, says Nietzsche, are written "Thou shalt" and "Thou shalt not." The dragon is whatever prevents us from fulfilling our own life. Often the dragon assumes the person of the law, of society, or of the establishment. For Paul, it was the Jewish Law; for Luther, the Catholic church; for Jesus, death itself.

This stage often occurs in early adulthood. We can see it in young people's rebellion against their parents. They need to break away from old ties and bonds so they can forge an identity for themselves. Childhood is a time of conflict and often of profound suffering. For many of us it will not be achieved through one mighty act; we will need to do battle many times throughout the course of our life.

On the Christian pilgrimage, the dragon is battled during the period of enlightenment (and elsewhere of course). We confront whatever in our life and thinking keeps us from full existence in the kingdom. As we have seen in Part Five of this guide the greatest confrontation here is with the world or the ego. Like Nietzsche, we must turn on the world's knowledge and throw it over, because we have come to see that it prevents us from truly living. The confrontation might also be with some disease such as alcoholism; it might be with a deep sense of worthlessness. Whatever the particulars, the dragon that keeps us back from fulfilling our lives must be slain. Only through this heroic deed can we pass into real life.

But what of the crucial role of surrender in this process? Nietzsche does not describe it here, but he constantly speaks of the Super Man as the servant of the overmind—that ideal which leads him on. We can see clearly the element of surrender in a more modern myth: *Star Wars*. The young man, Luke, must be trained by the old knight in the art of fighting. Luke tries his best, but his best is not good enough. He must learn to recognize and trust in the Force. This mysterious Force has many elements in common with our idea of God. At the film's climax, Luke is able to succeed in his almost impossible mission, not by relying upon his own skills or even those of his computer, but by closing his eyes and surrendering to the Force. Such surrender enables the hero to place his missile on target and slay the dragon.

Nietzsche says that once the dragon is slain, the lion is transformed into a young child. Echoes of this rebirth sing throughout all the great spiritual traditions. "Unless you become as little children you cannot enter the kingdom of God." In the film *2001: A Space Odyssey,* the man is transformed into a star-child as he passes into the next stage of human evolution. In neither case is this a simple child such as we know. This is the reborn child who, as Nietzsche says, lives from within herself. Unlike the newborn child who is totally dependent upon her parents for her needs, this reborn child lives like a wheel rolling from within itself. The new child is self-sufficient and operates from a power and wisdom within.

In terms of our Christian path, here is the fully developed Christian who has put aside ego and lives under the guidance of the indwelling Holy Spirit. She does not look outside for wisdom and direction, but recognizes this inner divine spark that draws her home to her Father.

This person is also what Jung calls the individuated being. She is the true realization of her own unique self. She is opposed to the individualists who are not really self-sufficient but use their supposed individuality as a crutch and a support to differentiate themselves from the crowd.

On the Christian path the person arrives at this stage of growth by the process of baptism which is considered a second birth. Now the Christian continues to work upon her life, for the process of transformation does not end here. From the raw material of her past, she forges a new world for herself and others which we have come to know as the kingdom.

EXPLORATION 48

THE SONG OF SONGS
time: twenty-five minutes a day for one week
materials: Bible (Song of Songs)

Any true spiritual teacher will provide two things for his disciples. First he gives them a vision. We have seen Jesus' vision of the kingdom of God and we have explored that kingdom to the extent that we wish we might enter that kingdom and partake of its life. So far, however, Jesus has been only a teacher presenting us with a vision. But a spiritual teacher also provides techniques whereby our life can be transformed so that we can enter the vision. Let's consider now and over the next few days one of the techniques for spiritual transformation.

The first technique, no longer available to us, is the powerful, charismatic personality of Jesus himself. Jesus is the Way, the Truth, the Light. We have seen transformations happen in a number of the stories and miracles, from that of Zacchaeus to the healing of blind Bartimaeus.

Jesus used his charisma to wake people from their spiritual slumber. See how he called Simon Peter to be a disciple. Simon was a fisherman, working with others to mend nets in preparation for the day's fishing. He was immersed in his world: Could the nets be mended? Would there be enough catch to pay this month's bills? Did he have enough help to bring in the catch? Could he sell the catch at a good market? These real concerns created the fabric of Simon's world.

But into that world broke a voice that disturbed Simon's "slumber." "Come follow me" demanded the voice. It was spoken in a way that brooked no questioning, no objecting. It was spoken in such a way that the mending of nets, fishing, and all the other particulars of Simon's life no longer seemed crucial or satisfying. Hearing the call, Simon could not go back to his ordinary world; he arose and dropped his nets and his workaday life in order to follow this voice. He was waking up; he was coming alive.

The earliest Christians employed a technique that later had to be abandoned because it made them seem rather foolish. They quite simply thought that the world was going to end. That thought was powerful enough to transform life. When one lived with such a disturbing thought, it became relatively easy to see through the world and into the kingdom. Granted, these people did not consciously use this idea as a technique, but the idea functioned as such. Later on in the Christian church, the monks returned to this technique. They practiced keeping their death always before them. To aid them in this practice they would sleep in their coffins. This sounds morbid, but it did aid many in remembering their mortality.

Today the consciousness of one's mortality plays a part in the preparation for baptism, which is a death and resurrection. We also witness its awesome power in people's lives as they discover they have but a short time to live. From the world's point of view such news is unbearable, for it signals the end of everything—there is no more time. And the world can only exist as long as time is assumed to be infinite rather than limited. But many of these people on the threshold of death do not despair. Instead their mortality gives them a fresh perspective on life. And they live the last days of this earthly existence as members of the kingdom rather than of the world. Friends and relatives often do not understand it when a dying person is serene and at peace, instead of angry and despairing; the person has passed over from the death that is the world into the life that is the kingdom.

Today we cannot see with human eyes the charismatic personality of Jesus, and we do not think that the world is going to end tomorrow; some would say that because of this, the Christian faith has lost much of its transforming power. Instead, we rely for the most part on one of the gentlest techniques imaginable. It does not have the awesome power of the end of the world nor the charisma of the guru; some would say it has little power at all. The technique is familiar to you; we have been using it throughout this pilgrimage and will use it in the future as well. It is the story: the stories Jesus told concerning the kingdom, and the stories told about Jesus as the reality of that kingdom.

Unfortunately, many of these stories, through over-familiarity and the smoothing over of rough edges in retelling, have lost some of their original power. But we can use Sufi stories to help us go back to the experience of primal impact. The parables of Jesus constantly show us that the world we take for granted as being real is only a figment of our fallen imagination. Sometimes these parables succeed in making us quite uncomfortable; they are intended simply to nudge us into a new way of seeing.

Unfortunately, we have heard the stories of Jesus again and again. They have lost their original shocking flavor. We have become anesthetized to them. And we assume we know what they are telling us. But we have really only missed the point. Consider the Sufi story:

> A man approaches the Mulla to test him. He has an egg in his pocket.
>
> "Of course," says the Mulla.
>
> "It is shaped like an egg," says the man. "It is surrounded by a white shell, it is runny inside, but if you cook it, it becomes firm with a white outer layer and yellow center. What is it?"
>
> "Why, that's obvious," says the Mulla. "It is a cake."

We, like the Mulla, think we know the stories and we often miss the point altogether.

For the most part, misunderstood or not, this is all we have from Jesus. Just these stories. Are they enough? Could they in their gentle subtle way be sufficient without all the charisma of Jesus' physical presence or his ability to wake the sleeping and the dead? There is a story from the Jewish heritage that gives us comfort and assurance.

Once upon a time, there was a village in which a very holy rabbi lived. Whenever trouble visited the village—whether it be plague, famine, or war—the rabbi would go into the forest. And in the forest he knew of a sacred place where he could find God. He would go to that sacred spot, and there he would build a special fire, and he would say the secret words and then God would spare the village.

The rabbi grew old, but before he died, he imparted the secret tradition of the sacred spot, the sacred fire, and the sacred words to his son who was rabbi after him. And there came a time during his son's lifetime when a plague threatened the village. So the son went into the forest but he could no longer remember the secret spot. So he picked out a spot and he built the special fire and said the sacred words. "God," he said, "I have built the fire and said the special words, but I no longer know where the secret place is. This will have to be enough." And miraculously the plague ceased; it was enough.

Before this son's death, he too passed on the secret knowledge to his son who succeeded him as village rabbi. And during that son's lifetime a famine struck the village. So the son went into the forest. But not only did he not know the sacred spot, he had also forgotten how to build the special fire; all he could remember were the sacred words. So he found a place and he said the sacred words and then he addressed God. "My village is in trouble and so I have come to you for your help. But I no longer know the secret spot nor how to build the sacred fire. All I know are the sacred words, but this will have to be enough." And shortly the famine lifted from the village; it was enough.

Before this rabbi died he passed along his knowledge to his son who succeeded him. And during his lifetime the threat of war and pogrom hung over the village. So the rabbi went into the forest. But not only did he not know the spot or how to build the fire; he had also forgotten the secret words. But he spoke to God. "My village is in great danger, and so I have come here as have my ancestors before me. But I no longer know the sacred spot, nor do I know how to build the special fire. I do not even know the sacred words anymore. But this will have to be enough." And before the rabbi could reach his home again he heard the good news that peace had been declared and the village was spared; it was indeed enough.

And do you know why it was enough? The rabbis say that it was because God loves a good story. If that is sufficient for God, it must also be enough for us.

- All of this reflection leads us into our activity this week. The story of Cana uses one of Jesus' favorite images of the kingdom: a wedding feast. This image is developed to its fullest not in any of Jesus' parables but in the Old Testament book of The Song of Songs, also called the Song of Solomon or The Canticle of Canticles. On the surface this is simply a very beautiful love poem, but in the Christian and Jewish heritage it has been read as a metaphor for the mystical experience.

During the next week read through this short poem. Allow its poetry, its images to enable you to taste the joys of the kingdom. Use the reading skills you have learned on your pilgrimage. It is not necessary to read the entire book, although it is quite short and could be read in a matter of minutes. Read in depth. If a passage appeals to you, use it in your meditation. Imagine the scene. Let the images take on power. Enter into the woman's experience for she represents humanity in this mystic marriage. For the next week taste the delights of the kingdom through this beautiful poem.

49 ENTERING THE STORIES
time: twenty minutes
materials: Bible (Acts 1:1-14)

There are certain crucial stories that lie at the heart of Christian life.
They are commemorated and celebrated by means of Christian feast
days. They are also used again and again as subjects for meditation.
During the exercises this week we will learn and explore a particular
way of meditating upon these stories. Our basis for this meditation is
the prayer from the Roman tradition called the rosary. We will look at
how the traditional rosary is set up, but we will also modify it for our
own purposes.

Today we shall begin by doing one of the rosary meditations. The
heart of the rosary is the fifteen meditations on scenes from the life of
Jesus. In the actual rosary these scenes are meditated upon briefly in
succession. Today, however, we shall look at just one of those scenes
and explore a technique of meditation with the scene.

• Begin by doing your preparation for meditation. When you are
ready, read over the account of Jesus' ascension in Acts. In this
extended meditation 49-49f begin by picturing the scene. Allow the
image to come into your mind. Now enter into the scene in some way.
Become a part of it, either as an invisible observer or as one of the
participants.

In our other meditations throughout this pilgrimage we have
actively explored the particular story for meditation. But for this prayer
we want to develop a less active meditation. We have no specific
purpose for this meditation. We are simply entering the scene and
allowing to happen whatever will happen. So once you have entered
the scene simply be with it and allow it to do what it will.

In our active meditations our mind and consciousness is a moving
force as it explores and seeks to mine the experience from the
meditation. The meditations for this exploration are more like our
dreams. We do not consciously control them. Rather we try to allow
ourselves to be open to them and to whatever they have to reveal to
us. This technique of being passive to the meditation will take time to
get used to and become comfortable with. But we begin today as we
spend the rest of our time experimenting with our current meditation
on the ascension.

As much as possible allow the story to unfold by itself. Try not to force anything. You have adopted a certain viewpoint to enter the scene. From this perspective, what does the scene reveal to you? As the scene plays itself out, what happens? We are not so much concerned here with acquiring any kind of knowledge. We are simply interested in being present to the scene. What are your feelings? What are the sights, smells, movements, words—everything that makes the scene present and alive? Allow yourself to be with the scene. Go with its flow. You are not here to learn but simply to experience this scene again.

EXPLORATION **49a**

ENTERING THE STORIES
time: twenty minutes   materials: Bible
(Luke 2:1-20) and rosary (optional)

• We could call this kind of meditation "pondering." Read over the story of Jesus' birth in Luke's gospel. The story concludes by relating how Mary treasured all the things that had happened and pondered them in her heart. In pondering we return to a thing again and again. We remember it. We relive it. We enjoy it and savor it again and again. The rosary is a Marian prayer form precisely because Mary is the model for this kind of meditation. She was able to open herself to God and to be the Lord's handmaid because she pondered the great events in her life and that of her Son. Her pondering nourished her, strengthened her, and allowed her to respond openly and lovingly to the presence and action of God in her life.

• Take just a few minutes right now to explore how this action of pondering is different from the other types of meditation we have used in this pilgrimage. You do not have to be verbal in your exploration. You can compare things like feeling, tone, your own expectations from the meditation, your relationship to the meditation material, how different kinds of meditations compare or contrast with experiences such as dream or reverie.

Pondering is an activity of quiet. It has no specific purpose. It involves not so much the mind but the heart. So in our pondering from now on we shall use a mantra to occupy the mind, because with the mind calmed we can more easily listen to our heart.

Traditionally the mantra used in the rosary is the prayer the Hail Mary which is a combination of the salute of the angel to Mary and her cousin Elisabeth's greeting to Mary (which we shall explore in another meditation). The prayer then concludes with an appeal for Mary's assistance. Here is the prayer in full:

> Hail Mary,
> full of grace!
> The Lord is with you;
> blessed are you among women,
>   and blessed is the fruit of your womb, Jesus.
> Holy Mary,
> Mother of God,
> pray for us sinners,
> now and at the hour of our death.

In the rosary this prayer is used as a mantra. It is said for its calming rhythm rather than for the meaning of each word. It is traditionally said quite quickly. The mantra calms and occupies the mind; it does not lift our attention from our meditation.

You may, if you choose, use the Hail Mary as your mantra in these meditations. That is the way it is traditionally done. However, since this prayer is quite long, some people have found that it gets in the way of their meditation. So, at least in the beginning you might want to work with a shorter mantra until you are experienced in pondering. As a beginning you can use the mantra we have been using throughout the pilgrimage: *Maranatha.* If you do use Maranatha for the meditation, chant it, using a long note for each syllable. Stretch out the word as long as possible.

• For our exercise today prepare as usual for your meditation. But when you come to the mantra, chant it aloud and stretch it out. Chant for a few minutes this way, keeping the mind on the sound in a relaxed way. If you are using the Hail Mary as your mantra, say it out loud quickly, without pausing or reflecting upon the words. You will notice a certain rhythm emerging from the prayer. Certain words also gain prominence, especially the names of Mary and Jesus. Allow the rhythm and those words to bring you into your heart so that you can ponder.

• After a few moments with the mantra to establish the rhythm and the calm, pause for a second. Announce the mystery you are going to ponder. Today we shall use the birth of Jesus, which we have just read about. Allow the scene to become present to you. Now enter it either as an invisible observer or as one of the members. Begin chanting the mantra again. Continue the chant throughout your meditation.

EXPLORATION **49b** ENTERING THE STORIES
time: twenty minutes   materials: Bible
(Luke 2:41-52) and rosary (optional)

• Read first the story of Jesus teaching in the Temple at age twelve. Later today this story will form the basis of our meditation. But to begin let us reflect upon what the boy could have taught those learned men. There is a teaching in many spiritual traditions that as children we know truth which we lose as we grow up and which we must then struggle to regain. In the adult world things become confused, and we mistake knowledge for wisdom or truth.

The meditations of the rosary are meant to lead us back to the truth. Here truth is not knowledge, which is of the mind, but wisdom, which is of the heart. We have already seen that by pondering we are getting in touch with that wisdom. But there is a knowledge to truth as well. For Christians that knowledge of the truth is summarized in the Creed. The Creed is a statement of what a person or group believes. In Christianity the shortest and most universally accepted Creed is called the Apostles' Creed, although it was finally formulated long after the Apostles.

When the rosary is prayed it begins with the Creed. Here is the knowledge we seek to penetrate and understand with our heart. If you have a rosary with you, find the cross or crucifix. We begin praying the rosary by praying the Creed.

You will be familiar with almost all of the meaning of the Creed by now. As you read it over and familiarize yourself with it, allow it to put all your Christian experience into perspective. The Creed is not necessarily the way that modern Christians speak of their faith. Today we might not use these same words or ideas. But when we affirm the Creed we are linking ourselves with the entire history of Christian tradition. We are saying that in spite of changes in thinking we hold to the same experience that reaches all the way back to Jesus.

> We believe in God
>> the Father almighty,
>> Creator of heaven and earth;
>> and in Jesus Christ,
>> his only Son,
>> our Lord,
> who was conceived by the Holy Spirit,
>> born of the Virgin Mary,
> suffered under Pontius Pilate,
>> was crucified,
>> died, and was buried.
> (He descended into hell;)*
> the third day he arose again from the dead.
> He ascended into heaven,
>> sits at the right hand of God,
>> the Father Almighty;
> from thence he shall come to judge the living and the dead.
> We believe in the Holy Spirit,
>> the holy Catholic church,
>> the communion of saints,
>> the forgiveness of sins,
>> the resurrection of the body,
>>> and life everlasting.

For our meditation today we will use the scene of the boy Jesus in the Temple. Prepare for meditation by chanting the mantra: either the traditional Hail Mary or *Maranatha.* When the mantra has established

*Not in the earliest versions of the Creed.

itself in your consciousness, pause a moment to allow the scene of Jesus in the Temple to establish itself with you. Move into the scene as we have done on previous days. Now continue the mantra as your heart ponders the scene.

EXPLORATION **49c**
ENTERING THE STORIES
time: twenty minutes
materials: Bible (Acts 2:1-13)

Today our meditation will be the great feast of Pentecost, when the Holy Spirit descended upon the disciples after Jesus had left the earth. This is the birthday of the Christian Church. As we read the story in the Acts of the Apostles we notice that the disciples had locked themselves in the upper room to pray for nine days.

When Jesus was still on earth the disciples had asked him to teach them how to pray. So Jesus had given them a model for prayer which has since become itself the most popular Christian prayer, the Lord's Prayer.

The Lord's Prayer is both a prayer and a model or blueprint for all Christian prayer. To whom should we pray? What should we pray for? What is the proper way to pray? All these concerns are spoken to in the few brief words of this prayer.

• For the first part of today's exploration learn the words of the Lord's Prayer if you do not already know them. Then spend some time with these words. What can they teach you about praying? What are the concerns Jesus tells you to bring to your Father in prayer?

> Our Father,
> who are in heaven,
> hallowed be thy name;
> thy kingdom come;
> thy will be done
>   on earth as it is in heaven.
> Give us this day our daily bread;

and forgive us our trespasses
    as we forgive those who trespass against us;
and lead us not into temptation,
    but deliver us from evil.
Glory be to the Father, and to the Son,
    and to the Holy Spirit;
As it was in the beginning,
    is now, and ever shall be,
    world without end. Amen.

As we pray the rosary we will use the Lord's Prayer to begin each meditation. And as we pray, let us allow its words to touch us and stimulate our own prayerful response to our Father. Unlike the words of the Hail Mary, we pay close attention to the words and phrases and meaning of this prayer. We pray the prayer very slowly so that we can flesh its words out with our own words or feelings.

•   After you have learned and explored this prayer today, begin to use the mantra so that you establish its presence in your mind. Then leave off the mantra and pray the Lord's Prayer once more. Allow its words to become your own. Be totally present to this prayer. After the Lord's Prayer announce the mystery for meditation: The Spirit descends upon the disciples at Pentecost. Allow the scene to build up before you; enter into it. Now use the mantra again and ponder the mystery. When you have completed the meditation, conclude with the Doxology, which means a prayer of praise. In it we give praise to God as Father, Son, and Holy Spirit. As you say the prayer, allow the feelings of praise and thanksgiving to flow from you toward this wonderful God who loves us and wishes to draw us homewards toward him.

Glory be to the Father,
    and to the Son,
    and to the Holy Spirit;
As it was in the beginning,
    is now,
    and ever shall be,
world without end.
Amen.

49d

ENTERING THE STORIES
time: twenty minutes
materials: Bible (various passages from Luke)
and rosary (optional but recommended)

Today we shall begin to put together into the full structure of the rosary all we have learned. It is not absolutely necessary that you have a rosary to do these meditations, but it is definitely helpful; for the beads of the rosary are a way of counting and timing the meditations. They also give your body a part in your meditation and prayer. We have seen the popularity of worry beads from Greece and the Middle East. These beads are fun to run through the fingers. They are something we can play with; if you have experience with them you know what a calming influence they can have. The rosary beads, in a much more structured way, provide a similar function.

The meditations we shall be doing in the next three days are timed in a way that our practice meditations so far have not been. The rosary beads are used as an unobtrusive way to mark the time of the meditation. You will notice that the rosary is basically a circle of large and small beads with a small chain of beads attached to the circle and a cross at the end of the chain. The beads are used to count the prayers and mantras. Each large bead signifies the Lord's Prayer; each small bead signifies a Hail Mary or whatever other mantra you use. As your fingers reach each bead you pray the appropriate prayer or mantra. Then you advance to the next bead in the circle.

The large bead next to the cross or crucifix signifies the Lord's Prayer. The next large bead (after the three small ones) and the four large ones inside the circle each signify not only an Our Father but the beginning of a meditation on a "mystery." The ten small beads then count off the mantras for the duration of the meditation. When you reach the link of chain after the tenth bead your finger signals that the meditation is completed; you pray the Doxology. Then you move to the next large bead and again pray the Lord's Prayer, announce the next mystery, and proceed with that meditation.

Of course you can also count the mantras on your fingers. But the device of the rosary lets you totally forget about such mundane matters as whether you began with your left or right hand in the count. It simply makes the process easier and more pleasant, as well, by giving your hands something to do.

Altogether there are fifteen mysteries associated with the rosary. They are divided into three groups: the Joyful, the Sorrowful, and the Glorious Mysteries.

• Today we shall explore the Joyful Mysteries. They all center upon the birth and childhood of Jesus. The first is the annunciation by the angel to Mary that she will bear the Savior (Luke 1:26-38). We have already meditated upon this scene in Exploration 14b. The second mystery is the visitation. After receiving the good news, Mary sets out to visit her cousin Elisabeth, for in her old age Elisabeth has become pregnant and will give birth to John the Baptist (Luke 1:39-56). Next Jesus is born in Bethlehem (Luke 2:1-20). In the fourth mystery Mary and Joseph take Jesus to the Temple to be circumcised in accord with the Jewish Law. There the old man Simeon and the prophetess Anna see Jesus and prophesy about him (Luke 2:21-40). The final Joyful Mystery occurs when Jesus is found in the Temple teaching the doctors of the Law (Luke 2:41-52).

Familiarize yourself now with these five scenes. If you are not already aware of them, read the passages in Luke's gospel.

• To begin our meditation today, pray the Creed which sums up the Christian faith. If you have a rosary, hold the cross as you pray the Creed. Now move to the first bead—a large one—and pray the Lord's Prayer. Next you will find three small beads. Use this time to establish yourself in the mantra. Use the number three here as only a suggestion. It might take you a longer time to establish the calm of the mantra. Take that time. There is no sense entering into the meditations before you experience a certain degree of peace. When the mantra is established, pause and conclude this introduction with the Doxology.

Now you will have arrived at the large bead just before the medal which joins the chain to the circle. Say the Lord's Prayer, then announce the first mystery, taking time to set the scene and enter it. Then begin the mantra, counting the first ten beads (or decade). Pause again, concluding the meditation and praying the Doxology. Proceed through the rest of the mysteries the same way. At the end of the final mystery take some time for personal prayer as you conclude your rosary.

At first it will be fairly difficult to keep all this knowledge in mind. But with some practice the procedure will become automatic, and you should find this a beautiful way to enter more deeply into the central mysteries of Jesus' life.

EXPLORATION **49e**

ENTERING THE STORIES
time: twenty-five minutes   materials: Bible (various references) and rosary (optional)

Today we shall explore the group of Sorrowful Mysteries. These scenes are all connected with Jesus' passion and death. The first is the agony in the garden of Gethsemane before Jesus is arrested. He asks his disciples to watch and pray with him. He prays to his Father for consolation, but the disciples fall asleep (Luke 22:39-46). In the second mystery, Jesus, after his arrest, is mocked, beaten, and whipped by the guards (Luke 22:63-65, 23:11-12). Next he is crowned with thorns (Matthew 27:27-31). The fourth mystery is the way of the cross. Jesus is forced to carry his own cross. He stumbles under its weight, and the soldiers force Simon of Cyrene to carry it for him (Luke 23:26-31). The final scene is the crucifixion and death of Jesus (Luke 23:32-49). Familiarize yourself with these scenes and then pray the rosary as you learned in the previous exploration.

EXPLORATION **49f**

ENTERING THE STORIES
time: twenty minutes   materials: Bible (various passages) and rosary (optional)

Today our meditations are the Glorious Mysteries, which focus upon the resurrection and our future life in the transformed world called the kingdom. The first mystery is the resurrection of Jesus from the dead (Luke 24:1-11). The second mystery is the ascension of Jesus to his Father (Luke 24:50-53; Acts 1:1-14). The third mystery is the descent of the Holy Spirit upon the disciples at Pentecost (Acts 2:1-13). The fourth mystery is the assumption of Mary. There is an ancient tradition that at her death Mary was received body and soul into the kingdom. We could use this scene to look forward to our own destiny. For we live in hope of that day when we shall all experience the resurrection of our bodies and the full coming of our Father's kingdom. The fifth mystery is the coronation of Mary as Queen of Heaven. This scene is the final action of history, which John in the Book of Revelation pictures as the descent of the heavenly Jerusalem and the marriage of the Lamb (Revelation 21-22). In your meditation you might use either of these great images.

As you can see, the mysteries of the rosary include not only the events of Jesus' life but, through the figure of Mary, the events past and future of our own life. As we return to these mysteries again and again in the course of our future pilgrimage they will journey with us and reveal more and more of the kingdom. In this prayer form lies one key to our continued growth. For our meditation here is of our heart—an exploration of God's love. As we have seen before on our pilgrimage, it is love that lies at the center of the universe—it is our encounter with that love that transforms us and brings us toward our final and perfect happiness.

50 WORK ON ONESELF
time: variable
materials: your life

Although Christianity relies heavily upon stories to carry its vision, Jesus shows us much more powerful techniques of transformation. Of course, it is not necessary to use Jesus' techniques; they are not the only ones available. In the Christian tradition many have become saints through the use of different kinds of techniques. The techniques are not important; the work of transformation is.

What is this work of transformation? It is that process of passing over from the world to the kingdom. It can also be described as the displacement of the ego and the enthronement of the Holy Spirit in one's heart. It is taking up one's cross. "By gaining his life a man will lose it; by losing his life for my sake, he will gain it" (Matthew 10:38).

This work may not be appropriate for you to undertake consciously at this time. Indeed, many never consciously engage in it at all—they are transformed by the simple process of living day to day. Only one thing is certain. One cannot enter the kingdom with ego fully intact. Someday this transformation must occur. What of those who never seem to undergo this transformation? Are they lost? No, they are not lost. There will be opportunities for everyone to complete the work. This is the reality behind the teachings about reincarnation or purgatory in the spiritual traditions.

This work of transformation is not necessarily religious. Indeed, in the teaching of Jesus it is quite secular and mundane, and often in opposition to religious practices. Many confronted with this work have no religion. They are compelled to work alone, with no guidance from God or guru and no consolation that this work is holy or even healthy. Or perhaps a person doing this work is religious but never realizes this task as spiritual.

Consider the possibilities for doing this work: You can do it through the process of dying; you can do it in grief when someone you love dies; you can do it by entering a relationship where you and the other person die to yourselves so that the marriage might come to birth and sustain you both; you can do it through a divorce or losing your job; you can do it through a struggle with alcohol or drugs; you can do it by simply facing and living through each and every day. Of course, you can also do it by postponing it till later, even if that later is purgatory. Or, finally, you can do it consciously as you experiment on your life. But only through this work of dying and rising, however accomplished, can we give our allegiance to the kingdom. In Christianity this dying and rising is made visible and celebrated in the sacrament of baptism. It is renewed in our acts of penance and forgiveness.

What are some of the ways then that we might consciously engage in this work? Jesus as a teacher is not primarily concerned with techniques, but that does not mean that he has none. He is more interested in the content of the work and the vision of the kingdom. After all, techniques are readily available, and there is no one technique that is the only way.

At the beginning of this journey, we found that the center of work was in our head. Our intellect, our thinking, our imagination were our tools. We were attracted by the care and love we heard Jesus promise as part of the kingdom. Our commitment was a thinking commitment. It did not involve logic or reason exclusively, but for one reason or another, we were able to affirm and accept Jesus as our teacher and lord.

We also discovered that this work will now continue by bringing the focus down to our heart. It is not enough to have a vision in our head. If the kingdom is to consist of anything more than comforting or challenging ideas, there must be action. We questioned how we would be able to live this life of love, service, and forgiveness. Where would we find the power to bring about this transformation? Our attention moves from our head to our heart. Paul has told us that we must confront our inadequacies and so experience in our heart the truth that we are loved, forgiven, and accepted. This work of the heart will unleash great amounts of energy. It will allow us to do things that were impossible before; they were prevented by our baggage of sins from the past, the inadequacies of the present, and the fears of the future. But once in touch with that transforming power, the center moves from the heart to the field of action.

Other spiritualities place the seat of action in the abdomen, a few inches below the navel. Christianity in the Middle Ages taught that the liver was the center of the active life, just as the heart was the home of emotions and the head of the intellect. Our work in this domain will involve the rest of our life.

Jesus introduces us to this work by teaching us to experiment upon ourselves. He calls us to work on our life; take it as it has been given to us and cultivate it. Most of us never do this work; we simply allow our life to happen. If anything, our life, or better, our fate, rules us rather than the other way around.

Perhaps one day we will wake up to realize that our lives are mostly past. We may be at that dreadful age of thirty or forty or whatever, and we discover we have not really been involved and active in creating our lives. We have been asleep, vulnerable to whatever has descended upon us. Sometimes there come moments when we glimpse the web which fate is weaving around us. Our response is to shrug our shoulders or allow our bodies and souls to tremble for an instant before we reach for the whiskey, the pills, the daily grind—anything that will soothe us to sleep again. We don't want to confront the menace of living, of taking charge of our lives.

Sure it's easy to sleep, but the security it gives is false. What if you wake up some day with only time left to prepare for death? That horror scares some people back into sleep. What if today you should have to confront the terrors of death? If you surrender your life to the Spirit, the horror will be gone.

How does Jesus recommend that we wake up? One of the primary techniques he himself used was the all-night vigil. Many people believe that Jesus was often in a trance-like state of prayer all night. Perhaps he was, but the purpose of the vigil for us is also to create conflict so that we might wake up in a deeper sense. Try staying awake all night in order to pray. What happens? The demons come out to play. "What are you doing?" they taunt you. "Don't you know you need your sleep? This is great for tonight, but what are you going to do at work tomorrow when you can't keep your eyes open? Perhaps you could call in sick and give yourself a chance to recover. You must be the only idiot in the world who would actually, consciously, and for no reason at all, deprive himself of a decent night's sleep. And all for what?"

All of those questions and whinings and pleadings are the voice of ego which doesn't like what is going on. It doesn't want to lose control over you.

You might respond to the whinings and pleadings of ego in this way: "You get a lot of mileage out of telling me I have to have eight ours sleep. Well, I'm tired of you having control over my life. The higher self is going to be in control from now on, and that higher self is going to receive strength from this night of prayer. That is my decision, I will handle the consequences."

As the conflict recedes and the demons realize they have lost control, the day dawns and you have won a bit more control over your own existence. You will make it through this day. You are not destroyed by lack of sleep. You may be tired but you will function. And what you have gained is worth the fatigue. You are a freer and more awake person than you were the night before. As you crawl into bed the next night, you are a different person, more aware of how you live and more in control of the ego that takes your living away from you. You have confronted demons that hamper your growth, that keep you tied to a bare animal existence, that oppose the dawning divinity of your soul.

Another technique Jesus used was fasting. There are many reasons to fast. Some people fast to lose weight. Christians often fast in penance for their sins. Some people fast to purify the body's systems. And Jesus fasted to do battle with the ego. Right after his baptism, the gospels say he went into the wilderness for forty days of fasting. There in the desert he confronted his ego, and his Spirit conquered. The ego came to him and asked to be fed. You cannot live without food, said the ego. "Man cannot live on bread alone; he lives on every word that God utters," said Jesus. (Matthew 4:4)

You may want to undertake a small fast, doing it for any of the above reasons. But if you wish to work on transforming yourself, the supremely important thing is to observe yourself. Listen to the different voices within you. Come to know them. Recognize them as ego or body. Can you also hear the small quiet voice of the Spirit, that word from the mouth of God that truly sustains your existence?

Almsgiving is a third technique recommended by Jesus for the work of transformation. In Christianity, almsgiving has become simply a matter of helping the poor, which, as aspirants to the kingdom, we should do. But it is also a way to work on oneself. To work in this way, your almsgiving must be done in secret as Jesus recommends. This way you will not receive ego-strokes from others for what you are doing. The ego-strokes will only defeat your purpose in weakening the ego. You should also give until it hurts. It does little good if you give only what you can afford. Give a little more than you can afford and observe the agitation of ego: "Why did you do that? How are we going to manage now? That was a dumb thing to do." When we use any of these discomforting techniques, it is relatively easy to hear the voice of ego. The difficulty lies in being able to disassociate our true self from this powerful voice of "reason."

All-night vigils, fasting, and almsgiving are rather artificial techniques that Jesus used himself and recommended to others. There are other more difficult practices we can do in the midst of our lives. "You have learned that they were told, 'Love your neighbor, hate your enemy.' But what I tell you is this: 'Love your enemies and pray for your persecutors; only so can you be children of your heavenly Father,' " (Matthew 5:43-45).

"The last thing we need," you answer, "is more guilt heaped upon our shoulders. We cannot live up to the Ten Commandments; why add new burdens?"

This, however, is not so much a commandment as an invitation to those who wish to work. Imagine the following situation: You are standing at a party when an acquaintance from the office approaches you. He's had a little too much to drink; he is loose, but not quite drunk. For the last few months you've noticed a certain tension between the two of you. Nothing major, no fights, but on the other hand, there is no warmth or comradeship either. Now you've both had a couple of drinks, and he decides it's time to get a few things off his chest. The conversation grows animated as your differences begin to surface. Pretty soon he has turned nasty.

How do you respond to this situation? Perhaps, as most people do, you do not really respond at all; you react. *Here I am, minding my own business, and this idiot comes to me,* you think. *He starts talking, saying things that aren't true. He makes insinuating remarks about me. Who does he think he is?* So, you retaliate. Your anger goes up a couple notches. He reacts to you in turn; more of his spleen shows. Now you are being attacked; your defenses are up; you show him just how low you consider him and his opinions. Now he brings out the big guns. He tells you things about yourself that you fear but hope no one else knows. Your life is on the line; you draw forth your own artillery and blast the bastard off the face of the earth. At this point the liquor will determine whether, like civilized beings, the two of you turn and walk away from one another or descend the evolutionary ladder and have at one another like savage dogs.

But what if you attempt to be on the alert during your encounter? You will then keep in mind that over the last few months your relation to this person has been icy. Something has not been well between you. You will think back on what you have done to feed his bad feelings. Is he talking to you or to the fictional enemy he believes you to be? When he begins the conversation and you enter into it, you are aware of what could happen, so you are sensitive to what and how you answer. As he becomes angry, you do not fall into the trap of reacting to his anger. Instead, you respond. *Why is he angry?* you ask yourself. *Is the anger real or is it toward something or someone he feels I represent? Has he a true case against me?* In most instances of anger there is no true case. We are not dealing with one another but with our own displaced feelings about ourselves. We may see another person as self-confident and assertive and see ourselves as cowards. But rather than face the issue, we become angry at our assertive comrade and avoid dealing with our own lack of confidence.

As this angry person then confronts you, you ask whether you should accept his gift of anger. *Should I allow myself to be drawn into his hurtful world by responding to him in kind? No.* Instead you decide to respond creatively. It will do him no good for you to become angry. He will only be more convinced of the truth. You might allow him to express his anger, but you refuse to absorb the anger yourself for you know that it is not truly directed toward you but only toward the fictitious opponent he believes you to be. Rather than take his anger, you let it fall to the floor where it hurts no one.

You can make a free decision to remove yourself from the situation also by finding a friendly way to end the conversation. As you leave, you do not carry with you his anger, his accusations, or your own reactive retaliations. No, you carry away your care and concern that this man will find ways to come to grips with his anger. If you have negative feelings, it is sorrow that these unnecessary barriers prevent you both from realizing your common humanity.

Rise to God's perspective and look at the other person, seeing him as yourself—an ordinary, weak human. Your opponent is angry because of his own emotional agenda. But now see the situation from God's eyes. Accept that anger; allow it to come at you. It will not destroy or hurt you; if you can take it away from him without reacting, he might walk out of here feeling a little better, too.

There are thousands of life-situations where we are involved in just this kind of behavior. The difficulty of the work of transformation is to do it when we are entangled in these powerful emotions. No one, in the midst of anger, ever wants to take a real look at it. Why should we? *Damn it,* we shout. *This anger is justified!* And so we allow it to take control. Meditation is much easier to do—we can make room for that. But to work on anger, or lust, or resentment, or depression is one of the most difficult tasks in the kingdom.

When we refuse to descend to instinct but instead rise to divinity, we begin to see ourselves for the first time in our totality. And we can begin to make slight adjustments. We can change the automatic programming that operates as we sleep through life. We can begin to make free choices in our responses. But to do this, we must be awake. Normal living provides more than enough occasions to practice this method.

Jesus puts forth these ways of work not so that we might become human, but that we might become divine. Our anger, lust, resentment, fear, worry, envy do not have to control our lives. By being observant, we can discover just how we create these destructive feelings. Then we can let them go and realize our true happy selfhood as the sons or daughters of our heavenly Father. It is difficult work, not just a matter of willpower. First and foremost, the work demands observation. Just what is going on in this situation? What am I responding to from my past? Such knowledge will go far toward freeing us from the past and future so that we might live in the only possible place life can occur: the present.

Jesus brings us swords and invites us to do battle with our lives. And the battle is more important than the victory. In the battle, we can come alive. As soon as we begin to work on ourselves, we work on our humanity. When we declare battle, our emotions do not go away but rather become even more intense. Now, instead of a nuisance, they are the laboratory where we can observe ourselves. They are the opposition we go forth against. They are the alarm clocks that can wake us up. They are the raw material out of which our godliness will emerge.

Courageous saints will go even further. They will actually choose to create conflict in their lives. Most of us, on the contrary, do everything in our power to avoid conflict. *Who needs it?* we say. Yet it can be helpful.

There is one major difference between the way of Jesus and the Buddha. The end toward which both aim may be the same, but the language in which they are expressed appear different. But the techniques Jesus and Gautama use to achieve that end are radically different, although not necessarily incompatible. Christianity has made far more use of Gautama's method of meditation than of Jesus' techniques. Gautama saw in the world the all-pervasive reality of suffering. "To exist is to be inextricably involved in suffering": That is the first Noble Truth of the Buddhist path. The Buddha's way then was a path out of suffering and illusion. His technique was meditation, the study of the mind's creation of illusion (which we call reality). To practice meditation demanded removal from the world if only for the time of the meditation. His pilgrimage was essentially inward.

Consider the figures of the Christ and the Buddha. The Buddha sits in the meditation pose—all the noises and distractions of the world are far from him. He has transcended the world and its suffering. Now look at the Christ on the cross, in the midst of suffering. He does not remove himself from it; he plunges through it.

Could it not be possible that Jesus actually planned his own crucifixion? Is this what he meant when he said he must go to Jerusalem and die? Did he consciously engineer this final battle with suffering and the world's illusions? If so, he did it not because of some masochistic tendency that might be psychoanalyzed. He did it because he knew that the one thing that most keeps us in the arms of spiritual sleep is the fear of death and death's machinery—human society. Like St. George confronting the dragon, Jesus rode into Jerusalem to confront the machinery of death—the Jewish/Roman state—with open eyes.

As we read the accounts of Jesus' trial and death, we can see something quite interesting. Christian piety pictures Jesus as the innocent lamb in the midst of wolves. But the evidence belies this picture. Pilate is so shaken that he performs the futile gesture of washing his hands of Jesus' blood. Here is no passive lamb led to the slaughter. Pilate is no fool; he knows he and these people are on trial today, not this man who, stripped of all power, is yet totally in control of the situation. On trial is the world and all its powerful illusions. Those illusions will finally be stripped away by Jesus just as the inner illusions of mind were revealed by Gautama.

On trial is a world that can only destroy truth. It cannot produce any of its own. "What is truth?" asks Pilate. For at this moment, he knows that he does not know. On trial are a people afraid to awaken to the light in their midst for fear that they would awaken only to their own approaching annihilation.

Pilate knows what is happening. Again and again he offers Jesus a way out of execution. Each time the invitation is offered Jesus plants himself ever more determinedly on the way to death. He will make that grim journey fully alive, fully awake. He will find a way through that journey that will reveal death as the ultimate illusion created by the world. If Pilate is unwilling to condemn him, he will condemn himself in the world's eyes. He will make the people cry out for his blood. For the spirit of this world—the ego, the Satan—knows that its last day is at hand. Its power is at an end. Someone has seen the joke. If they wish to put him to death as King of the Jews, so be it. Let the comedy proceed.

He does not approach this last confrontation as a novice. All through his life he has prepared for this day. After his baptism, he enters the wilderness and creates conflict in fasting. He alienates himself from his family and townspeople. He endures all-night vigils and confronts the early morning devils, sore with weariness. He nurses Judas in the midst of his chosen disciples, knowing that Judas will eventually turn on him and betray. He puts his trust in Peter, the weakest of the lot; he hopes Peter might grow but fears he might deny all.

Now Jesus moves through the last confrontation, that moment we fear and avoid all our lives. To save our own lives we would sacrifice anything and anyone. Jesus experiences all: betrayal, denial, the petty politics of Israel and Rome, and abandonment even by his Father. Yet he does not flinch. Somehow there is a way through the dark, a path through suffering into the kingdom.

Like the knight in the dragon story, there is a happy ending. The hero triumphs. Death is slain. And as a hero Jesus brings back boons for all humanity. There is now a path through death; he has blazoned it on the floor of the valley of death; we need fear no evil. The light dawning in the darkness will guide us through the perilous journey home.

Whether we like it or not, that same confrontation with death awaits us all. How will we prepare for the battle? Shall we follow the example of Jesus and confront head-on the problems of suffering, pain, and evil in our lives? Shall we bravely train our spirits through the conscious creation of friction in our life? The choice is ours. If Jesus' techniques frighten us too much, we can employ the seemingly more gentle process of the Buddha, even though the journey and its attendant dangers remain the same. With Jesus, the passage is made in this lifetime. With gentler techniques, who knows how many eons it may take? The choice is ours. Unfortunately, no matter what we choose now, we have no choice concerning that final confrontation.

• During this week why not undertake one of Jesus' techniques for creating conflict. Try either a fast, a vigil, or almsgiving. Decide the extent to which you will engage in the technique. For it to be a learning experience, you will want it to be mildly uncomfortable so that you feel the conflict. However, if you create something too uncomfortable at this point in your pilgrimage, you are also likely to fail; the experience will be so unpleasant that you will abort it and never return to it again. Find something uncomfortable enough to learn from but not so uncomfortable that nothing happens. And remember that what you do is not so important. What *is* important is to observe all the feelings and experiences that result from what you are doing. What can you learn about yourself by putting yourself into this conflict situation?

51 ATTITUDES OF BEING IN THE KINGDOM
time: twenty-five minutes a day for one week
materials: Bible (Matthew 5:1-12)

Now that we have seen some of the work Jesus invites us to undertake, we'll look at a person who in his life took Jesus' invitation seriously. He is Francis of Assisi, who in many people's minds was the man who talked to the birds. Some who have tried to penetrate behind that popular image have ended up agreeing that that was the best place for him to spend his time.

Francis is an enigma; he does not make sense. He takes Jesus absolutely at his word and acts out to an embarrassingly literal degree what Jesus demands. The rich young man in the gospels was told to sell all and follow Jesus. Any order in the church today knows unostentatious ways of fulfilling such instructions. One could even return home and quietly draw up a will. But Francis follows Jesus to the letter and the instant. In the village square before bishop, family, friends, and those who could not care less, he not only gives away all he owns but strips the clothes from his back. Standing before all without benefit of so much as a fig leaf, Francis surrenders completely to his Lady Poverty. The story goes that the bishop had the presence of mind to cover Francis with his own cloak. If he hadn't, Francis would have had the freedom, the simplicity, the idiocy and, yes, even the sanctity to walk naked out of the square singing poems to his Lady, as blindly in love as his fellow countryman, Romeo.

Francis is a saint because he naively insists on understanding Jesus literally. We fail to achieve sanctity because we have found thousands of ways to water down, romanticize, and make figurative Jesus' teachings. Christians have reinterpreted these teachings so they no longer say quite what they at first clearly seemed to say. The exhortation to turn the other cheek has been interpreted as a moral demand rather than a spiritual work. Christians have been able to engage in wars of defense and just wars, and even to prosecute wars they dare call holy.

Francis believed Jesus meant what he said. Sure Jesus told parables and Francis enjoyed a story as much as the rest. But Jesus also spoke directly using nonsymbolic language. Francis took him literally and, as a result, came closest to being the perfect Christian—another Christ.

Francis came from a rich family. He knew how to deal with wealth. Had Francis come to another teacher, imagine the exchange. The teacher, seeing this rich young man approaching, would immediately see Francis' dollars at work in the vineyard of the Lord. The money could be used to build hospitals and care for the poor. Such a teacher might gain our admiration. He or she loves humanity and transforms Francis into a great benefactor.

Jesus does not fit this teacher image, however. When he addresses the rich young man, he is not concerned about the money but about the youth himself. "Go, sell everything you have, and give to the poor, . . . and, come, follow me." (Mark 10:21). How the money is spent is irrelevant. His concern is with the person and his waking to life. "How can this man enter the joy of his Father's kingdom?" asks Jesus. He will not be able to do it by using his money, no matter how well. He already knows how to use money; it would be easy for him to be charitable. Without money, he could come alive and learn how to live. Where conflict is generated, growth can be fostered.

As we, too, approach Jesus, we find he makes us thoroughly uncomfortable. He raises our divinity by creating conflict where we sleep. Wherever the soft or sore spots, the Great Physician probes them into our attention. He is not interested in our talents. More important are our failings, those things we can't do at all. It is our death and failure he demands from us. And in Jesus' own life the way to resurrection lies through the agony of the cross. We are here not to feed our ego by building hospitals with our million dollars, but we are here to displace our ego by giving our million away and living on nothing.

Francis understands Jesus; there in the village square, acknowledging both diagnosis and treatment, Christ's troubadour casts everything off. Standing with nothing between him and the elements, he discovers freedom for the first time in his life. Entering the kingdom is quick and easy. Why spend lifetimes in meditation, paltry fasting, or acts of penance? The doors open immediately to those with the courage to die to whatever they were most dependent upon.

Having experienced the supreme joy of letting go, Francis continues his pilgrimage. How can he penetrate deeper into this wonderful kingdom? He reads in the gospel about the lepers. Jesus had a certain fondness for lepers, the very people others went miles out of their way to avoid. Francis, like a child imitating his father, decides that he too should befriend the lepers.

But Francis, unlike Jesus, can't cure the lepers so he will do the next best thing. He will embrace them and physically kiss them. Now wait a minute: Jesus we can forgive—he had something to offer these wretches. But what good will it do for these poor lepers to be embraced by this simple clown? Francis has gone too far. Simple acts such as disrobing in public have a certain shock value. But kissing lepers is downright repulsive not to say dangerous; it is inhuman.

Francis' action, if we are to discover the way of sanctity, forces us into his position. What would happen if I, as brother Francis, should come across a leper? My initial reaction might be to cross the street, run away, and, as soon as possible, take a thorough bath. I would be hurt and bruised just by the sight of lepers; they proclaim my own vulnerability. What if I should find myself in their situation?

If we really want to get in touch with this feeling, we should change the disease because we have no real experience of leprosy; it is an exotic, Biblical disease, outmoded and therefore even somewhat romantic. Our modern equivalent would be cancer. We are assured by medical authorities that it is not at all contagious. Yet, in its presence we are deathly afraid that we might in some magic way contract it. We are not here dealing with reality but with the fears that keep us from living. Meeting people with cancer creates conflict in our own lives. They proclaim our frailty, our inability to help or do anything. They make our death and suffering loom up before us. It is there now, lurking under the surface like a malignant shark, ready to rip us apart. Cancer could strike this minute putting an end to our plans, our projects, our lives. But Francis does not suppress this kind of fear; he charges forth to confront the dragon. He goes out of his way not to avoid the fear, but to embrace it.

He purposely creates conflict. He does not find leprosy attractive· in his early life he too lived in terror of it. But embracing it enables him to transcend his fears and become divine. It wakes him up. His embrace drags his fears out of the dark and into the daylight. Seen in that light, fears do not kill or destroy. They make life that much more precious. It is better to live with knowledge than ignorance. To embrace the lepers, to confront our fears is knowledge. But to suppress the things that scare us most makes real living impossible.

The story of perfect joy might at first lead us to designate Francis as the patron saint of masochists. But let's enter more deeply into this story and savor the mystery it offers us.

One day Francis and Brother Juniper, his straight man, are walking through the woods. Juniper asks the questions that enable Francis to expound his ideas. As usual Juniper begins with a question: "What is perfect joy, Brother Francis?"

"Brother Juniper, if I had all the wealth in the world and could dispose and use it as I wanted, that would not be perfect joy."

It was an interesting response, and as they continue their journey, Brother Juniper ponders the words. But after a while he realizes that Francis has not really answered his question. So he puts his query again.

"Brother Juniper, if I were the most beloved person in the world, and if everyone counted me their dearest friend, that would not be perfect joy."

I would have thought that should make me quite happy, thinks Brother Juniper. But as they continue, he tries to understand what Francis has said and why these friends would not bring perfect joy. Only after some thought does he realize once again that Francis has evaded his question. So once again he pesters his brother: "What is perfect joy?"

And once again Francis replies:

"If I had all the power in the world and could do anything I wanted, that would not be perfect joy."

Well, as in all good stories and wishes, replies must come in threes and by now even Brother Juniper is in on the game. He quickly jumps upon Francis' reply: "Brother Francis, I have asked you three times what perfect joy could be. Three times you have avoided my question; you have instead told me what perfect joy is not. I will admit that I might have considered it any one of those things you have mentioned it is not, and I thank you for correcting me. But I am no closer to an answer now than when we began our discussion. In fact, I am even more in the dark as to what perfect joy might be. If you know the answer, I ask you to give it me for my brain is by now quite muddled."

"Brother Juniper, let us say we are walking along as we are right now. But imagine it is cold and snowing. We have been travelling for three days now without food or shelter. We are chilled to the bone, ready to lie down in the snow and die.

"But just as we are about to surrender, we sight one of our brother monasteries. Thankful, we drag ourselves to the door and at the point of exhaustion, we knock. After a while a little window in the door opens and a brother sticks a rather unfriendly face out at us. 'What do you want?' he growls.

" 'We've been walking now three days without food or shelter. We are brothers in your order. Could you give us some food and shelter for the night, before we continue our journey tomorrow?'

" 'I don't believe you. Besides there is no room here. Be on your way!' And he slams the door in our face.

"It is impossible to continue as we are so we have no choice but to try again. We knock once more. The window opens a little more quickly this time, but the same mean face glares out at us. 'You two again. Listen, I know your kind. Now get out of here.'

" 'But we are at the point of death. Couldn't you spare us some room in the stables? We promise we won't ask for any more than that and we will not disturb the animals.'

"Slam! goes the little window in our face. What do we do now? What can we do? We have no choice; we knock a third time. But now our knocking is ignored. Apparently the brother thinks we will eventually go away. But we continue to knock.

"After a long time the door itself swings open. There is the brother we have seen twice before, but now he is not alone; two or three others have joined him, armed with clubs. They seize us, throw us on the ground and beat us bloody. When we are nearly dead they leave us unconscious in the snow, turn around, reenter the house and for the last time slam the door on us. Now, Brother Juniper, now we know perfect joy."

What are we to make of such a story? Can we take this man seriously or is this a tale told by an idiot? What is Francis doing here? He is embracing the cross of Jesus. In that cross, that instrument of torture and pain, he finds his joy, his perfection. He will pursue that pilgrimage toward the cross until at the end of his life he is "blessed" with the marks of the nails and spear in his hands and side.

The way to this perfection, the journey upon which Francis embarks, makes no sense in the ordinary world's mind. Logic and philosophy are of no use here. This experience does not proceed from and is not grounded in human reason or wisdom: It comes from God. In the world's eyes it is ultimate stupidity or insanity, but for Francis it is the pathway to divinity and happiness.

We might understand Francis' story as an illustration of Jesus' admonition to take up one's cross and follow. But it might also be a commentary upon one of the Beatitudes: "Happy are you when people insult you and persecute you and slander you for my sake." What are these beatitudes, these enigmatic phrases? They are definitions of real happiness, put at the beginning of Jesus' Sermon on the Mount as nine gates into the kingdom of God. Read Matthew 5:1-12.

We have been searching for that kingdom ever since we heard Jesus speak of it. We have entered it through imaginative meditation. We have looked at the ways of working to transform our lives in order to pass into the kingdom. Now we find these nine gates to the kingdom. There is not just one way in; rather, a wealth of possibilities is laid before us. Any one of these Beatitudes is capable of gaining us access; all we need do is enter into the saying.

Take a closer look at these sayings: "How happy are the poor in spirit; theirs is the kingdom of heaven. Happy the gentle, they shall have the earth for their heritage. Happy those who mourn; they shall be comforted" (The Jerusalem Bible). We have heard these words over and over again throughout our lives. Maybe they are no longer Beatitudes so much as platitudes.

Can we believe them? The more we really examine them, the more we bring our intelligence and heart to them, the less we feel we have any idea what they are saying. For example, how is it really possible and thinkable that I can experience true happiness through the process of mourning? All my experience says sorrow and happiness are at opposite ends of the experiential spectrum. How can one possibly lead to the other? If this Beatitude is true, then I do not understand what true happiness is.

For the present, let's lay aside the question of happiness. Take the second part that says that if I can truly mourn, I will be comforted. Is this true? Is it confirmed by my own experience? What does it mean to mourn? Why should I mourn? What should I mourn? Have I really mourned so that I can evaluate this Beatitude? What if I should give way to mourning and am not comforted but dissolve into my tears? There is much at stake; I might lose my life and still not enter into the kingdom of God.

If I cry, who will comfort me? This is a life and death question. Jesus says happiness, wholeness, life, the kingdom of God can be mine. It can happen through my sorrow and tears. We have accepted less from life than our Father is willing to give. We have made this bargain because we are afraid if we allow life to hurt us, we might dissolve in a puddle of tears.

Jesus says such is not the case. "Trust me" is the gist of his message. "Give in to the sadness. Do not repress it. Let it surface—feel the grief of your loss. It is all right for you to feel it. You've been hurt; tears can heal. And if you should surrender to mourning, know that comfort and healing will come as well. Through the tears, you open yourself to more of life than you have experienced so far. You will become whole, a full human being knowing the good and the bad. I do not offer just the happiness of humor and laughter. That has its place, but there is more to happiness than a smile or the chuckles. No, I offer you real life and real happiness."

Jesus in these Beatitudes offers a therapy that does not fit the molds of orthodox therapy today. Its aim is not to create a normal human being who can function in the world. No, its object is more grand; it aims to make us whole. At the end of this process, we will not say "I can cope" but rather "I am perfect as my heavenly Father is perfect." We will not be perfect in the sense of being morally righteous, of knowing it all, of having no problems left to deal with, or of being successful in all our endeavors, but we will be perfect in the sense of being complete, whole, harmonious, happy.

Fragmentation is the enemy. We respond from a fragment rather than the whole; we react to things rather than respond from a source of inner freedom and wisdom. The Beatitudes address our fragmentation and reveal ways for us to go through fragmentation into wholeness.

Although the Beatitudes are written in plain, simple language, there is a great barrier between them and us. It might be easier if they had been left in the original language; then we would at least know we do not understand them. Instead we assume we know their meaning. But do we? What does it mean to be poor in spirit? Is Jesus referring to the pious little twit who for far too long has been the image of the good Christian, when in reality he or she is truly the image of the good doormat and nothing else? This spineless wonder eaten away by passive aggression is certainly not the perfection of humanity.

How are we to understand these strange portals into the kingdom? Who will teach us? Jesus provides no commentary. There is no tradition of Christian gurus who might bring these words to life. In fact, Christianity rejects the whole idea of the guru who imparts secret knowledge to his or her disciples. The secret wisdom of Christianity is in the gospels for all to see. In spite of two thousand years of public proclamation, these sayings are still hidden; their true essence is as unknown to the general public as are the esoteric teachings of the Dalai Lama.

Who will be our teacher? No, this is the wrong question. We have a teacher in Jesus. He is sufficient, we need no other. But who will open us to these teachings; who will make them plain? Jesus says this is the domain of the Advocate, the Holy Spirit, this Spirit of God who already lives and breathes within us, this Spirit who sustains the entire creation in being. Wisdom does not need to be appropriated from some teacher. She is of God and already within us. But she is dormant, and the teachings of Jesus can awaken her. Then all will be revealed, not in books, but written upon our hearts.

● For the next week (and if you like much longer than that) select one of these enigmas of the kingdom for meditation. First acknowledge that it is indeed an enigma. We do not know what the Beatitude is truly saying. It is like a koan, a riddle, in the Zen tradition.

When the student approaches a Zen master for instruction, she or he might be given a riddle to work upon. The most famous koan is "What is the sound of one hand clapping?" The student receives this koan and works upon it constantly, both in meditation and during the rest of the day. He or she tries every way known to penetrate its meaning. Each day the student returns to the master with his or her answer. But each day the answer is rejected; the meaning has not been mastered. Finally when all the student's resources are exhausted, she or he surrenders and the answer floats into view.

We seem to know what the Beatitudes are saying. But if we are honest with ourselves, we really think they are nonsense, just as the sound of one hand clapping is nonsense. We have seen enough evidence in the world and in our own lives to convince us that mourning does not always involve comfort.

Yet these seemingly nonsensical phrases have great spiritual wisdom. Those who have penetrated through the gate into the kingdom have never disparaged them. So let's receive them as our koans from Jesus. Use them in your meditation. Sit with one of them through the confusion, the sterility, the winter, until it blossoms and you see into the kingdom. You might take the one that most disturbs you—that is a sure way to find your special Beatitude. You might want to take the one you least understand or the one that appeals to you most. Sit with it; wrestle with it; die with it. What does it mean? How is it true? It has power to awaken the sleeping Spirit within us. That Spirit will then make the Beatitude plain. When that happens, those words of nonsense will become a gate and passage into the kingdom.

52

THE SHAPE OF CHRISTIAN EXISTENCE
time: twenty-five minutes
materials: Bible (Matthew 14:13-21)

The Beatitudes and the work Jesus recommends are difficult and will necessitate heroic action at times. In the Christian church this kind of work is done by the entire community during the period of Lent. But there are other, everyday attitudes of life that Christians practice; it is not always necessary to struggle with the heroic. Christian existence could also be called one of thanksgiving; in our meditation today and our thinking throughout the next week, we will examine the shape of this thankful attitude.

In the story of the feeding of the five thousand, we can see very clearly the actions involved in thanksgiving. The story says that Jesus took the bread (or received it), gave thanks for it, broke it, and shared it with the multitude. How can these four actions, which form the basis for the Christian mystery of thanksgiving called the Eucharist, serve as a basic pattern for our lives?

• After preparation and reading of the story, pass over into the role of one of the disciples. You have accompanied Jesus today, and as usual, a large crowd has collected around him. It is getting late and you are a little concerned. These people are far from home. Who is going to feed them?

Approach Jesus with your concern. He asks you how much food you have. You tell him you only have enough food for your own small company. You didn't expect this crowd of five thousand, and you didn't expect Jesus to speak this long. Enter into the disciple's situation. How do you feel about what is happening? Are you afraid that the crowd might grow hostile as it gets hungry? Are you ashamed that you did not foresee this situation and plan accordingly? Do you feel you've failed as a disciple? Enter your thoughts and feelings at this moment of the story.

Now look at what is demanded of you in your own life. Do you often consider yourself inadequate to the task? Do you sometimes feel yourself drained of love? Do you feel stretched to the breaking point? Are people just demanding too much of you, so that you feel overcommitted? Allow these experiences to bring you into the disciple's experience.

Consider what you have learned of the kingdom and its ways. Certainly the program of Jesus does not seem easy. How are you going to find a way through death to life as he did? How can you come alive? How will you put aside your anger and judgmental attitude? There is a long path ahead on this pilgrimage. Is there some part of you that feels quite incapable and inadequate to the task? Bring these feelings now into this story.

As a disciple carry all this insufficiency with you as you bring Jesus the poor, miserly amount of bread and fish you had hoped would be enough for you and the other disciples. What are your feelings as you bring the food forward? Is there anger? Are you ashamed of what you have? Do you blame yourself for being inadequate?

• Now pass over into the figure of Jesus. He has been content to respond to the disciples' question. They wondered how they would be able to feed the crowd. Jesus asks how much food they have, and they tell him they don't have enough. But Jesus makes no judgment. He does not criticize them because there is not enough food. He does not enter into their fears that there will not be enough. He accepts what is present. Enter into Jesus' experience. Bring no feelings of fear, judgment, shame, hopelessness, or inadequacy with you. Simply be present to the situation. Accept it for what it is, and ask the disciples to bring whatever they have.

329

The baskets of food are brought before you. Receive whatever is given to you. Pause for a moment and give thanks to your Father for this food and this moment. It is all you have and it is enough.

• Let's do the same now with the rest of those things that concern us. Earlier we worried about our inadequacies and the difficulties ahead. Now let's look at what we have. Let's accept it and see it as good, as part of the gift our heavenly Father bestows upon us. He has provided us with sufficient for our needs. Let us trust that this is so and give thanks. Let's remove ourselves from judgment or blame or any groaning that this is impossible. Let's simply give thanks.

How does this action of thanksgiving feel? Is it quiet? Does it have a peaceful quality? Do you feel less agitated than before? How does this experience differ from your previous experience as a disciple? Did the feelings in the previous experience do you any good?

After Jesus gives thanks, he breaks the bread and fish and then gives it to his disciples to pass among the people. Once again there is no judgment. He does not look at the pathetically small amount of food and bewail the impossibility of the situation. He does not worry about what he and his disciples will now do to feed themselves once they have exhausted this small portion of bread and fish. Instead Jesus breaks up what he has and gives it away, simply trusting in the Father's providence. Enter into Jesus' action now, tasting this kind of faith and trust.

• Pass over into your own life and consider the things required of you: the ways you are asked to give of yourself, your time, your energy, your money. What would happen if instead of hoarding what little you have, you took Jesus' attitude—broke up what you have and shared it? If you feel you do not have enough time for yourself or other important matters, imagine taking that little time, giving thanks for it and then breaking it to share with all. If you feel fear or anxiety, tell it to leave you. Allow this action of Jesus to guide you in the breaking up and sharing of your life.

As the food is passed around, there is enough not only for all to eat, but for everyone to be satisfied. Afterwards, twelve baskets full of fish and bread are collected. Rather than suffer depletion, as the world teaches, the disciples discover that the multitude is fed and that they end up with more food than they first had.

Enter into the story once more as a disciple. You are now gathering the remainder. How do you react as you see all the bread and fish coming back? Are you surprised? Have you learned anything from this action? Have you begun to see the power in the simple action of giving thanks?

Can you imagine a similar miracle happening in your own life? Could a similar thing happen to you should you risk sharing the limited resources, love, and generosity you possess? In your life, what would be equivalent to this return of twelve baskets of bread?

In this meditation we have followed the four essential actions in the mystery of the Eucharist. The sacraments of Christian life are mysteries that, like the miracles and signs of Jesus, open to us the vision of the kingdom in the midst of our world. As fully realized Christians, we will not be perfect; our journey toward wholeness will consume the rest of our lives. Everything in our lives can teach us about the kingdom and its possibilities. Once initiated into the death and resurrection of Jesus through baptism, we will continue our journey led by the other sacramental mysteries of the kingdom. We will be able to see our way home by the light of the kingdom.

This miracle is not just something Jesus performs to convince the world of his powers. The actions of this story describe the shape of a truly fulfilled and happy human existence. By entering into these actions, we are drawn closer to the Father who in Jesus has sought and called us, and we enter into that wonderful celebration—that festival of the fatted calf, that marriage feast, that banquet that welcomes us back to our true home.

• Throughout the next week, be aware of opportunities to enter into these actions in your own life. If you are not willing to perform these actions yet, at least try to imagine what it might be like. In the story of the marriage at Cana, Jesus does not really do anything; his life is simply open to the power of the Father to make his glory manifest. If we place our lives in a similar position, perhaps the miracles of the kingdom will flow through us as well. There is really nothing to do or achieve; it is just the way things really and truly are.

53   THE EXPERIENCE OF GOD
time: twenty-five minutes a day for one week

The Christian understanding of God is expressed in the concept of the Trinity. God is one and, without any division to the Godhead, at the same time three persons—the Father, the Son, and the Holy Spirit. This idea is first and foremost a mystery; it can't be completely understood but it provides us with hints about the ultimate nature of things. Let's now consider seven different ways of approaching this mystery of existence.

First of all, we say that God is not divided by person. The Father is truly God; the Son is truly God; the Spirit is truly God. When we bear this unity in mind and look forward to the completion of our journey, we find that we are on the way to becoming divinized. The

Eastern Christians speak of this whole process as divinization. St. Athanasius said that in Jesus God became man so that through Jesus man might become God. But if God is not divided by person, then our end is not to become absorbed in some great, cosmic All, but rather to achieve perfection through our person. We can become who we are uniquely created to be and at the same time realize our divinity—the Holy Spirit—to its fullest.

The Trinity is not a static entity; it is not three acts in one show. The three persons are in relationship to one another and to creation. In our second image of the Trinity, we look at the relationships among the persons from our own viewpoint. During the course of this pilgrimage, we have learned the Christian action of prayer. Prayer is directed to our Father. It is our Father who created us and who, through his love, draws us home. When we enter into prayer, we enter into a dialogue with him. We make our prayer through the Son, for it is Jesus who has taught us how to pray and how to live. He is our teacher and our Lord, the pattern for our life; in him we find the perfection not only of the Father but of our humanity as well. Our prayer life is modeled after his prayer life. When we pray, we put ourselves into his experience and assume his stance toward the Father. We pray through the Son because the Son is our path home to the Father. And our prayer is made in the Holy Spirit. When we pray, we pray not as alien beings communicating to another being. In prayer there is divine unity between the Spirit that gives us our life and the Father from whom that life proceeds. The unity between the two is the Son who bridges creature and Creator. We make our prayer to our Father through the Son in the Holy Spirit. The Trinity is not something removed from us; it is the very foundation of all existence. We can say that the Father creates in the image of the Son by the power of the Spirit.

The early Christians meditated upon the mystery of the Trinity and discovered it was not limited to Jesus' teaching, but had been glimpsed darkly throughout the Old Testament times and in the natural world as well. We might glimpse the Trinity through the images of the Law, the Gospel, and the Spirit. In the course of Christian history, these three elements have often seemed in conflict with one another, but in essence they are the same. They proceed from only one God. We might call them three expressions of the same divinity. The Law speaks of the ordering of all creation. It includes not only the moral

332

law, but the order, the reason for creation itself. In the first chapter of Genesis we read that creation is brought forth by God out of chaos. On this pilgrimage we have named God that center of meaning in our lives, and we have come to believe and posit meaning even when we could not see it or comprehend it. The Israelite found this experience of the meaningfulness, the order, the reason of all existence in the Law. It provided meaning and order not only for the individual, but for the society, and, by extension, for the entire creation—all is one, all is the expression of the one Law.

While some have seen the Gospel as the antithesis or the replacement of the Law, Jesus calls himself the fulfillment or the perfection of the Law. If the Law regulated a person's exterior life and provided order among the creation, the Gospel is the interior regulator; it brings the order and meaning of the Law within the human person, and orders the human person and, by extension, society and the cosmos ever more closely to the one Law. If the Law proceeded through a conformity of the creation to it, the Gospel says that Jesus becomes identical to the Law. In doing this, he brings the Law to perfection and shows how the revelation of the Law was misunderstood in Israel. That Jesus and the Law come into conflict shows not that the Law is evil or inadequate but that it has been misunderstood and corrupted. It still stands as the external order of creation, but now in Jesus we receive the Gospel as the path toward identity with the Law. Jesus fulfills the Law—becomes the Law—and through his life enables all creation to do the same.

The Spirit is one with both the Law and the Gospel. The Spirit stands behind the Law and the Gospel and empowers them. Without the Spirit both Law and Gospel become letters that are dead and destructive to life. In the power of the Spirit, both Law and Gospel bring the creation into fulfillment and unity with the Godhead. When the Spirit stands against Law or Gospel, it must do so because our understanding of Law and Gospel has become benighted and corrupt, because we have lost the essence and cling to externals. The Spirit is the bond between ourselves and the ideals of Law and Gospel. It is the power that enables us to become conformed to the Law and identified with the Gospel. In the Law, we discover we are the creation of our Father; through the Gospel we become identified with the Son;

creation achieves perfection. This process is possible only because the Spirit already lives in our hearts and calls out to our Father as we journey homeward.

Once we have the eyes to see it, the entire creation proclaims this mysterious trinity. We might catch another glimpse of the Trinity as we look at something as simple as a song. Through this metaphor we can see the Father as music itself, all the possible music—the music beyond and underlying all the music we can hear. The Father is the music before any music is heard. But how will this music be heard by us? For this a song is necessary, and we could see the Son as the Father's infinite music given concrete expression in one song. We could then say that that song is the same music as the Father's music. We might say that through the music of that song all the other music we have ever heard was given shape and expression. But who will sing the song? The Spirit who sings the song a billion ways—through strings, winds, reeds, and throats. And when the singer sings, the singer, the song, and the music are one. There is no way to divide them, yet they are not the same; they are three in one.

Or consider the experience of love. There is first of all the lover and the beloved and the love that joins them. The Father loves and his love expresses itself in his creation. He creates in the image of his beloved Son. We and the rest of the entire creation exist in his image inasmuch as we allow it to be and do not turn away from our true nature. And the love that exists between the Father—the lover—and the Son—the beloved—is the Holy Spirit.

We have considered six metaphors for the Trinity. They are all metaphors. To take them literally, we miss the mystery and fall into chaos. Each one of these images gives us a certain entrance into this mystery—each one also falls far short of articulating the mystery.

• Search for a seventh image or metaphor of the Trinity in your own meditation this week, exploring any other metaphors and images of Trinity that come to mind. Prepare for your meditations as usual and then remain quietly with this mystery. Images will arise from the Spirit within us. Take them as images—some will provide much insight into this ultimate mystery, some perhaps only a smile. Each day end your meditation with prayer to your Father, through the Son, in the Holy Spirit. For the ultimate beauty of this mystery is not in contemplation but in the experience of prayer and life.

PART SEVEN
The Gift of Spirit

At the beginning of Part Six we found ourselves at the great feast of Easter. If, as we have suggested, we proceed by weeks from Easter, then seven weeks later plus one day we find ourselves at the other great Christian feast—Pentecost—the giving of the Holy Spirit to the disciples.

The Spirit is the ultimate gift and revelation of Jesus; the Spirit will bring us successfully through our pilgrimage. The Holy Spirit is our advocate, our guide, our comforter, our very real self. This Spirit, blowing where it will, sustains all creation in being. It cannot be imprisoned in forms, words, institutions. Through all creation, it is the freedom of God on the way home to the banquet the Father has prepared.

On Pentecost, Jesus sends the disciples out into all the world with the good news. But who is to say that the Spirit has not been there before? The spirit cannot be contained. It broke forth from the Law when the Law was misunderstood. It breaks forth from the Gospel when it becomes rigid. The Spirit is the spirit of truth, and truth is one as God is one. Where the truth is, there is the Spirit. It is in the unexpected places, just as in Jesus it was the unexpected Messiah. But with the good news of the gospel we might begin to discover its movements, its voice throughout the whole of creation.

Let's go out as disciples and pilgrims of Jesus with the company we have known here on pilgrimage: the members of our study group; the saints who have led us—John, Peter, Paul, Francis, and Mary; the artists whose imaginations light our way—Blake, Mahler, Verdi, Berlioz, Michelangelo; and our fellow-pilgrims from Chaucer and his goodly company to Dante, Alice, and Dorothy.

As we walk along, we see a huge gathering of people. The Lord Buddha, we are told, has promised today to give his greatest teaching so all of his disciples have gathered to listen. How opportune that the Spirit should lead us here on this special day.

• Since this will be a very deep teaching, prepare for meditation. When you are prepared, imagine the Lord Buddha walking into the deer park. All bow before him. He takes his seat and everyone becomes quiet, expectant. In his hand the Lord Buddha holds a lotus blossom. He looks at the lotus blossom. Anticipation is electric throughout the crowd. Feel the excitement. Time passes—a few minutes, twenty minutes, half an hour, an hour. Feel the time pass. What is happening to you? What are your feelings as you sit and wait? The Buddha is still gazing at the lotus blossom. What are your thoughts? Enter into that silence now for a few minutes and experience the scene.

Finally the crowd grows very restless. Someone dares break the silence and asks the Lord Buddha when he will deliver this teaching he has promised. The Lord Buddha looks up and says that he has just given the supreme teaching. How do you react? What are your thoughts and feelings? What does he mean?

Now your thoughts are interrupted by laughter from someone in your own group. You look around, embarrassed. The raucous, hilarious laughter continues. It is coming from someone in the back. Oh yes, you've noticed him, but he's not really a part of the group. He must be a knight, but he is a pathetic and ridiculous figure of a knight. His armor is rusty and ill-fitting. He himself is quite young and, as you've discovered in trying to talk with him, incredibly naive. Now in the midst of this solemn gathering and this supremely important moment, he is rolling on the ground with laughter. People around him are trying to keep him quiet, but he cannot control himself.

The Buddha motions him forward and he goes up to the Lord Buddha still shaking with laughter. The Lord Buddha hands him the flower and then speaks to the multitude. "Today I have given my greatest teaching and only this little one has understood."

The crowd begins to disperse. The little knight makes his way back to our group. He is still laughing, with the flower now placed in his helmet like a trophy. We are confused. What has happened here?

We have been on pilgrimage together for a long time. We have sustained one another through many adventures and know there is far to go before we reach home. What has this shabby knight learned today that we still do not know?

He approaches us again as we prepare to resume our journey. Finally someone asks him what this was all about. Turning to us, still laughing, he yells, "But where is the Grail?" and again bursts into peals of laughter.

At first we do not understand. But then someone else begins to laugh, and the laughter grows. "Where is the Grail?" Yes! That's it! "Where is the Grail? Why, it's been with us all along! We are already home. There's really nothing to do! We are fulfilled!" Blissful laughter prevails.

EPILOGUE

Where All Instruction Fails
and Art Can Only Point

Dante at the climax of the *Divine Comedy* describes it this way:

> How weak are words, and how unfit to frame
>   My concept—which lags after what was shown
>   So far, 'twould flatter it to call it lame!
>
> Eternal light, that in Thyself alone
>   Dwelling, alone dost know Thyself, and smile
>   On Thy self-love, so knowing and so known!
>
> The sphering thus begot, perceptible
>   In Thee like mirrored light, now to my view—
>   When I had looked on it a little while—
>
> Seemed in itself and in its own self-hue,
>   Limned with our image; for which cause mine eyes
>   Were altogether drawn and held thereto.
>
> As the geometer his mind applies
>   To square the circle, nor for all his wit
>   Finds the right formula, howe'er he tries,
>
> So strove I with that wonder—how to fit
>   The image to the sphere; so sought to see
>   How it maintained the point of rest in it.
>
> Thither my own wings could not carry me,
>   But that a flash my understanding clove,
>   Whence its desire came to it suddenly.

High fantasy lost power and here broke off;
    Yet, as a wheel moves smoothly, free from jars,
    My will and desire were turned by love,
The love that moves the sun and other stars.

Beethoven, at the end of his lifelong struggle with deafness, expressed it thus in his final string quartet:

Muss es sein?   Es muss sein!   Es muss sein!

340

In the Holy Scriptures the final words describe a vision seen by St. John:

Then I saw a new heaven and a new earth; for the first heaven and the first earth had passed away, and the sea was no more. And I saw the holy city, new Jerusalem, coming down out of heaven from God, prepared as a bride adorned for her husband; and I heard a great voice from the throne saying, "Behold, the dwelling of God is with men. He will be with them; he will wipe away every tear from their eyes, and death shall be no more, neither shall there be mourning nor crying nor pain any more, for the former things have passed away."

And he who sat upon the throne said, "Behold, I make all things new . . . . I am the Alpha and the Omega, the beginning and the end. To the thirsty I will give of the water of life from the fountain without payment. He who conquers shall have this heritage, and I will be his God and he shall be my son . . . ."

Then came one of the seven angels who had the seven bowls full of the seven plagues, and spoke to me, saying,

"Come, I will show you the Bride, the wife of the Lamb."
And in the Spirit he carried me away to a great, high
mountain, and showed me the holy city Jerusalem coming
down out of heaven from God, having the glory of God, its
radiance like a most rare jewel, like a jasper, clear as
crystal. . . .

The Spirit and the Bride say, "Come." And let him
who hears say, "Come." And let him who is thirsty come,
let him who desires take the water of life without price.

Amen! Maranatha!

Revelation 21:1-5a, 6b-7, 9-11; 22:17
Revised Standard Version

NOTES

The passage from the Prologue to the *Canterbury Tales* is from *The Poetical Works of Chaucer*, edited by F.N. Robinson (Boston: Houghton Mifflin Co., 1933), p. 19.

The words of the Buddha appearing on page 15 are taken from *The Dhammapada: The Sayings of the Buddha*, translated by Thomas Byrom (New York: Vintage Books, 1976), p. 4.

The quotation by Saint Augustine on page 20 is from *Selected Easter Sermons of St. Augustine*, edited by Philip T. Weller (New York: Herder and Herder, 1959), p. 142.

The comments of the young student of Islam on page 21 are from *The Book of Strangers* by Ian Dallas (New York: Pocket Books, 1978), p. 97.

The second quotation of the words of the Buddha is also from *The Dhammapada: The Sayings of the Buddha*, translated by Thomas Byrom.

Gustav Mahler's description of the fifth movement of his Second Symphony appeared in the program notes of a Dresden Concert in 1901.

The words of the poet Dante are taken from *Dante's Divine Comedy: Paradise*, translated by Dorothy L. Sayers (Baltimore: Penguin Books), Canto XXXIII, 121-145; pp. 346-7.

The musical passage cited on page 340 is from Beethoven's String Quartet No. 16 in F, Op. 135, Fourth Movement.